Development of the Industrial U.S.

Almanac

Development of
the Industrial U.S.
Almanac

Sonia G. Benson

Jennifer York Stock,
Project Editor

U·X·L
*An imprint of Thomson Gale,
a part of The Thomson Corporation*

THOMSON

GALE ™

Detroit • New York • San Francisco • San Diego • New Haven, Conn. • Waterville, Maine • London • Munich

THOMSON
GALE
™

Development of the Industrial U.S: Almanac
Sonia G. Benson

Project Editor
Jennifer York Stock

Editorial
Sarah Hermsen

Rights Acquisitions and Management
Shalice Shah-Caldwell, Kim Smilay

Imaging and Multimedia
Randy Bassett, Lezlie Light,
Daniel Newell, Denay Wilding

Product Design
Pamela A. E. Galbreath

Composition
Evi Seoud

Manufacturing
Rita Wimberly

For permission to use material from this product, submit your request via Web at http://www.gale-edit.com/permissions, or you may download our Permissions Request form and submit your request by fax or mail to:

Permissions Department
Thomson Gale
27500 Drake Rd.
Farmington Hills, MI 48331-3535
Permissions Hotline:
248-699-8006 or 800-877-4253, ext. 8006
Fax: 248-699-8074 or 800-762-4058

Cover photographs of Ford Model T assembly line and Eli Whitney's cotton gin, © Bettmann/Corbis.

While every effort has been made to ensure the reliability of the information presented in this publication, Thomson Gale does not guarantee the accuracy of the data contained herein. Thomson Gale accepts no payment for listing; and inclusion in the publication of any organization, agency, institution, publication, service, or individual does not imply endorsement by the editors or publisher. Errors brought to the attention of the publisher and verified to the satisfaction of the publisher will be corrected in future editions.

LIBRARY OF CONGRESS CATALOGING-IN-PUBLICATION DATA

Benson, Sonia.
   Development of the industrial U.S. Almanac / Sonia G. Benson ; Jennifer York Stock, project editor.
      p. cm.
Includes bibliographical references and index.
ISBN 1-4144-0175-2 (hardcover : alk. paper)
   1. Industries–United States–History–Juvenile literature. 2. Industrial revolution–United States–History–Juvenile literature. [1. United States–Economic conditions–To 1865–Juvenile literature.] I. Stock, Jennifer York, 1974- II. Title.

HC105. B454 2006
330. 973'05–dc22   2005015915

Printed in the United States of America
10 9 8 7 6 5 4 3 2 1

Table of Contents

Introduction

I ndustrialization is the widespread development of profit-making businesses that manufacture products on a large scale, using labor-saving machinery. Understanding the history of the development of industrialization in the United States, which took place over two centuries, involves learning about some of its technical elements, such as technology and the economy. But the history of U.S. industrialism is also a dramatic story of people rising and falling from power or struggling desperately to make the world a better place. Industrialization fueled the national culture, economy, daily life, and politics, creating such tremendous social changes that it is impossible to imagine what life in the United States would be like without it.

Though the Industrial Revolution, a period of rapid industrial growth causing a shift in focus from agriculture to industry, first began in England and Europe in the middle of the eighteenth century, industrialization did not begin to take root in the United States until after the American Revolution (1775–83). Even then American industrialization had a slow start, due to overwhelming obstacles. At the time, the vast majority of

Americans lived independent lives as farmers in remote areas. For the most part, they had little connection with anyone but neighboring farmers, since there were few good roads or systems of communication. Most people did not even own clocks; time was determined by the seasons and the rising and setting of the sun. Few people worked for wages, and those manufactured goods Americans could afford generally came from Europe. The new nation had vast natural resources, such as land, timber, metals, minerals, water power, and ports, but without transportation or manufacturing it was nearly impossible to make industrial use of them.

Once begun, the American Industrial Revolution took on its own character, differing from that of other countries. This was primarily because Americans themselves had been shaped and selected by a unique set of forces. After fighting hard to gain independence from England, most Americans were passionate about the ideals of liberty and equality for all (although to many Americans at the time this meant only white males), and they were determined to create a society in which any individual could rise and prosper through his or her own efforts. They were also driven by the desire for wealth. Though many Europeans immigrated to America to find religious or social freedom, the majority came seeking riches. Many had faced bitter hardships and were prepared to take major risks to obtain wealth. Another key trait of Americans was a spirit of innovation; it had been a necessary attribute for emigrants who left Europe in the seventeenth century, for they would have to reinvent the most basic aspects of their daily lives in the New World. The combined spirit of individualism, greed, and innovation came to characterize U.S. industrialism.

In the years between the American Revolution and the American Civil War (1861–65), innovation and invention were highly esteemed by the American public. Most industrial designs and ideas came initially from Europe, but once they reached the machine makers, or "mechanicians," of American shops, they were improved until they became distinctly American, suited to the land and its people. The times produced an extremely talented group of inventors and innovators, and from their workshops, which were mainly located in the northeastern United States, the "American System," or mass production and the use of interchangeable parts, emerged. It would forever change the nature of manufacturing worldwide.

With new advances in technology, some enterprising business people built the first U.S. factories, and most of them flourished. However, from the start the stark division in wealth and position between industry owners and their workers was at odds with the popular belief in American liberty and equality. Despite early factory owners' efforts to humanize factory work, workers faced low wages and poor working conditions. Many claimed they were slaves to wage labor. It was not long after the first industrial workforces were hired that the first labor strikes took place. The conflict between employers and employees continued, and the factory owners' early attempts to create ideal circumstances for workers were abandoned. Professional managers were hired to get as much work from the workforce as possible. A huge influx of immigrants from Europe and Asia from the 1840s until the 1920s supplied inexpensive labor, but labor strikes continued.

After a slow beginning in the Northeast industrialization began to spread at a rapid pace with the nationwide building of transportation and communications systems. The construction of the transcontinental railroad spanning the nation from one coast to the other—a mammoth undertaking—signaled the start of a new way of life for all Americans. Where railroads went, towns and cities with bustling new commerce arose. The construction of the railroads spawned giant new industries in steel, iron, and coal. Railroads brought farmers' crops to distant markets and were instrumental in bringing the industrial society to the West.

For the railroads to be built and industry to advance, capital, or vast quantities of money, was required. The art of raising large amounts of capital and applying it to industry was mainly accomplished by a generation of extremely capable industrialists who built the gigantic industries that dominated the nation and ruled its economy. These legendary men, admired as the "captains of industry" by some and loathed as ruthless crooks, or "robber barons," by others, included railroad owner Cornelius Vanderbilt, steel empire founder Andrew Carnegie, Standard Oil tycoon John D. Rockefeller, investment banker J. P. Morgan, and many others. Though some of them came from wealthy backgrounds, many were born in humble circumstances and rose to wealth and power through their own efforts. These industrialists created new systems of doing business that are still in place today. Their tactics almost always included creating monopolies, huge corporations that dominated their industry nationwide and limited attempts at competition by others. As the industrialists prospered, most of the wealth of the nation fell into their hands. This period became known as the Gilded Age, the era of industrialization from the early 1860s to the turn of the century in which a few wealthy individuals gained tremendous power and influence. During the Gilded Age the power of industrialists and their corporations seemed unstoppable.

The number of U.S. companies dwindled from thousands to hundreds as the most powerful industrialists bought out or crushed their competitors. Once again, the national spirit of liberty and equality was aroused. Farmers, laborers, poor immigrants, and labor unions as well as middle class reformers sought relief from the power of the corporations, giving rise to the Progressive Era, or the period of the American Industrial Revolution that spanned roughly from the 1890s to about 1920, in which reformers worked together in the interest of distributing political power and wealth more equally. It was during this time that the strong hand of the federal government was finally felt in American industry, as it began to leave behind its laissez-faire, or non-interference, policies in order to regulate businesses, curb monopolies, and protect workers.

By the twentieth century, the United States was the richest and most powerful industrial nation in the world, but the process of industrialization continued. During the twentieth century industry was shaped by scientists like Frederick Winslow Taylor, who devised measurable methods of business management designed to produce top levels of efficiency. The best-known follower of "Taylorism" was Henry Ford, who began to mass produce affordable automobiles in 1909. The Great Depression (1929–41) and World War II (1939–45) both had profound effects on American industrialism, causing government controls and assistance to individuals to increase even more. In recent decades, computers and globalism have been the active agents of change in U.S. industrialism.

Finally, it is worthwhile to note that the development of U.S. industrialization is not finished. It took more than one hundred years for the United States to transform from a farming society to an industrial world power. Adjusting to industrialism has already taken up another century and will continue for many years to come.

Sonia G. Benson

Reader's Guide

The United States began as a nation of farmers living in remote areas, but over a period of two hundred years the country became the wealthiest and most powerful industrial nation of the world. During the American Industrial Revolution inventors and innovators created new and improved machines for manufacturing, while a new breed of American businessmen created revolutionary methods of conducting business and managing labor. The road to industrialization was not always heroic. Ruthlessness and greed were often key ingredients in advancing industry. While a few found wealth and power, multitudes of workers and farmers suffered, and small businesses were crushed by the powerful new corporations. Reformers, unions, and protestors against big business played a crucial role in the industrialization process as they pressed for the rights of workers and regulations on business to help farmers and consumers. The diverse people and events that forever changed the nation from a rural farming economy to an industrialized urban nation create a dramatic story that lies at the heart of U.S. history.

Coverage and features

Development of the Industrial U.S.: Almanac presents an overview of the history of American industrialization. Its fourteen chapters cover the first American factories, inventors, the rise of big business and railroads, urbanism, labor unions, industrial influences in places such as the South or the Great Plains, the Gilded Age, the Progressive Era, the post-industrial era, and much more. Each chapter of the *Almanac* features informative sidebar boxes highlighting glossary terms and issues discussed in the text and concludes with a list of further readings. Also included are more than sixty photographs and illustrations, a timeline, a glossary, a list of suggested research and activity ideas, and an index providing easy access to subjects discussed throughout the volume.

U•X•Development of the Industrial U.S. Reference Library

Development of the Industrial U.S.: Almanac is only one component of the three-part U•X•L Development of the Industrial U.S. Reference Library. The other two titles in the set are:

- *Development of the Industrial U.S.: Biographies* profiles twenty-six significant figures who participated in American industrialization. The biographies cover a wide spectrum of people, from the creators of the first factories, such as Samuel Slater and Francis Cabot Lowell, to inventors and innovators, including John Fitch, Elijah McCoy, and Thomas Edison. Industrialists Andrew Carnegie, J. P. Morgan, and John D. Rockefeller are profiled, as are reformers and educators such as Jane Addams, Florence Kelley, and Booker T. Washington. *Biographies* also includes labor advocates such as Eugene Debs and A. Philip Randolph. The volume features more than fifty photographs and illustrations, a timeline, a glossary, and sources for further reading.

- *Development of the Industrial U.S.: Primary Sources* presents eighteen full or excerpted written works, speeches, and other documents that were influential during American industrialization. The volume includes excerpts from the writings of Thomas Jefferson and Alexander Hamilton reflecting their debate on industrialization; excerpts from legislation regarding industrialization, such as the

Interstate Commerce Act and the Sherman Antitrust Act; segments of popular novels by Horatio Alger and William Dean Howells depicting the effects of industrialization on American society; political cartoons; a popular labor song; an excerpt from an essay by William Graham Sumner presenting the concept of social Darwinism, and much more. Nearly fifty photographs and illustrations, a timeline, sources for further reading, and an index supplement the volume.

A cumulative index of all three volumes in the U•X•L Development of the Industrial U.S. Reference Library is also available.

Comments and suggestions

We welcome your comments on *Development of the Industrial U.S.: Almanac* and suggestions for other topics in history to consider. Please write: Editors, *Development of the Industrial U.S. Almanac,* U•X•L, 27500 Drake Rd., Farmington Hills, Michigan, 48331-3535; call toll-free: 1-800-877-4253; fax to: 248-699-8097; or send e-mail via http://www.gale.com.

Timeline of Events

1780: American mechanics in the Northeast begin to apply principles learned from the English Industrial Revolution in their innovations on tools and machines.

1781: Oliver Evans invents machines to replace human labor in flour mills.

1790: Eighty percent of the nation's population is made up of farmers and ninety-five percent of the population lives in rural areas.

1790: Congress passes the first patent law.

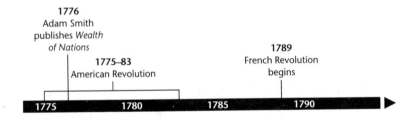

1776
Adam Smith publishes *Wealth of Nations*

1775–83
American Revolution

1789
French Revolution begins

1775   1780   1785   1790

1798: Eli Whitney proposes to make 4,000 muskets for the U.S. government, using new machine-making tools and interchangeable parts.

1807: Robert Fulton's steamboat, the *Clermont,* makes its maiden voyage from New York City to Albany, New York.

1807: Eli Terry builds four thousand clockworks on a tight schedule using the latest principles of mass production.

1817: Congress authorizes the construction of the National Road, the first road to run west across the Appalachian Mountains.

1817–1825: The Erie Canal is built, connecting Albany and Buffalo, New York.

1825: The New York Stock Exchange opens its new headquarters at 11 Wall Street.

1826: The first U.S. railway, the Baltimore and Ohio (B & O) is launched.

1831: Cyrus McCormick invents the first workable reaper.

1836: Two thousand women workers go on strike for better wages and conditions at the Lowell textile mills.

1837: John Deere invents the steel plow.

1840: The *Lowell Offering,* a journal written by the women workers of the Lowell mills, is launched.

1840s: Immigration to the United States from Europe increases significantly. Between 1840 and 1920 37 million immigrants will arrive in the country.

1844: Samuel F. B. Morse sends the first official telegraph message from Washington, D.C., to Baltimore, Maryland.

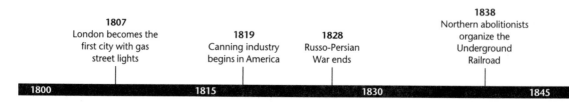

| 1807 | 1819 | 1828 | 1838 |
| London becomes the first city with gas street lights | Canning industry begins in America | Russo-Persian War ends | Northern abolitionists organize the Underground Railroad |

| 1800 | 1815 | 1830 | 1845 |

1846: Elias Howe patents his sewing machine. Isaac M. Singer will market a more practical sewing machine within four years.

1851: U.S. technology exhibits impress visitors at the Crystal Palace Exhibition of London, the first world's fair.

1852 Samuel Colt opens a large arms manufacturing factory, using advanced mass-production techniques.

1859 The first successful effort to drill for oil gives rise to the oil industry.

1860: Shoemakers in Lynn, Massachusetts, launch a massive strike for better wages and working conditions. The strike will spread to factories over a wide area and include as many as twenty thousand men and women workers.

1862: The Pacific Railroad Act calls for building a transcontinental railroad from Omaha, Nebraska, to Sacramento, California.

1862: Congress enacts the Homestead Act, which provides small pieces of public land to settlers in the West for farming; industry soon expands into the new territories.

1864: The first Bessemer converter, a new process for making steel, is introduced in the United States.

1866: The National Labor Union (NLU) is formed to promote the eight-hour workday.

1867: In the first cattle drive, organized by James G. McCoy, cattle are driven from Texas to Abilene, Kansas, where they are shipped by railroad to Chicago, Illinois.

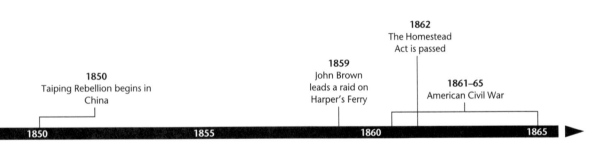

1850
Taiping Rebellion begins in China

1859
John Brown leads a raid on Harper's Ferry

1862
The Homestead Act is passed

1861–65
American Civil War

1850   1855   1860   1865

1867: The National Grange of the Patrons of Husbandry (usually called the Grange) is founded to advance the interests of farmers.

1869: The two railroad companies, the Union Pacific and the Central Pacific, commissioned to build the transcontinental railroad meet at Promontory Point, Utah, marking the completion of the first transcontinental railroad.

1869: The Knights of Labor, one of the early national labor unions, is founded.

1869: On September 24 or "Black Friday," the price of gold fell due to the speculations of James Fisk and Jay Gould, creating a financial panic.

1869: A fire in the Avondale coal mine in Pennsylvania kills 108 men and boys.

1872: Hunters and railroad workers have killed millions of buffalo on the Great Plains, reducing their numbers from 15 million to 7 million. The extermination will continue until less than one thousand buffalo remain in the 1890s.

1873: One of the nation's largest banks, owned by Jay Cooke, fails, causing business failures and unemployment. A nationwide depression follows.

1875: The National Farmers' Alliance is founded. It quickly divides into two groups, the Northern Alliance and the Southern Alliance.

1877: A large railroad strike begins in West Virginia to protest wage reductions. Within a few weeks, it spreads throughout the nation with about ten thousand participating workers. More than one hundred are killed by federal troops and about one thousand are jailed before the Great Strike is suppressed.

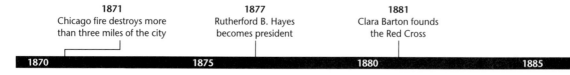

1871 Chicago fire destroys more than three miles of the city	1877 Rutherford B. Hayes becomes president	1881 Clara Barton founds the Red Cross
1870	1875	1880	1885

1886: The Haymarket Riots erupt in Chicago, pitting striking workers against police.

1886: The American Federation of Labor (AFL) reorganizes under the leadership of Samuel Gompers as a federation of trade unions formed to improve wages and working conditions, shorten working hours, abolish child labor, and provide for collective bargaining.

1886: The Colored Farmers' Alliance is founded.

1887: Congress passes the Interstate Commerce Act to regulate the railroads. It is the first regulatory act designed to establish government supervision over a major industry.

1889: James Buchanan Duke merges his tobacco company with four others to create the American Tobacco Company, controlling 90 percent of the U.S. tobacco industry.

1890: Congress enacts the Sherman Antitrust Act to prohibit companies from restricting competition or creating monopolies.

1890: The People's Party, better known as the Populists, is formed to combine the interests of farmers in the South and West and laborers nationwide to combat the powers of the Eastern industrialists.

1892: In the Homestead Strike, the workers at Andrew Carnegie's steel mills strike to protest low wages and the hiring of nonunion workers. A violent battle ensues, and the union in the steel mills is crushed.

1893: A financial panic, mainly due to the collapse of hundreds of railroad companies, results in a nationwide depression.

1894: When the workers at the Pullman factory go on strike for better wages, 125,000 railroad workers in the

1890 Battle of Wounded Knee | 1893 Lizzie Borden trial | 1896 Supreme Court rules on *Plessy v. Ferguson*

1890   1892   1894   1896

American Railway Union (ARU) join the strike to support the Pullman workers.

1900: New York City becomes grossly overpopulated, with about 1.2 million people, or about 75 percent of its population living in overcrowded tenement buildings without adequate water, air, sewage, or garbage removal.

1900: About 1.7 million children under the age of sixteen are working in factories.

1900: Industrial accidents kill about 35,000 workers each year and disable 500,000 others.

1900: African Americans begin to migrate from the South to Northern industrial cities. By 1910, 366,880 African Americans will migrate to Northern cities from the South. From 1910 to 1920 between five hundred thousand and one million African Americans will make the trip north.

1900: Several U.S. magazines present a new form of journalism called muckraking, which investigates corruption in big business and government.

1903: President Theodore Roosevelt creates a federal Department of Commerce and Labor to investigate the operations and conduct of corporations.

1903: Frederick Winslow Taylor publishes an essay about making the workplace more efficient that will quickly become the basis of a new movement of scientific business management, or Taylorism.

1904: The U.S. Supreme Court rules that the Northern Securities Trust, a combination of several railroads owned in a trust under the management of James J. Hill, Edward H. Harriman, and J. P. Morgan, is in violation of the Sherman Antitrust Act. It is the first major trust to be dissolved under the act.

1900	1901	1903	
Boxer Rebellion begins in China	President William McKinley is assassinated	Wright brothers make historic flight	
1900	1901	1903	1904

1907: A federal law against child labor is introduced to Congress, but it is defeated. Three years later, an estimated 2 million American children are still employed by industries.

1910: In the South, 80 percent of African American farmers and 40 percent of white farmers are either sharecroppers or tenant farmers struggling to survive.

1911: The U.S. Supreme Court rules that the Standard Oil Trust and the American Tobacco Company are in violation of the Sherman Antitrust Act and order them to dissolve.

1911: A fire at the Triangle Shirtwaist Company, a garment factory, kills 146 workers, mostly poor immigrant women and girls.

1914: Congress enacts the Clayton Antitrust Act, which updates the Sherman Antitrust Act and includes an important provision allowing workers to unionize and strike.

1920: For the first time in the United States, more people live in the city than in the country.

1927: Charles A. Lindbergh makes his famous 2,610-mile transatlantic (spanning the Atlantic Ocean) solo flight from Long Island, New York, to Paris, France, launching the aviation industry.

1932 Franklin Delano Roosevelt initiates his New Deal reforms, creating federal jobs, assisting farmers, protecting citizens from losing their homes to mortgage foreclosures, and enacting the Social Security Act to create an old-age pension system and paying benefits to the disabled and widows with children.

1938: Congress passes the Fair Labor Standards Act (FLSA), which sets a minimum wage for all workers, sets a maximum workweek of forty-four hours, and prohibits

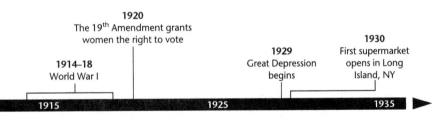

1920
The 19th Amendment grants women the right to vote

1914–18
World War I

1929
Great Depression begins

1930
First supermarket opens in Long Island, NY

1905   1915   1925   1935

interstate shipment of goods produced by children under the age of sixteen.

1945: During American participation in World War II, the number of workingwomen rises to 18.6 million, a 50 percent increase from the 11.9 million workingwomen of 1940.

1946: The first real computer, the Electronic Numerical Integrator and Computer (ENIAC), is introduced to the public, starting the computer age.

1969: The first personal computers are introduced.

1980s: Companies begin scale back production and staffs, and American factories begin to deteriorate as investors build factories in other countries to benefit from lower labor costs.

1990s: The U.S. workforce experiences a widespread shift from industrial labor to service labor, marking the start of the postindustrial era.

2000: Multinational corporations account for about 20 percent of the world's production.

1939–45
World War II

1957
Russian satellite *Sputnik 1* is launched

1975
Vietnam War ends

1986
Space shuttle *Challenger* explodes

1940   1955   1970   2000

Words to Know

A

anarchist: An individual who advocates the use of force to overthrow all government.

antitrust laws: Laws opposing or regulating trusts or similar business monopolies.

apprentice: Someone who is bound to work for someone else for a specific term in order to learn a trade.

aristocracy: A government controlled by a wealthy, privileged social class.

artisan: A person who is skilled at a particular trade or craft.

assimilation: The social process of being absorbed, or blending into the dominant culture.

aviation: The operation and manufacture of aircraft.

B

bankruptcy: A state of financial ruin in which an individual or corporation cannot pay its debts.

boiler: A tube (or several connected tubes) in which water is heated to steam.

bond: A certificate of debt issued by a government or corporation that guarantees repayment of the original investment with interest by a specified date.

boycott: Consumer refusal to buy a company's goods in order to express disapproval.

bureaucratic structure: An organization with many levels of authority, in which people specialize in their jobs and follow set rules of operation.

C

capital: Accumulated wealth or goods devoted to the production of other goods.

capitalism: An economic system in which the means of production and distribution are privately owned by individuals or groups and competition for business establishes the price of goods and services.

capitalist: A person who invests his or her wealth in business and industry.

compulsory attendance: Mandatory obligation to go to school.

Confederate states: The eleven Southern states that withdrew from the United States in 1860 and 1861.

conservation: Planned management of natural resources to prevent their misuse or loss.

consolidation: A process in which companies purchase other companies and fold them into one large corporation.

conveyor belt: A moving belt that carries materials from one place to another.

corporation: A company, or organization of employers and employees that is permitted by law, usually owned by a group of shareholders and established to carry out a business or industry as a body. Corporations have legal rights usually reserved for individuals, such as the right to sue and be sued and to borrow or loan money.

cylinder: A tube-shaped chamber or tank.

D

depression: A period of drastic decline in the economy.

directorates: Boards of directors of different companies that have at least one director in common.

E

entrepreneur: A person who organizes a new business.

evolution: Evolution is the process by which all plant and animal species of plant and animal change over time because of variations that are passed from one generation to the next. The theory of evolution was first proposed by naturalist Charles Darwin (1809–1882).

F

factory: A building or group of buildings in which manufactured goods are made from raw materials on a large scale.

feudalism: A system in which most people live and work on farms owned by a noble who grants it to them in exchange for their loyalty.

foreclosure: A legal process in which a borrower who does not make payments on a mortgage or loan is deprived of the mortgaged property.

G

gauge: Distance between the rails of a railroad track.

Gilded Age: The era of industrialization from the early 1860s to the turn of the century in which a few wealthy individuals gained tremendous power and influence.

grain elevators: Huge storage bins built next to railroad tracks to hold grain until it is loaded into train cars.

grant: A transfer or property by deed or writing.

Great Plains: An area of grassland that stretches across the central part of North America eastward from the Rocky Mountains, from Canada in the north down to Texas in the south.

gross national product (GNP): The total of all goods and services produced each year.

H

holding company: A company that is formed to own stocks and bonds in other companies, usually for the purpose of controlling them.

horizontal expansion: Growth occurring when a company purchases rival companies in the same industry in an effort to eliminate competition.

hydroelectric power plants: Plants that produce electricity from waterpower.

I

industrialism: The social system that results from an economy based on large-scale industries.

industrialists: People who engage in profit-making enterprises that manufacture a certain product, such as textiles or steel.

industrialization: The development of industry.

Industrial Revolution: A period of rapid industrial growth causing a shift in focus from agriculture to industry beginning in the late eighteenth century and continuing through the nineteenth century. During this time new manufacturing technologies and improved transportation gave rise to the modern factory system and a massive movement of the population from the countryside to the cities. The Industrial Revolution began in England around 1760 and spread to the United States around 1780.

industry: A distinct group of profit-making enterprises that manufacture a certain product, such as the textile or steel industry.

infant mortality: The percentage of babies born in a year that die before they reach the age of one.

intellectual: A person devoted to study, analysis, and reflection, using rational intellect rather than emotions in pursuit of enlightenment.

interchangeable parts: Standardized units of a machine that could be used in any machine of that model.

interstate commerce: Trade that crosses the borders between states.

L

labor union: An organization of workers formed to protect and further their mutual interests by bargaining as a group with their employers over wages, working conditions, and benefits.

laissez-faire: An economic doctrine that opposes government regulation of commerce and industry beyond the minimum necessary.

loom: A frame or machine used to weave thread or yarns into cloth.

M

machine tool: A machine that shapes solid materials.

machinist: A worker skilled in operating machine tools.

magnate: A powerful and influential person in an industry.

manufacture: To make something from raw materials, usually as part of a large-scale system of production using machinery.

mass production: The manufacture of goods in quantity by using machines and standardized designs and parts.

mechanize: To equip with mechanical power.

mediation: Intervention to help two opposing sides of a dispute reach an agreement.

monopoly: The exclusive possession or right to produce a particular good or service.

muckrakers: Journalists who search for and expose corruption in public affairs.

N

New Deal: A set of legislative programs and policies for economic recovery and social reform initiated in the 1930s during the presidency of Franklin Delano Roosevelt.

O

omnibus: A horse-drawn coach for hire.

overhead expenses: The costs of running a business not directly related to producing the goods, such as rent or heating and lighting the workspace.

overproduction: An economic condition that occurs when there are more goods on the market than there are consumers to purchase them, usually leading to lower prices.

P

patent: A legal document issued by a government granting exclusive authority to an inventor for making, using, and selling an invention.

pension: A fixed sum paid regularly, usually as a retirement benefit.

philanthropy: The desire or effort to help humankind, as by making charitable donations.

pools: Agreements among rival companies to share their profits or divide up territories to avoid destructive competition and maintain higher prices.

postindustrial era: A time marked by the lessened importance of manufacturing and increased importance of service industries.

productivity: The amount of work someone can do in a set amount of time.

Progressive Era: The period of the Industrial Revolution that spanned roughly from the 1890s to about 1920, in which reformers worked together in the interest of distributing political power and wealth more equally.

public domain: Land held by the federal government.

pulley: Simple machine consisting of a wheel with a groove through which a rope passes. The pulley is used to move things up, down, or across, such as a flagpole or a curtain rod.

R

refinery: A building in which a raw material is processed to free it from impurities.

reservations: Land set aside by the U.S. government for use by Native Americans.

robots: Machines that automatically perform routine, often complex, tasks.

S

settlement houses: Places established and run by educated, and often wealthy, reformers to provide social and educational services to the residents of poor urban immigrant communities.

sharecropper: A tenant farmer who works the land for an agreed share of the value of the crop, minus the deductions taken out of his share for his rent, supplies, and living costs.

shuttle: A device that carries threads across a loom in the weaving process.

slums: Severely overcrowded urban areas characterized by the most extreme conditions of poverty, run-down housing, and crime.

speculator: A person who takes a business risk in the hope of making a profit, particularly when buying or selling stocks or commodities (economic goods) in order to profit from shifts in the market.

socialism: An economic system in which the means of production and distribution is owned collectively by all the workers and there is no private property or social classes.

solidarity: Unity based on common interests.

steam engine: An engine that burns fuel to heat water into steam, which becomes the power that turns the parts of the engine.

stock: An element of ownership of a corporation that has been divided up into shares that can be bought and sold.

stock market: A system for trade in companies, ventures, and other investments through the buying and selling of stocks, bonds, mutual funds, limited partnerships, and other securities.

strike: A work stoppage by employees to protest conditions or make demands of their employer.

sweatshop: A factory in which workers work long hours in poor conditions for very low wages.

T

tariffs: Government-imposed fees on imported goods.

telegraph: Any system that transmits encoded information by signal across a distance.

tenant farmer: Someone who farms land owned by someone else and pays rent or a share of the crop for the use of the land.

tenement: Urban dwellings rented by impoverished families that barely meet or fail to meet the minimum standards of safety, sanitation, and comfort.

textile: Cloth.

transcontinental: Spanning the continent from one coast to the other.

transcontinental railroad: A railroad that spans a continent, from coast to coast.

trusts: A group of companies, joined for the purpose of reducing competition and controlling prices..

turnover: Employees quitting their jobs and others being hired to take their place.

turnpike: A road which people have to pay to use.

V

ventilation: Air circulation or access to fresh air.

vertical expansion: Growth that occurs when a primary company purchases other companies that provide services or products needed for the company's business, in order to avoid paying competitive prices.

W

wage worker: A person who works for others for pay.

Wall Street: Financial district and home of the nation's major stock exchanges in New York, New York.

warp yarn: The threads that run lengthwise on a loom.

waterwheel: A wheel that rotates due to the force of moving water; the rotation of the wheel is then used to power a factory or machine.

woof: The threads that run crosswise on a loom.

work ethic: A belief in the moral good of work.

workers' compensation: Payments made to an employee who is injured at work.

Y

Yankee: A Southern word for Northerners.

Research and Activity Ideas

Research: Invention and innovations

Choose one of the following American inventors: Eli Whitney, Oliver Evans, Samuel Colt, Robert Fulton, Samuel F. B. Morse, or Cyrus McCormick. Research his life and invention at the library and/or on the Internet. Then write a one- or two-page essay on the inventor, focusing mainly on his invention and how it advanced industrialism in the United States. Be sure to discuss the inventor's business efforts with the invention.

Activity: Business monopolies

Form a group of four. Prior to the day of the activity each member should read about the rise of big business monopolies from the early 1860s to the 1920s. Then the group should play the board game *Monopoly*. Afterward, discuss among your group the principles of business monopolies that arose in the game. Begin by discussing what a monopoly is. Who in the game achieved a monopoly, or came close? What was the effect of the monopolies? What kinds of competition were presented in the game? How did competition affect each player?

Research: Social Darwinism

Research the concept of social Darwinism, or the "survival of the fittest" in the social and economic world. Write a paragraph briefly explaining what social Darwinism is. Then write one paragraph discussing the reasons that some people thought it was a good way of thinking about society. Next write a paragraph discussing the reasons that some people thought it was wrong. Finally, write a brief paragraph stating what you think about social Darwinism.

Group Activity: Robber barons

Prepare for this activity by reading about such major industrialists as Cornelius Vanderbilt, John D. Rockefeller, Andrew Carnegie, J. P. Morgan, Jay Gould, James J. Hill, Daniel Drew, James Fisk, and others. Separate into two groups for a debate. One side should argue that these men were "robber barons," a ruthless and greedy bunch that would stop at nothing in pursuit of their own fortunes. The other side should argue that these men were the "captains of industry," responsible for making the United States the richest industrial nation of the world.

Research: The Model T

Write a report on Henry Ford's Model T, first produced in 1909. Be sure to address some of the following questions in your report: What was new and different about the way that the Ford Motor Company made this car? How did the assembly line work? How did the manufacture of the Model T change U.S. industry? Try to find a picture of the Model T to accompany your report.

Classroom Discussion: Collective bargaining

Prepare for this activity by reading about labor unions and the major industrial strikes of the late nineteenth and early twentieth centuries. For this exercise, the class becomes a manufacturing company—the name of the company and the product it makes can be decided by the class. Divide the class in two. On Side 1 are the company's workers, who are part of a labor union. On Side 2 are the company management. A strike is looming.

Side 1: Workers. The workers are dissatisfied with their pay of $2.00 per day and want to be paid $3.00 per day. They want to work eight hours a day instead of the twelve-hour days they are now working. Machinery in the factories is in bad condition, causing accidents and the workers want the machines fixed or replaced. For the workers a strike will mean a loss of wages, but they are willing to face the hardships for what they believe are fair demands.

Side 2: Management. The company's owners and managers have refused to grant the union's demands. They fear that if the company increases workers' salaries, decreases working hours, and fixing or replacing machines, it will not be able to keep up with its competitors and could even collapse at some point in the future. Furthermore, management knows it can hire people who have recently immigrated to the United States to do the job for less pay than its union workers. They wish to avoid the strike, which will stop their production, but they are unwilling to allow workers to dictate their own terms of employment.

The two sides are about to meet one final time to try to come to a compromise and avoid a strike. Each group should meet separately for fifteen minutes and prepare to negotiate with the other side. Pick a leader to state your side's position, presenting strong arguments for its position. When the two sides meet to negotiate, the two leaders will present their summaries. Then debate and negotiations can begin, involving all members. Try to work toward a compromise, while remembering your side's interests.

Research: Progressive Era
Write an essay describing the Progressive Movement. Include the following information. When did the movement begin, approximately? What American groups were part of it? Who were its leaders? What did the Progressives want? What kinds of reforms did they advocate? What were some of their accomplishments? When, approximately, did the Progressive Movement end?

Research and classroom discussion: Microsoft and Bill Gates
Research the history of Microsoft and its founder, Bill Gates, at the library and on the Internet. Discuss in the classroom the way that Gates transformed the personal computer industry

and some of the ways that Microsoft came to dominate the personal computer software industry. What made Microsoft so successful? How did Microsoft deal with its competitors? Also discuss Gates's philanthropy. Compare and contrast Gates to industrialists Andrew Carnegie and John D. Rockefeller.

Development of the Industrial U.S.

Almanac

Industrialism Takes Root in the United States

At the time of the American Revolution (1775–83; the American colonists' fight for independence from England) the earliest elements of another revolution—the Industrial Revolution—were taking root in the farms, workshops, businesses, and towns of the new nation. These elements included the development and use of labor-saving machines, the production of goods on a large scale, the employment of many laborers in one large operation, new management systems, and the efficient transportation of raw materials and manufactured goods. Industrialism was to have a profound effect on the way people lived in the United States, dramatically changing the nation's economy and way of life and transforming the United States from a rural (country) farming society into an urban (city) industrial society. Most historians agree that the Industrial Revolution took place over more than a century of U.S. history. The early roots that developed between the American Revolution and the American Civil War (1861–65; a war between the Union [the North], who opposed slavery, and the Confederacy [the South], who were in favor of slavery) unfolded slowly and only in certain sections of the country, but they set the stage

The first Slater mill, in Pawtucket, Rhode Island. *(© Bettmann/Corbis.)*

for a powerful and rapid industrial expansion that, over the next half century, would make the United States the wealthiest and most powerful industrial nation in the world.

The Industrial Revolution in England

Though the United States would eventually become the most industrialized nation of the world, the Industrial Revolution first took shape in England in the early eighteenth

Words to Know

apprentice: Someone who is bound to work for someone else for a specific term in order to learn a trade.

artisan: A person who is skilled at a particular trade or craft.

capital: Accumulated wealth or goods devoted to the production of other goods.

economic depression: A period of low economic activity and increasing unemployment.

factory: A building or group of buildings in which manufactured goods are made from raw materials on a large scale.

industrialism: The social system that results from an economy based on large-scale industries.

loom: A frame or machine used to weave thread or yarns into cloth.

manufacture: To make something from raw materials, usually as part of a large-scale system of production using machinery.

mechanize: To equip with mechanical power.

shuttle: A device that carries threads across a loom in the weaving process.

textile: Cloth.

century. England had long been a farming country. During the seventeenth century, however, it had experienced a dramatic increase in population. There was not enough land for everyone to farm and most farmland passed into the hands of the wealthy aristocrats. Many of the poorest people moved to the cities to try to find work. Some of England's artisans (people who are skilled at a particular trade or craft) set out to discover better ways to feed the growing population. The artisans designed new farm machinery that could do large amounts of work with fewer people. New tools for farming created larger crops that could feed the growing populations in the cities and towns.

The English textile industry

English workers who could no longer find work on farms began to spend more time at other trades, particularly the production of textiles, or cloth. Prior to the 1730s most English textiles were produced in the home. People called spinners spun thread from raw fibers like cotton, wool, or flax on a spinning wheel or by hand. They sold the thread to cloth merchants, who brought it to the homes of weavers to be woven into cloth. This process took so long that the cloth merchants could not keep up with the demand for their goods. Then, in the 1730s English engineer John Kay (1704–1764) designed the flying shuttle to speed up the pace of weaving. A shuttle is a device that carries threads across the loom (a frame or machine used for weaving thread or yarns into cloth). With the new flying shuttle a weaver simply pulled a cord and the shuttle shot across the loom by itself. Using the flying shuttle, fabrics could be woven twice as fast as they could be woven manually.

Spinning was mechanized (equipped with mechanical power) in 1764 when English weaver James Hargreaves (1720–1778) perfected an existing design for a machine called the spinning jenny, which could spin several threads at a time. At around the same time English inventor and manufacturer Richard Arkwright (1732–1792) designed his spinning frame, a spinning machine powered by a water-driven wheel. Around 1771 Arkwright built a waterwheel-operated mill (a building with machinery to produce a certain product) to power his spinning frame. The new spinning machine could spin thread by mechanically reproducing the motions ordinarily made by the human hand. Arkwright's cotton mill is often considered the world's first factory. A factory is a building or group of buildings in which many people work to manufacture goods, generally with labor-saving machines powered by a central source.

The English iron and steel industries

New ways of producing iron and steel transformed life in England in the eighteenth century. In order to convert iron ores to iron and steel, manufacturers heated the raw materials using charcoal as fuel. Charcoal is made by burning wood in a kiln. After many years of cutting down trees for this purpose, wood had become scarce in England and iron and steel producers had to look for another fuel. They found this fuel in coke, which is what coal turns into when it is heated in the absence of air. Coke was cheaper to produce than charcoal and more efficient because it could be packed more tightly into a furnace, therefore allowing a larger volume of iron to be heated. But there was a problem with coke. It required a flow of air to pass

The spinning jenny, designed by James Hargreaves. *(UPI/Corbis-Bettmann.)*

through the furnace that was more intense than any machine available could create. The answer to this problem lay in the latest designs of the steam engine.

The early steam engine

The steam engine provided the vital new power source of the Industrial Revolution. A steam engine burns wood or other fuel to heat water into steam. The steam then becomes the power that turns the parts of the engine. The first steam engines had been designed in the seventeenth century to pump water from mines. In 1712 English engineer Thomas Newcomen (1663–1729) greatly improved the steam engine, and in 1765 Scottish engineer James Watt (1736–1819) improved Newcomen's design. Watt's steam engine was equipped with a cooling system that could cool down the steam and transform it back into water, using much less fuel than previous designs. The Watts

James Watt working on improvements to the Newcomen steam engine.
(© Stefano Bianchetti/Corbis.)

steam engine could be used to power mills, so factories no longer needed to be near a source of moving water to power a waterwheel. By the last decade of the eighteenth century, steam-engine-powered factories were being built throughout England. Using steam engines, iron and steel production became a thriving new industry.

Social changes in England

England prospered from its new industrialism. The country was able to produce the goods needed by its citizens with plenty left over to export to other nations. Many industrialists grew rich and invested in new mills, creating more goods and more jobs. People were able to purchase goods for less money because these products were cheaper to manufacture. Running a household became less laborious because less time was spent making the household goods. But industrialization was not beneficial for everyone. The people who worked in the factories often found their living conditions much worse than in a farming environment. They now faced repetitive, unhealthy, and sometimes dangerous work, long working hours, low pay, and miserable living conditions in the factory towns.

The new United States

In 1790 the newly formed United States lagged far behind England in industrialization. Of the five million people living in the country at the end of the century, more than 80 percent were farmers. Only two cities, New York and Philadelphia, had populations over twenty thousand people. One reason that industrialism was slow to develop in America was that England had always supplied the colonies with manufactured goods, but there were many other difficulties to overcome before the United States could become a productive industrial nation.

Early Americans found transportation a difficult problem, due to the size of the nation and its primitive road system. There were few roads before the Revolution, and those that existed were rugged dirt paths unsuitable for anything beyond foot or horse traffic. The Ohio and Mississippi rivers were principal transportation routes. But most manufactured goods were brought into the East Coast port cities from Europe. Transportation was so limited in the United States it was easier and cheaper to ship materials thousands of miles across the Atlantic than to cross a few hundred miles of land.

American farmers were much more isolated than European farmers and had to rely on their own abilities to farm and raise animals, make and fix their tools, and keep their families supplied with the goods necessary for their survival. For most rural Americans, shopping meant an occasional stop at the one store in town, called a mercantile. The store was stocked with every foreseeable need of the people—clothing, food, animal feed, pots and pans, farm tools, seeds, and much more. The manufactured goods, for the most part, came from England. The English merchants made a profit on them and so did the owner of the mercantile, making the goods too expensive for most people to be able to afford them. In order to be able to buy tools and other necessities, many farmers took up another occupation in the off-seasons of farming, making goods such as cloth or shoes to sell or trade. The farmers in the new nation were a particularly self-reliant group. They were full of new ideas and inventions, but there were few networks through which their breakthroughs in farming or manufacturing technology could spread.

Another factor delaying industrialism in the United States was a lack of money. There were some very wealthy people in the young nation, but there were very few people who could afford to risk great amounts of capital (accumulated wealth or goods devoted to the production of other goods) for the untested industrialization of the United States.

Visions of the future United States

Industrialization was not universally desired by the people of the new nation. Well before the American Revolution, there was controversy over whether the nation should maintain its farming economy or move toward an industrial economy like England's. The founding fathers of the young nation had decided not to follow in England's political footsteps. Instead they created a democratic republic, a society in which government gets its authority by popular vote. Many saw a possibility for a new kind of society in which everyone, no matter what social class they were born into, had equal rights. Some believed that if the United States were to follow in England's economic footsteps, it would lead to the kinds of inequalities among social classes that existed in England.

After the American Revolution, England resumed its practice of exporting manufactured goods to the United States. The United States was forced to pay the prices England demanded but had little to trade. An economic depression (a period of low economic activity and increasing unemployment) ensued, stimulating debate over whether the United States should produce its own goods in efficient factories or continue upon its farming course, allowing England to drain the country of its money and resources. Two of the best-known arguers of this debate were the U.S. statesmen Thomas Jefferson (1743–1826) and Alexander Hamilton (1755–1804).

Thomas Jefferson's pro-agricultural vision

Thomas Jefferson served as secretary of state under the first U.S. president, George Washington (1732–1799; served 1789–97). Jefferson was always a supporter of poor, laboring Americans, though he was a very wealthy slave owner himself. He firmly believed that the way to provide a prosperous and dignified life for all Americans was to create a society of independent farmers. Jefferson argued that farming was the one truly virtuous occupation. As land-owning farmers, every man, woman, and child could determine their own destinies and participate in the nation as equal citizens.

Jefferson argued that factory systems led to an unequal class system in which the working class would always be viewed as brute workers, inferior to, and with fewer rights than, their employers. He feared that workers in an industrial system would become vir-

Thomas Jefferson argued that America should maintain its farming economy, rather than follow in England's industrial footsteps. *(© Bettmann/Corbis. Reproduced by permission.)*

tually enslaved to the industrialists, who would most probably try to pay them the lowest possible wages in order to turn a large profit. The workers, having no better opportunities, would be forced to take whatever tiny wages their employers decided to give them. Having witnessed miserable conditions in England, Jefferson urged Americans to avoid dooming the working poor to the dreadful environment of the factory. In his book, *Notes on the State of Virginia* (1785), Jefferson argued: "Let us never wish to see our citizens occupied at a work-bench, or twirling a distaff [an implement for holding fibers when spinning].... For the general operations of manufacture, let our workshops remain in Europe." Many Americans agreed and sought to preserve the agricultural basis of the nation.

Alexander Hamilton's pro-manufacturing vision

Alexander Hamilton, who played a large role in the shaping of U.S. economic policy as the secretary of treasury under Washington, was an outspoken proponent of industrialization. He argued that American dependence on manufactured goods from England and Europe weakened the economy and lowered the international status of the United States. He sought to replace the home crafts system of producing necessary goods with machine-driven factory production. Hamilton argued that an urbanized and industrial economy would not enslave the workers but rather create many new opportunities for them. In 1791 Hamilton presented to Congress his famous report, *Report on Manufactures*. He recommended that the government nurture "infant industries," or those U.S. businesses that were just getting started, by placing tariffs (taxes) on imports from overseas. If these products became too expensive for the public to buy them, it would stimulate production at home of necessary goods. Although his recommendations were not immediately put into practice, Hamilton's vision of a powerful industrial United States accurately forecast things to come.

English restrictions on U.S. industry

England had never been willing to allow the United States to participate in its successes as an industrial nation. It did not want competition and did not want to lose the American colonies as the primary market for English goods. Before the American Revolution, England had imposed many restrictions upon the colonies to prevent industrialization. A 1719 law, for example, forbade the practice of metalworking. A 1750 law was more restrictive, explicitly prohibiting the use of a mill "or other engine for slitting or rolling iron, or any plating forge to work with a tilt hammer, or any furnace for making steel." These restrictions angered the colonists and helped to fuel the revolution. After the United States gained its independence in 1783, England tried to preserve its dominant control over modern textile manufacturing. The English government refused to allow plans or models of industrial machinery to leave the country. It also prohibited the emigration (departure) of skilled workers who might share the secret designs of their machinery with industrialists in foreign lands.

Samuel Slater and the early U.S. textile industry

In the late 1780s a number of businessmen sought to industrialize the production of textiles in the United States. They found that England thoroughly controlled the industry and was not about to share the secrets of the trade. Several American textile companies began to offer rewards to mill workers who would immigrate to America, bringing their knowledge of textile machinery with them. One of the Englishmen lured across the ocean in this way was Samuel Slater (1768–1835).

When Slater was fourteen, his father died and Slater was apprenticed (bound to work for someone for a specific term in order to learn a trade) to a neighbor, textile industrialist Jebediah Strutt (1726–1797). Just a few years earlier, Strutt had entered into partnership with inventor Richard Arkwright (1732–1792) to construct the first spinning frame powered by a waterwheel. Strutt employed Slater as the supervisor of one of his textile mills. For six and a half years Slater learned about the process of manufacturing cotton yarn. At the end of his apprenticeship he decided to immigrate to the United States. Since it was illegal to export textile technology, such as parts, designs, and sketches, Slater memorized the construction plans for the Arkwright factory. He did not tell anyone of his decision to leave the country; even his family did not learn of his departure until receiving a letter a few days after Slater left. At the docks, Slater told authorities that he was a farm laborer so they would allow him to leave the country.

Slater arrived in Philadelphia in 1789. He found textile production in the United States to be very crude and inefficient. Within a few months Slater made contact with Moses Brown of the Almy and Brown textile firm. Brown offered to make Slater a partner in the firm if he would convert one of Brown's existing mills into an English-style textile factory. Slater accepted. At Brown's old mill in Pawtucket, Rhode Island, Slater designed and built the essential machinery for a cotton mill; his machines were almost identical to machines found in English mills. In 1793 Slater's mill began producing high-quality cotton yarn. The unskilled workers in his mill were generally children between the ages of four and ten. They were paid wages for their work, but very low wages.

Slater's Early Cotton Mills

In his first mill in Pawtucket, Rhode Island, Samuel Slater revolutionized the new U.S. textile industry by building several machines—three carding machines, two water frames, and a carding and roving machine—that mechanized the spinning process. When cleaned, raw cotton fibers were brought into a textile mill. The first step of the spinning process was carding, a process of combing fibers and gathering them into a loose rope. Before mechanization, carding had been done by laboriously pulling cotton fibers by hand through wire teeth mounted on a board. The ropes of carded cotton fiber were then combined, twisted, and drawn out into a roving, a tightened and aligned roll of the cotton fibers. Slater's new carding machine was equipped with a large cylinder (a tube-shaped chamber or tank) covered with slightly bent teeth sticking up from its surface. There were corresponding teeth protruding from flat surfaces just above the cylinder. The roving was fed into the teeth, and when the cylinder rotated, the roving was tightened and aligned between the two sets of teeth. The machine replaced hand carding and did the work much more quickly.

Prior to mechanization, spinners used a spinning wheel, which twisted and drew out the roving and wound the yarn onto a bobbin. The person operating the spinning wheel had to continually draw out the yarn by hand. Slater's mechanized spinning frame did the same job. The roving passed through a system of rolls and spindles that reduced them to the required yarn size. Then they were wound onto small bobbins (spindles or cylinders on which threads or yarns are wound). The machine could produce forty-eight lengths of yarn at the same time without human assistance. Operating the spinning frame required no skill; the operator simply fed it with roving and made sure that no threads broke and the machine remained running.

Slater's mill was powered by a waterwheel. Water from the river on which the mill was situated was channeled into a canal that flowed to a drop-off point. There, a waterwheel equipped with buckets caught the water as it fell to a lower level. The buckets filled with water, propelling the wheel around. The power from the wheel's rotation was then transferred to the mill's many machines via shafts running from the wheel to each floor of the mill. The process was slow and noisy, but it was far more efficient than spinning cotton yarn by hand.

In 1789 Almy, Brown, and Slater opened a second mill, then a third, and eventually controlled the production of cotton yarn in much of Rhode Island, Massachusetts, and New Hampshire. Slater is considered the founder of the American cotton-textile industry. By bringing English technology to the United States, he played a crucial role in setting the wheels of U.S. industrialization in motion.

For More Information

Books

Bagley, Katie. *Let Freedom Ring: The Early American Industrial Revolution, 1793–1850.* Mankato, MN: Bridgestone Books, 2003.

Bailey, Thomas A., David M. Kennedy, and Lizabeth Cohen. *The American Pageant.* 11th ed. Boston, MA: Houghton Mifflin, 1998.

Hindle, Brooke, and Steven Lubar. *Engines of Change: The American Industrial Revolution, 1790–1860.* Washington, DC and London: Smithsonian Institution Press, 1986.

Kornblith, Gary J. *The Industrial Revolution in America.* Boston, MA: Houghton Mifflin, 1998.

McCormick, Anita Louise. *The Industrial Revolution in American History.* Berkeley Heights, NJ: Enslow Publishers, 1998.

Web Sites

Hamilton, Alexander. "Report on Manufacturers." (December 5, 1791). *The Founders' Constitution.* Edited by Philip B. Kurland and Ralph Lerner. http://press-pubs.uchicago.edu/founders/documents/v1ch4s31.html (accessed on June 30, 2005).

Jefferson, Thomas. "Notes on the State of Virginia." (1st edition 1785). *Electronic Text Center, University of Virginia Library.* http://etext.lib.virginia.edu/toc/modeng/public/JefVirg.html (accessed on June 30, 2005).

Kreis, Steven. "The Origins of the Industrial Revolution in England." *The History Guide: Lectures on Modern European Intellectual History.* http://www.historyguide.org/intellect/lecture17a.html (accessed on June 30, 2005).

2

Transportation and Communication Systems in the New Nation

W hen the United States gained its independence from England in the American Revolution (1775–83), the majority of American colonists lived within one hundred miles of the East Coast. They received manufactured goods, such as clothing, tools, and pottery, from Europe and paid for them with American raw materials, particularly timber, tobacco, fish, and grain. But as the nineteenth century began, available farmland along the East Coast of the United States was decreasing and large numbers of people began moving to lands west of the Appalachian Mountains. There were few roads in the western United States and it was highly expensive and time-consuming to transport goods there. Not only did farmers in the West need manufactured goods from the East, but East Coast merchants also needed crops from the West, and early textile industrialists needed cotton from the South. What was sorely lacking was the means to efficiently move goods where they were needed.

Most Americans understood that building transportation systems was essential to the prosperity of their new country, but the size and complexity of the job ahead of them was

Early U.S. roads were rough and muddy, making travel difficult and dangerous. *(© Bettmann/Corbis.)*

daunting. It was not clear whether private individuals, states, or the federal government would pay the tremendous expenses. Furthermore, as the century began, many forms of transportation that would prove useful in the future—particularly steamboats and railroads—had either not been invented or had not been adapted to the needs of the rugged American landscape. Despite the obstacles, roads, canals, steamboats, and railroads spread throughout the young nation over the next fifty years, built by the initiatives of the local and federal governments, private investments, and rising new businesses. Communication systems, connecting people across the vast country through letters, newspapers, and, later, telegraph messages, followed the path created by transportation systems.

Roads

At the time of independence, the only roads available to most Americans outside of the northern East Coast states were rough rural roads, many of which had been created by Native Americans in eras before the colonists arrived in the New World. The existing roads were muddy, prone to flooding, and filled with stumps and boulders, making travel by stagecoach or wagon difficult and dangerous. A few wealthy businessmen in the East had invested in turnpikes, roads built for profit, which people had to pay to use. But the turnpikes were expensive to build and usually did not make a profit. Additionally, none of the turnpikes crossed the Appalachian Mountains, which left the West and much of the South without good road systems.

In 1817 Congress authorized the construction of the National Road, also called the Cumberland Road, from western Maryland to the Ohio River at Wheeling, Virginia (in present-day West Virginia). It was the first road to run across the Appalachian Mountains and into the territory known as the Old Northwest, which was composed of the modern-day states of Ohio, Indiana, Illinois, Michigan, and Wisconsin. The National Road, the largest single road-building project to occur before the twentieth century, caused considerable controversy, as many people firmly believed the federal government should leave internal improvements to the states.

Nonetheless, by 1818 a useful roadway had been built, with gravel surfaces graded, or leveled off, to limit water damage and stone bridges to cross waterways. For a few decades, the National Road operated very much like a modern interstate highway. Every day commercial carriers, family passenger vehicles, and public conveyances maneuvered for room on its 30-foot-wide surface.

River traffic

For many Americans in the early nineteenth century, water transportation along the nation's river systems was the only way to move goods and produce. Before 1840 most of the produce grown in the Old Northwest was carried to market by flatboats on the Ohio and Mississippi Rivers. Flatboats were light, shallow boats about eight to ten feet wide and thirty or forty feet long with a cabin on deck. Rivers presented a very basic problem: traveling downstream was relatively easy, as flatboats were built to travel downstream, but moving upstream was extremely slow and difficult. Keelboats, constructed around a rigid timber in their center, were equipped with sails and built to go upstream. However, there was little wind in the heavily forested Mississippi Valley, so keelboats often relied on the muscle power of eight- to twenty-man crews to pole, row, or drag (using ropes flung over tree limbs) them upstream. Flatboats and keelboats were the most common kinds of river craft used in the early part of the century. Each year between 1815 and 1840 an average of 2,500 flatboats carrying the surplus grain, flour, pork, whiskey, and lumber of the Ohio Valley sailed down the smaller rivers of Indiana, Illinois, Kentucky, and Ohio and on into the Mississippi River, bound for the markets of the South or for the bustling city of New Orleans.

Steamboats

By the late eighteenth century, many engineers in the United States were exploring the idea of powering boats with steam engines. Steam engines burn fuel to heat water into steam, which becomes the power that turns the parts of the engine. In 1787 U.S. mechanic John Fitch (1743–1798) demonstrated to potential investors the first working American steamboat, a boat equipped with twelve paddles propelled by a small steam engine. By 1790 Fitch had established passenger steamboat service on the Delaware River, providing service between Philadelphia, Pennsylvania, and Burlington, New Jersey, on steamboats that traveled at a rate of about four miles an hour. Invention was only half the battle, though. Finding the money to fund the new enterprise was more difficult. Like many other inventions of the early industrial era, Fitch's venture failed financially before the public understood its value.

Other inventors continued to work on the design of the steamboat. In 1787 inventor James Rumsey (1743–1792) created the world's first boat moved by jet propulsion. His boat was equipped with a steam engine, which powered a pump that took water in at the helm and expelled it from the stern (rear) in a jet stream, thus achieving a forward push. In 1804 engineer John Stevens (1749–1838) built a successful steamboat with a new high-pressure steam engine and twin screw propellers. He made plans for a bigger boat that he hoped to use to carry passengers and freight across the Hudson River between New York City and Albany, New York. However, steamboat builder Robert Fulton (1765–1815) accomplished this task before Stevens.

Fulton succeeded where others had not because he promoted his steamboat well and worked with talented and influential people. He managed to secure a monopoly (the exclusive possession or right to produce a particular good or service) on Hudson River steam transportation, as state governments were generally happy to grant monopolies as incentives for individuals to create much-needed services and products. Fulton imported an engine built by Scottish inventor James Watt (1736–1819) and used it to power a 133-foot steamboat, the *Clermont*. On August 17, 1807, Fulton's boat made its maiden voyage from New York City to Albany in thirty-two hours. Fulton continued to improve his design and add boats to his fleet.

By the 1830s steamboats crowded the inland waterways of the United States. Steamboats expanded trade to towns and

Robert Fulton's steamboat the *Clermont*. *(Bettmann/Corbis.)*

cities located along navigable waterways (deep and wide enough for boats to pass). St. Louis, Missouri, for example, utilized the steamboat to develop trade throughout the entire Mississippi and Ohio River Valleys. Steamboat construction became a thriving industry, with towns such as Louisville, Kentucky, Pittsburgh, Pennsylvania, and Cincinnati, Ohio, becoming centers of technology that supplied most of the steam engines.

Canals

Still, many of the best farming districts in the Old Northwest had no river access to the markets back East. Canals, man-made waterways built for inland transportation, seemed to provide a solution. After much controversy over the practicality of building a canal to connect New York City to the Old Northwest, in April 1817 the state of New York authorized funding for the construction of the Erie Canal, a 363-mile canal linking Albany on the Hudson River with Buffalo, New York, on Lake Erie.

Upon its completion in 1825 the Erie Canal was already carrying monumental traffic along its 4-foot-deep and 40-foot-wide channel. The canal opened an inexpensive route for Western goods, especially lumber, grain, and flour, to flow into the Hudson and then out into world markets from the New York ports of Manhattan and Brooklyn. Moving in the other direction, manufactured goods swept west along the new channel. The Erie Canal cut the cost of sending goods from Buffalo to New York City from its prior cost of about $100 a ton to less than $8 a ton. Between 1830 and 1847 well over half of all American imports traveled through New York City's harbor, making it the biggest port in the country.

Along the canal new towns and industries were established. The canal provided access to the Great Lakes, which were soon crowded with hundreds of steamships. Small towns on the banks of the Great Lakes, such as Chicago, Illinois, Detroit, Michigan, and Cleveland, Ohio, grew into massive cities. Due to the success of the Erie Canal, many states rushed to build their own canals. Between 1810 and 1840 canal mileage in the United States increased from 100 miles to over 3,300 miles.

Railroads

As the canals were being built, the most revolutionary effort to expand U.S. transportation was underway: the construction of railroads. Most of the first railroads in America hauled goods short distances, often from ships to warehouses, using horses or oxen for power. The concept of the railroad as a means of long-distance transportation may have originated with John Stevens, the inventor who developed one of the first steamboats. In 1825 Stevens built a half-mile circular track on his estate in New Jersey and created the first steam locomotive to run on rails in the United States. Though his invention was not ready for commercial use, the idea sparked interest among other inventors. Around this time, English engineer George Stephenson (1781–1848) designed a successful steam locomotive in England. The world's first steam-powered, public passenger train, the British Stockton & Darlington Railway, soon began operation, and railroads quickly took over as England's major transportation system.

A Baltimore & Ohio locomotive. *(© Bettmann/Corbis.)*

In 1826 a group of Baltimore, Maryland, businessmen began looking for a way their city could compete with the now-bustling port city of New York. They decided to launch the first American railway, named the Baltimore and Ohio (B & O) because it extended between Baltimore and the Ohio River. The businessmen estimated that they would need about three million dollars to fund the venture. They received approval from the state of Maryland to create a corporation—a legal arrangement in which many individuals owned portions, or shares, of one large company. The three million dollars needed to support the venture was to be raised by the sale of stock shares to the public. The public was very enthusiastic about the railroad, and the stock sold in twelve days, distributed among twenty-two thousand individuals. In the end, nearly every family in the state had purchased stock in the company.

Incorporation

An enterprise as costly as building a railroad or creating a factory with heavy machinery and a large work force demanded more money than any one individual could invest. Prior to 1809 people wishing to participate in joint economic enterprises usually formed partnerships, in which each partner was personally liable, or responsible, for the entire debt of the organization. Corporations became the solution for financing such large-scale business ventures after 1809, when courts began to recognize the right of private enterprises to incorporate. State charters set the terms by which these early corporations would be run.

Corporations offered many benefits to industrialists. The corporation was, and still is, a limited-liability organization. That is, each investor risked only the capital (accumulated wealth or goods devoted to the production of other goods) he or she put into it. Corporations were stable, secure, and protected by state laws. They could endure over long periods of time because they did not have to legally reorganize every time an owner died or transferred his ownership. Additionally, a corporation was treated by the courts as a legal "person"; it could establish contracts, sue and be sued, and own property just like an individual person.

Corporations were essential to the rise of industry in the United States because they could raise huge amounts of capital by "going public," that is, selling ownership shares to anyone who wanted them. The huge amounts of capital made available by public sales made it possible for businesspeople to finance large projects like establishing railroads and factories, which would have been impossible under the old partnership agreements.

After the success of the B & O, other new companies also began building railroads. However, many problems arose during these first years of train travel. The land was vast and the railroad companies did not have a lot of money. Consequently, American tracks were rough and hastily built. The roadbeds were poorly graded and the tracks were often uneven, causing trains to derail. Accidents were frequent. Additionally, most railroads could only afford to build single-track lines. When two trains were scheduled for the same line, one had to get off on a siding (a short track connected to the main track) and wait for the scheduled train to pass before continuing. This resulted in great delays. Other problems existed because the railroad companies all used different gauges, or widths of track, and the competing lines did not connect. Philadelphia, for example, was served by five different railroads, and passengers and shippers had to hire wagons to carry their belongings from one company's station to another.

The iron-covered wooden rails used on early railroad routes simply could not handle the heavy locomotives needed to pull trains over the rugged mountain ranges and deep ravines of the Appalachians. Solid iron rails were the most obvious solution, but the American iron industry had just begun and could not supply enough iron or skilled ironworkers. In 1830 mechanical engineer Robert Livingston Stevens (1787–1856; son of inventor John Stevens) solved the problem by designing a solid iron T-shaped rail. The shape of the rail provided it with more strength than the British rails and did not require the work of skilled metalworkers on site during construction. Initially, Stevens had the rails manufactured in Wales and shipped to the United States. The Stevens T-rail quickly became the standard.

American railways grew from about three thousand miles of track in 1840 to thirty thousand miles of track in 1860—more growth than the rest of the world's rail systems combined. Railroads reduced the price of shipping goods by as much as 95 percent between 1815 and 1860. These lower costs stimulated production and growth in all areas of the nation's economy. In addition, the demands of rail construction and finance expanded the nation's industry. Iron, and later, steel, production rose, and corporation stocks increased in value as a result. The dramatic growth of long-distance railroads signaled the growth of the United States as an industrialized nation. Railroads made industry possible by efficiently moving goods throughout the large nation. The railroad developers were equally vital in setting an example of the tremendous possibilities that arose when large amounts of capital, coupled with innovation, were used to create and improve large, complex enterprises.

Communication

In the far-reaching geography of the United States, communication between distant people presented as many challenges as did transportation systems. In 1789 it took twenty days for a letter to get from Savannah, Georgia, to Portland, Maine, and another twenty to get a reply. The nation's federal postal service had existed before it won independence from England in 1783. The postal service contracted stagecoach drivers to carry the mail and required that the mail be carried into the West and

The Steam Locomotive

In its simplest form, a steam locomotive consists of a firebox (a box in which the fire burns), a boiler (a tube or set of connected tubes, in which water is heated to steam), a cylinder (a tube-shaped chamber or tank), and wheels, all of which are mounted on a rigid frame. The flames in the firebox heat water in the boiler to create steam. The steam is directed into a cylinder where its force is used to push a plunger (a mechanism that plunges, or is thrust). The plunger is attached to the driving wheel of the engine by a connecting rod. Driving wheels are the wheels that move a train along, as opposed to carrying wheels, which distribute the weight of the engine. The force of the plunger causes the drive wheels to turn, which moves the engine along the track.

Americans relied almost entirely on English steam locomotive technology for their first trains. For example, in 1830 Robert Livingston Stevens (1787–1856), the son of John Stevens and president of New Jersey's Camden and Amboy Railroad, went to England to visit the best steam locomotive factory. Stevens ordered a train, the *John Bull,* and had it sent in parts to the United States. The *John Bull* was by far the most advanced steam locomotive in the country, but it was not adapted to the United States. Because U.S. railroad tracks had been built much more roughly than European tracks, the high-performance British locomotive, with its fixed, four-wheel suspension, did not fare well on them, derailing and breaking axles on the uneven rails. To make the *John Bull* hold to the tracks, mechanics added a bogie truck, a set of four leading carrying wheels that could swivel independently on the track and prevent derailing. With this adaptation, the *John Bull* was classified as a 4-4-0, meaning it had four leading wheels, four drivers, and no trailing wheels. This design became standard to the American engine, along with other adaptations, such as spark-arresting stacks to prevent fires, cow catchers (implements that pushed objects out of the train's way), and bells and whistles to warn people of their approach. U.S. manufacturers soon took over construction of American steam locomotives in large new factories filled with complex machinery and staffed by highly skilled workmen.

Southwest. About 70 percent of the mail's weight was in newspapers, which had a low postage rate. For most people living in the West at the turn of the nineteenth century, the mail and news provided their only contact with the rest of the nation.

The telegraph

The nation sought more immediate ways of communicating over long distances than the mail. In England in 1837 a successful electric telegraph system was invented by William

Fothergill Cooke (1806–1879) and Charles Wheatstone (1802–1875). The telegraph system transmitted encoded information by signal across a distance. But even before the English telegraph system was in place, an American scientist, Joseph Henry (1797–1878), had been experimenting with electromagnets (a type of magnet in which the magnetic field is created by a flow of electric current; when the current ceases the magnetic field disappears) and was able to send controlled clicks, or signals, through a mile-long wire to a distant receiver. In 1831 Henry met American artist and scientist Samuel F. B. Morse (1791–1872) and shared his findings with him. Morse and his partners conducted more experiments and introduced new designs to the electromagnetic telegraph before demonstrating the product in 1837.

Morse's telegraph consisted essentially of a battery for electricity, an electromagnet, and an electric switch known as the key. To send a message, the operator pressed down on the key. Electricity flowed out of the telegraph, into external electrical wires, and then to waiting receivers in other parts of the world. The electrical current flowed through the electromagnet, creating a magnetic field. The magnetic field caused the receiver's key to be attracted to the plate beneath it. As the key came into contact with the plate, it made a click. The sender could vary the sound of the click by holding the key down for a shorter or a longer period of time. To read the code, the receiver used Morse's code in which short clicks (dots) and long clicks (dashes) represented letters and numbers.

Morse did not invent the telegraph by himself, but he was largely responsible for establishing it as a communication system in the United States. In 1843 he convinced the U.S. Congress to provide $30,000 to fund a telegraph line from Washington, D.C., to Baltimore. The line was completed on May 24, 1844. In front of a crowd in Washington, D.C., Morse sent to Baltimore the first official telegraph message, which read: "What Hath God Wrought."

Within a few years there were fifty telegraph companies in the United States. No other industry, not even the railroad, experienced more rapid growth. In 1848 every state east of the Mississippi except Florida was connected to the growing network. By 1852 more than twenty-three thousand miles of

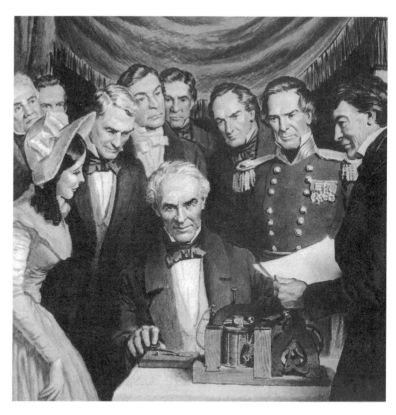

Samuel F. B. Morse sending the first telegram. *(© Bettmann/Corbis.)*

telegraph lines had been built. Newsgathering, business, financial, and transportation interests were revolutionized by the new means of instant communication. The telegraph, like the railroad, symbolized the advent of the new era in which the distances between people, institutions, and political units were drastically reduced.

For More Information

Books

Bailey, Thomas A., David M. Kennedy, and Lizabeth Cohen. *The American Pageant.* 11th ed. Boston, MA: Houghton Mifflin, 1998.

Hindle, Brooke, and Steven Lubar. *Engines of Change: The American Industrial Revolution, 1790–1860.* Washington, DC and London: Smithsonian Institution Press, 1986.

Kornblith, Gary J., ed. *The Industrial Revolution in America*. Boston, MA: Houghton Mifflin, 1998.

McCormick, Anita Louise. *The Industrial Revolution in American History*. Berkeley Heights, NJ: Enslow Publishers, 1998.

Web Sites

Railroad Museum of Pennsylvania. http://www.rrmuseumpa.org/index.shtml (accessed on June 30, 2005).

"Steamboats of the Hudson River." *Hudson River Maritime Museum*. http://www.ulster.net/~hrmm/steamboats/steam.html (accessed on June 30, 2005).

The Machine Makers

A period of rapid advances in technology started soon after the United States gained its independence in 1783 and continued through the mid-nineteenth century. It was driven by a remarkable group of inventors and innovators who created the machines that served industry. Most of these machine makers, who called themselves "mechanicians," received their training as apprentices (people who are bound to work for someone else for a specific term in order to learn a trade) in machine shops, where the tools of industry were made. In these shops, American machinists learned from each other by trading ideas and sharing their designs. Their goal was to reduce human labor by mechanizing (equipping with mechanical power) the work done in industries and on farms.

Though the nation repected its inventors, the systems by which they were rewarded, notably patents (government grants of exclusive authority to an inventor for making, using, and selling an invention), were poorly designed. Even the most famous inventors found it difficult or impossible to stop others from reproducing their creations for a profit. Part of the problem lay in the way most people conceived of invention—as the

Apprentices in a machine shop. *(© Schenectady Museum; Hall of Electrical History Foundation/Corbis.)*

creation of an individual working alone. In truth, there were very few single inventors. The discovery and design of new machines were usually the result of the innovations of many people. In fact, most of the ideas for U.S. machines originated in England and were adapted by U.S. machinists to conform to American needs. Over time, these products went through a variety of changes to meet the diverse requirements of the nation and to accommodate new power sources.

Words to Know

apprentice: Someone who is bound to work for someone else for a specific term in order to learn a trade.

boiler: A tube (or several connected tubes) in which water is heated to steam.

Great Plains: An area of grassland that stretches across the central part of North America eastward from the Rocky Mountains, from Canada in the north down to Texas in the south.

interchangeable parts: Standardized units of a machine that could be used in any machine of that model.

machine tool: A machine that shapes solid materials.

mass production: The manufacture of goods in quantity by using machines and standardized designs and parts.

mechanize: To equip with mechanical power.

patent: A legal document issued by a government granting exclusive authority to an inventor for making, using, and selling an invention.

pulley: Simple machine consisting of a wheel with a groove through which a rope passes. The pulley is used to move things up, down, or across, such as a flagpole or a curtain rod.

The American system

Many manufactured items before the turn of the nineteenth century were painstakingly crafted by a highly skilled artisan, or craftsperson. Products such as guns, clocks, and tools were made one at a time by a single person. They were very expensive and no two finished products were alike. If a part broke, the product would either have to be replaced or sent back to the craftsperson for repair. Because of this, only the wealthy could afford most manufactured items.

By the turn of the nineteenth century, U.S. machinists and inventors had rejected these traditions of craftsmanship and were busy designing machines to perform simple tasks more efficiently. In factories they studied how to break down complex hand operations into a series of simple tasks that could then be performed by machinery operated by workers with little training.

One of the great innovations of the age was the production of interchangeable parts. By using a machine tool, which shaped solid materials to make uniform (completely alike) parts for machines and other manufactured goods, a manufacturer could produce large quantities of each part. Rather than making one machine at a time, manufacturers were able to assemble many machines from the parts, which led to great savings in cost, labor, and quality. From the 1810s on, machinists and inventors introduced interchangeability of parts into several key American industries. Their labor-saving methods came to be called the "American system of manufactures" and were responsible for the techniques of mass production (manufacture of goods in quantity by using machines and standardized designs and parts) still being used worldwide at the beginning of the twenty-first century.

Eli Whitney and the American system

Pioneering American industrial inventor Eli Whitney (1765–1825) was already renowned for his labor-saving cotton gin when he became interested in the principles of mass production. (For more information on the cotton gin, see later in this chapter.) In late 1798 Whitney made the bold proposal to the U.S. government that he would manufacture four thousand muskets (a type of gun) in less than two years. At that time guns were constructed one at a time, with each part made individually and fitted to the connecting part. No single craftsman would be able to make so many guns in a lifetime.

Whitney had invented a system of milling (cutting and shaping) uniform parts of a musket in quantity, then assembling muskets from the parts. In 1799 he built and equipped a water-powered factory on the Mill River in Connecticut, where he intended to use his gun manufacturing system to fulfill his contract. At first he hired men skilled at making guns to work in his factory, but he quickly learned that it was easier to train unskilled labor to work in easy repetitive steps in the new manufacturing methods he was devising than to argue with skilled workers who were set in their own ways. Whitney built housing near his factory for his workers, and the resulting village was called Whitneyville.

During his first years in the factory, Whitney made tremendous advances—but not in making guns. He first needed to make machines to do the work. He made drilling and boring (piercing) machines to make holes, a screw machine to screw parts, a filing jig to guide the filing of the metal, and stencils to guide the workmen to drill holes in the right places. As he developed new machines, Whitney established an entire manufacturing process staffed by workers who were, for the most part, trained to do only one step of the process. Overseen by the inventor himself, the machines and their operators could efficiently make all the parts necessary to assemble muskets in quantity.

It took Whitney ten years to deliver on his contract. Other inventors and industrial planners such as gunsmith John Hall (1781–1841) were more successful in putting Whitney's theories into practice. Though Whitney never achieved commercial success as a gun manufacturer, Whitneyville was a forerunner of modern American factories and mass production. Many historians consider Whitney's concept, the American system of manufactures, to be the greatest technological innovation in U.S. history.

Oliver Evans automated most of the work in his flour mills.
(Photo by MPI/Getty Imags.)

Oliver Evans's automated flour mills

In 1780, after apprenticing in several other industries, machinist and inventor Oliver Evans (1755–1819) went into the flour-milling business with his brothers. At that time, water-powered flourmills required large amounts of human labor. Heavy bags of flour were carried into the mill and poured into a tub, which was hoisted up into a second floor granary, or storehouse, by strong men. Once the flour had been ground, it was cooled by being spread on the floor and raked by a person called a "hopper boy." When it had cooled, mill workers carried out the heavy loads of ground flour and loaded them onto wagons.

Evans began replacing human labor in the mill with machines, focusing in particular on the movement of grain

Patents

A patent is a legal document issued by a government, granting exclusive authority to an inventor for making, using, and selling an invention. The U.S. patent system was developed as a way for the government to encourage innovation by helping the inventor to profit from his or her invention. The U.S. Constitution (1787; Article I, Section 8) vaguely provided for federal patents on inventions, stating "Congress shall have the Power . . . To promote the Progress of Science and useful Arts, by securing for limited Times to Authors and Inventors the exclusive Right to their respective Writings and Discoveries." In 1790 Congress passed the first patent law, written mainly by Secretary of State Thomas Jefferson (1743–1826), which granted to an inventor the exclusive right to make or sell his or her invention for a period of fourteen years. There were only three patents granted the first year after the patent system was established, but each following year the number of applications grew rapidly. Congress repeatedly revised its organization of the U.S. Patent Office as abuses of authority occurred frequently, usually at the expense of the inventor.

Despite the government's good intentions, a legal patent was often insufficient protection against having others duplicate and receive rewards for the patent holder's invention. Inventors John Fitch (1743–1798) and James Rumsey (1743–1792) both received patents on their steamboats in the same year (1791) and spent the rest of their lives unsuccessfully disputing each other's claims. Oliver Evans (1755–1819), who held several patents for his factory machines and his improvements on steam engine designs, was so discouraged by his long legal battle over royalties that he burned all the records of his inventions. Eli Whitney made no profit on his patent for the cotton gin.

through the mill. His grain elevator, a leather strap equipped with cups to hold the product, raised the flour vertically into the granary by means of pulleys (simple machines used to move things up, down, or across, made up of a wheel with a groove through which a rope passes). Evans built conveyor belts that moved horizontally through the mill transporting the flour from machine to machine. His descender transported the flour on a downward slope. Another machine, named after the "hopper boy," cooled and raked the hot flour. In the end, flour from his automated mill was finer, drier, and easier to store than flour milled by hand. His inventions mechanized the flour mill to the point that it could be run by one person.

Eli Terry's mass-produced clocks

Eli Terry (1772–1852) adapted mass production methods to clock making in the early 1800s, a period in which few people had clocks in their homes. Built individually by skilled clock-makers, they were very expensive. Terry opened a clock shop in 1793. He had heard about Eli Whitney's methods of using interchangeable parts and decided to try it in his own business. He hired several workmen to cut the individual clock parts and then assembled the parts to make finished clocks. Within three years Terry was producing ten to twenty clocks at a time. In 1807 he received an order to build four thousand clockworks (inner workings of clocks) in three years. No one thought it possible to fill this huge order, but Terry formed a partnership with two other clockmakers and, using his new system, finished the job on schedule. Later Terry invented the wooden shelf clock, or mantle clock. His innovative methods allowed him to build as many as twelve thousand of these clocks per year. A large group of peddlers sold them door-to-door all over the northeastern United States. Because they were inexpensive, it was soon common for even the most humble homes to be equipped with clocks.

Samuel Colt's firearms manufacturing

As a young man Samuel Colt (1814–1862) designed a firearm known as a revolver, a rapid-fire handgun with rotating cylinders. He opened a factory and began to manufacture his guns, but the endeavor failed financially and he eventually closed the business. Ten years later the U.S. Army gave Colt a $28,000 contract to supply them with a thousand of his firearms. He lost money on the first order, but Colt's weapons became standard in the army, and from that point on Colt had to continually increase his production to meet public and private demand.

In 1852 Colt opened a giant factory in Connecticut where he combined arms manufacturing with advanced mass-production techniques. He was able to produce truly interchangeable weapons parts mainly because specialized machines, which had the precision to cut and form perfectly uniform parts, were being designed by the mechanics in his factory. Machine tools were in high demand, and Colt ended up selling both the weapons and the machines needed to make them.

Elisha K. Root

Colt employed Elisha K. Root (1808–1865), one of the best mechanics of the age, to design tools and machines for his plant. Root had begun his career as an apprentice in a textile mill, but at age fifteen he became an apprentice in a machine shop and soon earned a reputation for his innovations. In 1849 Root was building machines to produce a renowned line of axes when Samuel Colt turned to him to run his firearms factory. Root transformed the factory, building nearly four hundred machines. These precise machines produced the interchangeable parts that made the Colt factory a model of industrial efficiency. Historians credit Root's mechanical genius for making the Colt firearms company a success. Among Root's most successful machine tools was the "Lincoln miller," a tool that performed a great variety of metal-cutting operations, each of which previously required a separate machine. More than 150,000

Samuel Colt, holding a Colt revolver. *(© Bettmann/Corbis.)*

Lincoln millers were sold, making it the most commonly used machine tool in America. Root also designed the advanced drop hammers (powered hammers that are raised and then released to drop), boring machines, gauges (measuring implements), jigs (tools that keep work materials and tools at a precise distance from each other), and other machine tools that made the Colt revolver the first handgun in the world to be produced with truly interchangeable parts. Root mentored many other U.S. inventor-mechanics of the nineteenth century, spreading the concepts of the American system nationwide.

Commercial and mechanized farming

In the beginning of the nineteenth century the vast majority of Americans were farmers. For the nation to become industrialized it was essential that most farmers run commercial farms—farms that produced large crops to be sold—rather than subsistence farms, which only provided food for the use of the farmer and his family. The nation's crops, particularly wheat and cotton, were needed to feed the working people in the cities and to provide the factories with materials for manufactured goods. As the cities grew, so did the demand for the farmers' products. Although the farmers had more than enough land to farm, they did not have the necessary supplies of labor. Starting in the early nineteenth century, American machinists sought to solve this problem by mechanizing farm labor.

Eli Whitney's cotton gin

In 1792, after his graduation from Yale University, Eli Whitney moved to Savannah, Georgia. There he watched slaves as they carried out the time-consuming task of cleaning cottonseeds from cotton fibers by hand. Whitney began experimenting with building a machine designed to accomplish the job more efficiently. By 1793 he had built his cotton gin, which worked by turning a crank that caused a cylinder covered with wire teeth to revolve. The teeth pulled the cotton fiber, carrying it through slots in the cylinder as it revolved. The slots were too small for the seeds to pass through, and they were left behind. A roller with brushes then removed the fibers from the wire teeth.

With the use of the cotton gin, the increase in the production of processed cotton was remarkable: one large gin could process fifty times the amount of cotton that a laborer could process in a day. Soon southern plantations and farms were supplying huge amounts of cotton to the new textile mills in the Northeast and to Europe. Cotton production underwent a massive increase with the arrival of the cotton gin. In 1790 the United States produced 4,000 bales of cotton. By 1820 production was 73,222 bales, and by 1840 the figure had risen to 1,347,640 bales. Whitney had hoped that by making the task of cleaning cotton so inexpensive he might help eliminate slavery. But with the growing demand for southern cotton, southern slaveholders pushed westward to acquire more land for growing cotton and purchased many more slaves to keep up with the demand.

Illustration of two slaves working the first cotton gin. *(Courtesy of The Library of Congress.)*

Cyrus McCormick's reaper

As the population of the United States grew, the demand for wheat from western farms increased greatly. Wheat farmers of the fertile lands in Ohio, Indiana, Illinois, Michigan, and Wisconsin had trouble keeping up with the great demand for their wheat. They could easily expand their acreage, but they did not have enough farm labor to harvest all the wheat they could grow. Harvesting was time-consuming work and resulted in much waste. It was estimated that prior to mechanization, one farm worker could cut only about two acres a day. To solve this problem, inventors and mechanics of the early nineteenth century began to experiment with building reapers, machines that helped farmers harvest their grain.

Cyrus McCormick (1809–1884) is generally credited with inventing the first workable reaper, though his first machine, made in the summer of 1831, was not very useful. He would spend the next decade improving it, and during that time other inventors were also making advances on reapers. (McCormick also incorporated the design improvements of other inventors on his own new models.) The McCormick reaper was pulled by horse. It was equipped with a straight blade protected by guards linked to a drive wheel (the wheel that moves the machine). As the drive wheel turned, the blade moved back and forth in a sawing motion, cutting through the stalks of grain, which were held straight by rods. The cut grain stalks then fell onto a platform and were collected with a rake by a worker. The McCormick reaper could handle from twelve to fifteen acres a day, and required fewer workers than harvesting by hand. It more than tripled the acreage harvested. In 1830 the total wheat crop in the United States amounted to approximately 40 million bushels. Within nine years this figure had doubled, and in 1860 it exceeded 170 million bushels, becoming the most important cash crop (a crop produced to be sold) in the United States. McCormick's reaper profoundly changed the nature of farming in the United States, and his business quickly became the largest farm implement factory in the world.

John Deere's steel plow

The first farmers in the American colonies made their own plows out of wood. Plows are tools used to cut, lift, and turn over soil for farming. Wooden plows had many disadvantages: they did not cut well, they broke easily, and mud stuck to them. By the end of the eighteenth century, cast iron (an iron mix that is formed in a mold) plows were available, but these also broke easily. In 1836 John Deere (1804–1886) opened a blacksmith's shop in Illinois, a shop where iron was forged, or molded. Customers complained to him about their wood and iron plows. Using the steel from an old circular saw, Deere began tinkering with a plow with a smooth surface, and in 1837 he invented the steel plow. By the mid-1840s Deere and a business partner were manufacturing one thousand steel plows each year. Deere's invention played a major role in opening up the Great Plains (an area of grassland that stretches across the central part of North America eastward from the Rocky mountains, from Canada in the north down to Texas in

U.S. Iron and Steel Production Prior to 1865

Iron production had its roots in England, and even at the end of the eighteenth century, British ironmakers had little competition from their American colonies. Then, in the early part of the nineteenth century, the arrival of the steam age created a huge demand for iron in the United States. The use of steam to power machines and for transportation created a demand for iron boilers (tubes, or several connected tubes, in which water is heated to steam). In addition, more than thirty thousand miles of railroad track with iron rails were laid in the United States between 1830 and the beginning of the American Civil War (1861–65; a war between the Union [the North], who were opposed to slavery, and the Confederacy [the South], who were in favor of slavery). Iron was not the ideal material for either enterprise.

Using iron boilers, as the railroads and paddle-wheel riverboats of the time did, was dangerous; the iron was not strong enough to contain the steam pressure and iron boilers often blew up, frequently causing destruction and death. Iron rails frequently warped, resulting in train derailments.

Steel is an alloy (a substance created by fusing a metal and another substance together) of carbon and iron that is harder and stronger than iron. Though steel was being made in England prior to the 1860s, the U.S. steel industry did not develop on its own until after the Civil War. Up until that time steel was too expensive to manufacture by the methods available, so the United States imported nearly all of its steel. The conversion process invented by Henry Bessemer in 1856 would finally make American-made steel affordable.

the south) to farming. Though iron and wood plows were no match for the rich, heavy soil of the Great Plains, Deere's steel plow could cut through the earth with speed and efficiency.

The Crystal Palace Exhibition of London, 1851

In 1851 the first world's fair, the Crystal Palace Exhibition, took place in London, England. More than six million people from all over the world visited the fair that year. Everyone expected the technologically advanced England to display noteworthy machines, but the observers were amazed at the more than five hundred exhibits entered by the United States. Many U.S. exhibits won prizes, among them McCormick's reaper and Samuel Colt's revolver. England was so intrigued with the U.S. products on exhibition that it sent a commission

Visitors study the exhibits at the Crystal Palace Exhibition of 1851. *(© Corbis.)*

to the United States to investigate American industry. After the Crystal Palace Exhibition, England and other European countries began to regularly order machines from the United States. The United States was on its way to becoming the world's leading industrial nation, largely due to the group of "mechanicians" who had shaped the American system.

For More Information

Books

Cochran, Thomas C. "An Innovative Business System." In *The Industrial Revolution in America*. Edited by Gary J. Kornblith. Boston, MA: Houghton Mifflin, 1998, pp. 12–23.

Hindle, Brooke, and Steven Lubar. *Engines of Change: The American Industrial Revolution, 1790–1860*. Washington, DC and London: Smithsonian Institution Press, 1986.

McCormick, Anita Louise. *The Industrial Revolution in American History.* Berkeley Heights, NJ: Enslow Publishers, 1998.

Wallace, Anthony F. C. "The Fraternity of Mechanicians." In *The Industrial Revolution in America.* Edited by Gary J. Kornblith. Boston, MA: Houghton Mifflin, 1998.

Web Sites

Hoke, Donald. "Ingenious Yankees: The Rise of the American System of Manufactures in the Private Sector." http://www.thebhc.org/publications/BEHprint/v014/p0223-p0236.pdf (accessed on June 30, 2005).

"The National Inventors Hall of Fame." *Infoplease.* http://www.infoplease.com/ipa/A0004638.html (accessed on June 30, 2005).

The First Factories

Factories are buildings or sets of buildings in which manufactured goods are made from raw materials on a large scale. Work in factories is usually accomplished with labor-saving machinery operated by wage workers, or people who work for others for pay. The entire manufacturing process, including humans and machines, is usually directed by professional managers hired by the owners or their representatives. The first U.S. factories were built around the turn of the nineteenth century. Most were located in the northeastern states, and they were usually established by a group of local businessmen who remained involved in their day-to-day operation at some level. Though these early industrialists were interested in making a profit on their investment, some expressed concern about the way their industries would shape the social world. Americans had heard about the miserable, dangerous, and unhealthy conditions for workers in British factories. Several leading businessmen hoped to create an industrial environment that was, at least in their own judgment, fair and safe for workers.

There was no existing group of workers to staff the first factories. Most Americans in the early nineteenth century were

Textile mills in Lowell, Massachusetts. *(© CORBIS. Reproduced by permission.)*

Words to Know

capital: Accumulated wealth or goods devoted to the production of other goods.

entrepreneur: A person who organizes a new business.

factory: A building or group of buildings in which many people work to manufacture goods, generally with labor-saving machines powered by a central source.

loom: A frame or machine used to weave thread or yarns into cloth.

overhead expenses: The costs of running a business not directly related to producing the goods, such as rent or heating and lighting the workspace.

shuttle: A device that carries threads across a loom in the weaving process.

strike: A work stoppage by employees to protest conditions or make demands of their employer.

turnover: Employees quitting their jobs and others being hired to take their place.

wage worker: A person who works for others for pay.

warp yarn: The threads that run lengthwise on a loom.

waterwheel: A wheel that rotates due to the force of moving water; the rotation of the wheel is then used to power a factory or machine.

woof: The threads that run crosswise on a loom.

work ethic: A belief in the moral good of work.

farmers. Men and women on farms were used to toiling from dawn to dusk, but they set their own schedules in accordance with the sun. If they had a good season, they reaped the benefits. When people left the farms to work in factories, they found themselves in a very different work situation. Factory managers, bells and whistles, and the driving pace of machines directed their actions. The work was repetitive and did not change with the seasons. Employers determined their pay. Learning to do factory jobs was only a portion of the education process in their new occupation; they were also required to conform to a way of life and labor that was foreign to them. Like the industrialists, the first factory workers had no existing work traditions or organizations to guide them. Though much hard work was accomplished in these first U.S. factories, the relations between the industrialists and the industrial workers remained somewhat experimental as each group tested the system.

The first factory system

In the 1790s textile mechanic Samuel Slater (1768–1835) successfully mechanized the spinning, or yarn-making, process when he introduced British spinning machines to a mill in Pawtucket, Rhode Island (see Chapter 1). Other businesspeople in the area soon followed his example. These New England mills are considered the first true factory systems of the United States because they mechanized spinning and organized the work processes of the unskilled wage workers.

By 1828 Slater owned three factory compounds—factories and the villages surrounding them—in the area of Dudley, Massachusetts. In his first mill Slater hired very young children between the ages of seven and twelve to work the machines, but he soon found that American farming families resisted sending their young children to work for his low wages. In his later mills Slater hired young women, entire families, and newly arrived immigrants. Slater played a personal role in his mills. Though he hired several levels of managers to oversee operations, he visited his factories regularly. He tried to instill a new work ethic, or a belief in the moral good of work, in his workers, presenting them with detailed schedules and rules about absenteeism, punctuality, and behavior toward bosses. He demanded exhausting workdays and conformity to the company's rules and in return paid very low wages. Slater's paternalistic attitude (an authoritative attitude in which someone tries to control the conduct of his or her inferiors, like a father might try to control his children) toward his employees probably annoyed some, but most historians agree that he succeeded in avoiding the poor working conditions that existed in the textile mills of England. His workers, for the most part, did not resist his rules or work schedules.

Lowell establishes the textile industry

In 1810 wealthy Boston businessman Francis Cabot Lowell (1775–1817) visited England's textile mills. He was impressed with British technology, particularly an auto-mated weaving machine called the power loom (a frame or machine used to weave thread or yarn into cloth) that was not available in the United States. Lowell studied the looms, making sketches and memorizing mechanical

Francis Cabot Lowell, who established the first textile mill to include all the processes of making cloth from raw cotton under one roof. *(Courtesy of The Library of Congress.)*

details. Back in Massachusetts, he was able to create his own version of a working power loom with the help of a highly skilled mechanic. Then he began to study all the processes of textile production to determine how to carry out large-scale production at low cost.

To build a factory required large amounts of capital (accumulated wealth or goods devoted to the production of other goods), so in 1812 Lowell formed the Boston Manufacturing Company, also called the Boston Associates, with several wealthy businesspeople, each providing large sums of money. Two years later the company had built the water-powered mill Lowell had envisioned. For the first time in the United States, raw bales of cotton could be transformed into bolts of cloth under one roof. The production process became known as the "Waltham-Lowell System." By reducing the cost of cotton cloth, Lowell's mill put out a cheaper product than other cloth makers, thus assuring the company's success.

Lowell died in 1817, but the Boston Associates went on to build a complete factory town along the powerful Merrimack River in Massachusetts, naming it Lowell in his honor. They built more mills on the Merrimack at Lawrence, Massachusetts, and Manchester, New Hampshire. Soon the largest waterwheel in the nation was built on the Merrimack, supplying power to a dozen large factories. A waterwheel is a wheel that rotates due to the force of moving water, and the rotation of the wheel is then used to power a factory or machine. The new textile industry prospered. In 1832, 88 of the 106 largest American corporations were textile firms. By 1836 the Boston Manufacturing Company employed

The Lowell Machines

The Boston Associates hired the best machinists they could find to build the advanced textile machinery that filled the company's four-story brick mills in Waltham, Massachusetts, and Lowell, Massachusetts. Waterwheels powered the mills from the basement, with belts running up to all floors to run the machines. Cotton, delivered to the mill in bales, traveled through the entire building, going through a different part of the manufacturing process in each room until exiting as finished cloth. The first stop for the cotton bales was just outside the mill at the cotton-picking machines, which opened the bales and removed foreign matter from the cotton. The cotton fiber was then sent along to the first floor carding machines, which combed the fibers and gathered them into a loose rope of strands called a sliver. The sliver passed through two more machines to be made into a more uniform strand called a roving. The roving then went to the second floor spinning machines to be drawn out into yarn. After spinning, the warp yarn (the threads that run lengthwise on a loom) was further processed and then closely bound on a spool.

Next the yarn went up to the third floor for weaving, a process in which the crosswise, or woof, threads were interwoven with warp threads on a loom to make cloth.

The operator first set up the power loom with the warp yarn, which was mounted on a beam. Each piece of yarn was then drawn through a harness, which raised and lowered the warp threads on the loom, and onto a front roller. Then the filling yarn was mounted on shuttles (devices that carry threads across a loom in the weaving process) on the loom. After being set up the looms worked automatically. Hammers knocked the shuttle across the warp threads at a rate of about one hundred times per minute, while a movable frame called a reed separated the warp threads passed back and forth across the loom, beating strands of filling cloth into the woven material. The tubes holding the warp threads automatically unwound, releasing more thread to be woven, and the beams holding the woven cloth wound it into rolls.

The machines in the Lowell textile mills only made one kind of cloth and they were easy to operate without much training. The operators fed the threads into the machine and then allowed it to do the work, stopping the process only if threads broke or there was a malfunction. It was not easy to be a mill worker, though. In order for the total mill operation to run smoothly, all the machines had to be operating at the same time and at a steady speed. Factory work allowed for little independent action. Hours were long and the work was repetitive.

six thousand workers at the Lowell mills, and by 1848, the city of Lowell itself had a population of about twenty thousand and was the largest industrial center in America. Its mills produced fifty thousand miles of cotton cloth each year.

The Lowell girls

Lowell found an ideal workforce for his mills—the unmarried daughters of New England farm families. In the first decades of the nineteenth century, many young women were eager to work in the mills, viewing it as a chance to be independent or to provide income for their families. The "Lowell girls," as they were called, usually ranged in age from about sixteen to thirty. Most worked two or three years at the mill before returning home to marry and start a family. By 1831 women made up almost forty thousand of the fifty-eight thousand factory workers in the textile industry.

The women who operated the machines in the Lowell mills earned $2.40 to $3.20 a week plus room and board. The pay was more than double that of domestic servants and seamstresses, the two most common occupations for working women. Still, it was only one-half to one-third the wages paid to men for similar work. The Boston Associates tried to attract the young women to work for them by providing decent work and living conditions. They built factories that were clean and well lit. Understanding that single women living on their own feared for their safety and avoided circumstances that would stain their reputations, they established the country's first planned industrial communities, setting up rows of boardinghouses near the factories for their workers. The Associates paid responsible older women to run these boardinghouses and to enforce strict discipline on the residents, imposing curfews, requiring church attendance, and demanding chaperones for male visitors.

Work routines were strict at Lowell, with a twelve- to fourteen-hour day starting at seven in the morning and only a half-hour lunch break at midday. Factory bells announced times for leaving and entering the plant, and the employees were fined for lateness as well as breaking other rules. The work did not demand great physical strength, but it did require constant attention. In winter work began before sunup and lasted into the darkness, when smoky whale-oil lamps illuminated the interior of the factories. Because cotton thread breaks more readily in dry air, overseers sealed windows shut and sprayed water in the air to keep the humidity high, frequently creating an uncomfortable working environment.

The *Lowell Offering*

So many of the young women who worked at the Lowell mills wrote memoirs, letters, and stories about their experiences that readers today know more about them than numerous other historical groups. Many of the "Lowell girls," as the women who worked in the Lowell mills were called, were eager to experience independence from family for the first, and perhaps the only, time in their lives and they made the most of their time away from their rural homes. Though they had almost no free time, as work consumed up to fourteen hours of each day, it was common for young mill operators to spend their evening hours participating in reading groups, attending night school, going to lectures, or just reading on their own.

In October 1840 some of the women from the mills got together to produce and publish a sixteen-page journal called the *Lowell Offering,* the nation's first journal to be written solely by women. The *Offering,* which sold for about six cents a copy, published poems, articles, and stories contributed by mill women. In all, twenty-eight volumes of the journal were published, and it was hailed worldwide, even receiving praise from English novelist Charles Dickens (1812–1870), who had been impressed by it on a visit to the mills.

Title page of the December 1845 issue of the *Lowell Offering.* (© *THE BETTMANN ARCHIVE/NEWSPHOTOS, INC./Corbis.*)

In the 1840s tensions mounted between the management and workers of the Lowell mills. The workers stopped reading the *Offering.* They believed the journal was serving the company and not its workers, since it would not publish articles about the worsening working conditions at the mills. The paper soon closed down.

Workers rebel

The success of the Lowell mills encouraged other industrialists. Soon many new textile mills were producing cloth, and by the 1830s the supply of cloth on the market had become greater than the demand for it. Though profits were down, the

Boston Associates greatly increased operations between 1836 and 1847 in an effort to cut costs. The cost reductions were made at the expense of the workers, who were forced to tend more looms and spindles at once and to operate them at a faster speed. To reduce expensive turnover (employees quitting and others being hired to take their place) caused by the demanding new workload, workers were required to sign yearlong labor contracts. While these changes increased productivity dramatically, wages did not increase. In fact, in 1836, with profits down, the Lowell managers actually reduced workers' wages and raised their boarding fees. Two thousand women walked off their jobs in protest. The company fired the leaders of the strike (work stoppage by employees to protest conditions or make demands of their employer) but called off the pay reductions.

In 1837 the workers established the Lowell Female Labor Reform Association (LFLRA) and petitioned the Massachusetts state legislature to limit the workday to ten hours. No action was taken in response to their protest, but it signaled the end of the young women's workforce at the mills. The Boston Associates soon started to replace them with poor immigrants who were willing to tolerate harsher conditions and lower pay. By 1860 one-half of Lowell's mill workers were impoverished Irish immigrants and Francis Cabot Lowell's early experiments with making a kinder and nobler industrial society were quickly fading from memory. (For more information on immigrant labor, see Chapter 5.)

The ready-made clothing industry

In the Northeast at the turn of the nineteenth century the time-consuming process of making clothing was often divided between a tailor's shop, which provided seamstresses with precut pieces of cloth, and the seamstresses, who stitched the pieces together in their homes for a very low price for each finished piece. In an 1867 magazine article journalist Sarah Hale (1822–1879), as quoted by Joan Perkins in *History Today,* estimated that "to make an average shirt by hand required 20,620 stitches; at a rate of thirty-five stitches a minute, a competent seamstress could complete a shirt in ten to fourteen hours." Most home seamstresses were married women with children who were supplementing their husbands' income, but sewing was also a common occupation for widows, unmarried daughters, and elderly women. Seamstresses working at home made so little money that many were forced to work long hours six or seven days a week. Clothing industrialists were happy to exploit this labor source, which provided service at low cost with no overhead expenses (those costs of running a business not directly related to producing the goods, such as rent or heating and lighting the workspace).

The garment industry began its shift from custom tailor shops to ready-made clothing stores in 1831, when prominent New York businessman George Opdyke (1805–1880) established a clothing store in New Orleans, where southern plantation owners were eager to purchase ready-made clothing for their large households, particularly for the slaves. Opdyke could not keep up with the demand for his inexpensive cotton clothing, so he went back to New York and established what is considered the first ready-made garment factory, in order to ensure a steady supply of goods. Soon other entrepreneurs, or people who organize new businesses, in New York established ready-made clothing factories, though many also continued to employ seamstresses who worked at home as well. The new garment factories employed young, unmarried women— sometimes as many as several hundred. At first, all work in the factories was done by hand.

In the 1850s the invention of the sewing machine greatly reduced the amount of work involved in sewing garments. Sarah Hale estimated that a seamstress with a machine could sew three thousand stitches per minute and complete a shirt in about an hour. The labor reduction did not mean that seamstresses worked any less, however. In the garment factories of New York, they were carefully monitored in relentless work schedules, producing many garments in their workday. Since one person could produce many times the number of garments, labor costs dropped at a great rate, bringing the price of ready-made clothes down with them. The value of the American ready-made clothing industry, on the other hand, increased from $40 million in 1850 to over $70 million in 1860. Still, most sewing continued to be done by local tailors and seamstresses. This would change during the American Civil War (1861–65; a war between the Union [the North], who were opposed to slavery, and the Confederacy [the South], who were in favor of slavery).

The Sewing Machine

Sometime between 1832 and 1834 inventor Walter Hunt (1786–1859) invented the first U.S. sewing machine, but he never promoted it. According to some sources he was concerned that his machine might put needy seamstresses out of work. It was not until 1846 that inventor Elias Howe (1819–1867) patented (secured a legal document from the government granting exclusive authority to an inventor for making, using, and selling an invention) a sewing machine. However, Howe's design was not very practical and by that time there were many competitors already in the field who could make a better machine. In 1850 Isaac M. Singer (1811–1875) began to market the first practical sewing machine in the United States. Singer and his company perfected the machine and went on to develop mass marketing techniques for its sale. Sewing machines were sold by an aggressive force of nearly three thousand salesmen for use in homes and factories in the Northeast. The industry was producing some 111,000 sewing machines annually

Elias Howe's sewing machine. *(© Bettmann/Corbis.)*

by 1860. In time, the garment shops began to demand that seamstresses who worked at home purchase their own sewing machines and lowered their payments for piecework accordingly. The sewing machine had a tremendous impact on the way that clothing and shoes were produced.

The shoe and boot industry

Prior to the nineteenth century, shoes and boots were made in farmers' homes or by a traveling shoemaker. These shoes were unlike the shoes we know today. There were no standard sizes and there was no left or right shoe. Though handmade to order and finely crafted, the shoes had to be worn a long time before they became more flexible and comfortable. They were also very expensive.

Jan Ernst Matzeliger and the Lasting Machine

By the mid-nineteenth century, machines had been invented that could cut, sew, and tack (fasten) shoes, but the "lasting" process was the final one to be mechanized in shoe factories. In lasting a shoe, its leather uppers are stretched over the last, a foot-shaped model. After the leather is correctly lasted, it is sewn to the inner sole. The labor required in the lasting process slowed production and added significantly to the cost of a shoe. One day, in a shoe factory in Lynn, Massachusetts, a young Dutch-African American worker named Jan Ernst Matzeliger (1852–1889) overheard coworkers claim that no machine could ever last shoes as well as humans. Matzeliger had apprenticed in his father's machine shop and had also worked in a shoe factory in Philadelphia, Pennsylvania. An avid machinist and inventor, he took these words as a challenge.

Matzeliger spent his free time designing a lasting machine. By the fall of 1880, he found financial backers and began to build a machine. After about five more years of development, Matzeliger had a model appropriate for factory testing. It could last the leather, arrange it over the sole, and drive in the nails, finishing the shoe in about one minute. Before Matzeliger's lasting machine, a worker of average skill could last about thirty-five to fifty shoes per day. With adjustments, Matzeliger's machine could make between 150 to 700 pairs a day, depending on the leather's quality. Matzeliger's invention cut the cost of shoes in half.

Around the turn of the century, merchants in the Northeast began to organize the shoemaking process into a system like that of ready-made clothing. Precut parts of shoes were sent from central shops out to farmers who then put together the finished shoes for a set fee per piece. These farmers had learned the shoemaking trade as apprentices and worked at it part time, usually in the slow seasons on the farm, to supplement their income. They usually had small shoemaking shops called "ten-footers" (denoting the size of the shop) on their farms, and if there was enough business they trained assistants to help them. In the early decades of the nineteenth century the demand for manufactured shoes grew. With enough work to sustain them year-round, some rural shoemakers in the Northeast moved into town to work in the central shoe shops. The basic work process and tools for making shoes did not change.

A worker in "Shoe City," Massachusetts, pastes the sole lining into a pair of children's shoes. *(© Corbis.)*

The shoe industry expanded around 1845, when machines replaced hand tools for pounding sole leather into dense and long-lasting material. Soon the sewing machine was adapted to shoemaking. Enterprising shoe manufacturers also invented important marketing devices, such as standardizing shoe sizes and creating differently shaped shoes for the right and left feet. In the new shoe factories, some tasks required little training while others demanded specialists; the pay scales reflected the skill level of the worker. The owners of the factories hired professional managers. Some were paid to keep the productivity level of the other employees high through strict discipline. Others oversaw the operation, upkeep, and new design of machines.

In 1860 about one hundred million shoes were manufactured annually in the United States, with about 123,000 people working in the industry, mainly in New England and Philadelphia. Lynn, Massachusetts, the "Shoe City," was a major center of the shoemaking industry.

The factory workers in Lynn had watched as profits soared while their wages remained the same. Barely able to make a living and receiving no indication that their employers would begin to pay fair wages, they joined forces in a labor struggle against the factory owners and managers. In February 1860 shoemakers in Lynn walked off their jobs, starting a massive strike that eventually spread over a wide area, including factories in New Hampshire and Maine. By some estimates as many as seventeen thousand to twenty thousand men and women workers participated in the strike. The work stoppage cost their employers dearly, and the strikers eventually won the wage increase they demanded.

The Lynn strike was the largest labor movement in the United States before the Civil War and a sign of times to come in relations between industrialists and industrial workers. The protective care of the early industrialists had proved insufficient when the economy slumped or there were pressures in the market. The workers, though often powerless to accomplish change individually, had proved their strength when united.

For More Information

Books

Dublin, Thomas. "Factory Employment as Female Empowerment." In *The Industrial Revolution in America*. Edited by Gary J. Kornblith. Boston, MA: Houghton Mifflin, 1998, pp. 53–62.

Faler, Paul. *Mechanics and Manufacturers in the Early Industrial Revolution: Lynn, Massachusetts, 1780–1860*. Albany: State University of New York Press, 1981.

Hindle, Brooke, and Steven Lubar. *Engines of Change: The American Industrial Revolution, 1790–1860*. Washington, DC and London: Smithsonian Institution Press, 1986.

McCormick, Anita Louise. *The Industrial Revolution in American History*. Berkeley Heights, NJ: Enslow Publishers, 1998.

Prude, Jonathan. "Social Conflict in the Early Mills." In *The Industrial Revolution in America*. Edited by Gary J. Kornblith. Boston, MA: Houghton Mifflin, 1998.

Web Sites

Lubar, Steven. "Managerial Structure and Technological Style: The Lowell Mills, 1821–1880." *Business and Economic History Online*. Vol. 13, 1984. http://www.thebhc.org/publications/BEHprint/toc131984.html (accessed on June 30, 2005).

"Shoes of the 19th Century." http://people.deas.harvard.edu/~jones/mckay/history.html (accessed on June 30, 2005).

The Gilded Age

The foundations of industrialism (the social system that results from an economy based on large-scale industries) were established in the United States during the first wave of industrialization, or the development of industry, which occurred between the American Revolution (1775–83; the American colonists' fight for independence from England) and the American Civil War (1861–65). Even by the time of the Civil War, however, these advances were limited to only a few sections of the country. Eighty percent of the nation's factories and 70 percent of its railroad mileage were in the northern states, while the South, with its economy built around slave labor and exporting farm products, had maintained a far more rural culture, that is, a culture based on farming and country life. Even in the northeastern United States most industries were family owned and catered to a local market rather than operating nationally. The nation remained primarily rural; in fact five out of every six Americans lived in rural areas and the vast majority of Americans were farmers. Only a few U.S. cities had populations over one hundred thousand. Nonetheless, in 1860 the United States stood poised and ready to begin an era of remarkably rapid industrialization, that would transform the country into an urban society that relied heavily on industry.

The second wave of industrialization occurred between the Civil War and the turn of the century. People living in that era were well aware that the nation was changing dramatically and some had trouble accepting the direction it seemed to be taking. Though rapid industrialization made the United States the richest and most powerful nation in the world, it was not always viewed as a positive thing. For the American public, the least appealing aspect of industrialization was probably the corresponding rise of big business on a dramatic scale. Businesses working to gain massive profits found ways to control politicians and crush competitors. A new class of millionaires paraded their wealth, while industrial workers earned only a small salary for their hard labor. The facts of daily life conflicted with the democratic ideals instilled during the American Revolution—that all men are created equal. During the late nineteenth century the power of money gained what seemed to be unlimited influence over the nation.

The era of rapid industrialization came to be known as the "Gilded Age." The term was coined by American writer Mark Twain (1835–1910) and his coauthor Charles Dudley Warner (1829–1900) in their satirical 1873 novel *The Gilded Age: A Tale of Today*. The novel's characters set out to get rich quick through questionable railroad and land deals in an age presented by Twain and Warner as "gilded" or glittering on the surface but corrupt underneath. The use of the term Gilded Age labels the era of industrialization as a time when democratic values appeared to give way to the power of money, corporations, and unprincipled political machines, or groups of unelected leaders that control political parties.

The Gilded Age presents only one view of the era. Many observers at the time argued that, despite the extreme poverty that existed during the era, the country remained true to its ideals by presenting opportunities for personal advancement to all its citizens. Writer Horatio Alger (1832–1899) gained a large popular following with books portraying "rags to riches" themes, in which poor young men rose from poverty to wealth through determination and hard work. Other defenders of the era argued that the unrestrained activities of some immoral business tycoons may have been a crucial factor in the United States's rise as the world's industrial leader.

Words to Know

bond: A certificate of debt issued by a government or corporation that guarantees repayment of the original investment with interest by a specified date.

bureaucratic structure: An organization with many levels of authority, in which people specialize in their jobs and follow set rules of operation.

capital: Accumulated wealth or goods devoted to the production of other goods.

capitalism: An economic system in which the means of production and distribution are privately owned by individuals or groups and competition for business establishes the price of goods and services.

corporation: A company, or organization of employers and employees that is permitted by law, usually owned by a group of shareholders and established to carry out a business or industry as a body. Corporations have legal rights usually reserved for individuals, such as the right to sue and be sued and to borrow or loan money.

entrepreneur: A person who organizes a new business.

factory: A building or group of buildings in which manufactured goods are made from raw materials on a large scale.

industrialism: The social system that results from an economy based on large-scale industries.

industrialization: The development of industry.

industry: A distinct group of profit-making enterprises that manufacture a certain product, such as the textile or steel industry.

laissez-faire An economic doctrine that opposes government regulation of commerce and industry beyond the minimum necessary.

manufacture: To make something from raw materials, usually as part of a large-scale system of production using machinery.

monopoly: The exclusive possession or right to produce a particular good or service.

speculator: A person who takes a business risk in the hope of making a profit, particularly when buying or selling stocks or commodities (economic goods) in order to profit from shifts in the market.

stock: An element of ownership of a corporation that has been divided up into shares that can be bought and sold.

stock market: A system for trade in companies, ventures, and other investments through the buying and selling of stocks, bonds, mutual funds, limited partnerships, and other securities.

tariffs: Government-imposed fees on imported goods.

transcontinental: Spanning the continent from one coast to the other.

This family was able to establish a farm in Nebraska thanks to the Homestead Act of 1862, which provided small pieces of public land to settlers in the West. *(Bettmann/CORBIS. Reproduced by permission.)*

Republican legislation during the Civil War

The era of rapid industrialization started at the same time that the American Civil War began. In 1860 bitter conflicts between the North and South led the Southern states to secede, or withdraw, from the Union. Slavery was only one issue of disagreement between the regions; the southern farming economy and the northeastern manufacturing economy had many conflicting political and economic interests. Each group fought to promote its own interests. The Southerners in the Democratic Party backed an agricultural and slave-based economy, and the Northerners in the Republican Party, which stood firmly against slavery, supported business and industrial interests. When the South seceded from the Union, the Republican Party was suddenly free to promote its interests without the restraints of the

Democrats in Congress. Some of the bills passed during the war provided necessary stimulation for the industrialization process.

In 1861 Congress authorized an increase in tariffs (government-imposed fees on imported goods) for the first time in two decades. The tariffs made goods imported from Europe more expensive than American-made goods, allowing U.S. manufacturers to set their own prices. Though tariffs were a great help to U.S. industry, Southerners had long fought tariff increases, fearing that foreign markets would respond by placing tariffs on imports of U.S. cotton. The United States passed several other bills that were favorable to businesses during the war years. The Homestead Act of 1862 provided small pieces of public land to settlers in the West for farming, and industry soon expanded into these new territories as well. Although it was intended to help poor families, the Homestead Act sometimes placed land in the hands of speculators (people who take business risks in the hope of making a large profit, particularly when buying or selling in order to profit from shifts in the market) who then sold it to incoming farmers for a profit. This was just one of many instances in which government assistance led to fraud and corruption.

Legislation of the railroads and big business

In 1862 President Abraham Lincoln (1809–1865; served 1861–65) signed a bill that authorized the federal government to assist railroad companies in the massive project of building a transcontinental railroad, which spanned the continent from one coast to the other (see Chapter 6). Over the next ten years the federal government gave railroads millions of dollars in aid and more than one hundred million acres of land to advance construction. Railroad expansion began at a rapid pace. In 1860, only about thirty-three thousand miles of track had been available for use, but by 1900, two hundred thousand miles of track covered the United States—more than existed in all of Europe. Railroad service enabled businesses to sell to a national rather than a local market, greatly stimulating industry of all types.

As the railroad network expanded, the individual rail companies found the scale of their business and financial structures growing as well. Starting in the 1850s railroad companies became the biggest businesses the country had ever known, funded by hundreds of millions of dollars and employing tens of thousands of workers nationwide. The railroad companies

The National Bank Act of 1863

The United States became engulfed in a financial crisis as soon as it entered the Civil War. The treasury, where government funds are kept, was almost empty and there was not enough money to cover the heavy expenses of the war. At that time there were no national banks, and if the government needed to borrow money it offered government bonds to private bankers. A bond is a certificate of debt issued by a government or corporation that guarantees repayment of the original investment with interest by a specified date. In 1861, however, bankers were reluctant to commit their money to government bonds, as they were unsure whether the Union would survive to pay the debt. Financier Jay Cooke (1821–1905) solved the crisis when he proposed that the government borrow money directly from the American people by marketing its bonds to the public. He and his business associates were largely responsible for the sale of over one billion dollars in government bonds that paid interest to American investors and helped finance the war years.

This federal financial crisis pointed to a need for a national bank system. In 1862 there were more than fifteen hundred state banks in operation, all of them issuing their own bank notes, which formed the majority of currency circulating in the United States. The value of the notes varied and doing business on a national level was difficult. A national banking system was proposed to provide the country with a truly national currency and to facilitate federal loans. A bill to provide for such a banking system was introduced into the Senate in January 1863. Many people objected, fearing that the national government would gain too much control by stepping into local government roles. Still, the national banking system was created and it was a distinct improvement over the uncontrollable state banking systems. The national banking system provided much-needed financial stability in the age of industrial expansion.

formed the first systems of sophisticated industrial management, developing a large, bureaucratic structure. A bureaucratic structure is an organization with many levels of authority, in which people specialize in their jobs, and there are set rules for operation. This highly organized business structure was quickly adopted by other basic industries such as steel, oil refining, meatpacking, food processing, and electrical machinery.

Immigration legislation

In 1864 Congress passed the Contract Labor Law to encourage people from other countries to immigrate to the United States and join the country's industrial labor force. The law stated that immigrants could enter the country under

The writings of English economist Adam Smith influenced many U.S. leaders, who adopted a laissez-faire policy toward industry during the Gilded Age. *(© Bettmann/Corbis.)*

contracts with potential employers in which they pledged their first year's wages in return for passage to the United States. Between 1860 and 1900 about fourteen million immigrants, many with little or no money, arrived in the country in search of a better life. Many wound up working in factories for low wages. The rush of new immigrants swelled the populations of the eastern cities, where overcrowding produced slums and unsanitary living conditions. For a variety of reasons, second- and third-generation citizens of the United States often treated the new immigrants with contempt. Much of their attitude was based on prejudice. The new immigrants often arrived poor and needy. Some were from different religions or looked different or spoke a different language than the earlier settlers. Because immigrants were often desperate for work, they usually accepted lower wages than people who had been working in the country for many years. This raised a powerful fear that the immigrants would lower wages for everyone. Yet this was also the reason businesses welcomed the new Americans.

Laissez-faire policy

The Republican policy toward businesses and corporations changed during the Civil War years. During the war, the government stopped interfering with industries, at times even looking the other way when it was clear that companies had acted illegally. Many of the country's leaders adopted the views of British economist Adam Smith (1723–1790), who, in his book *An Inquiry into the Nature and Causes of the Wealth of Nations* (1776), reasoned that economies operated best under the "natural law" of free competition without the disruption of government intervention. The proper role of the national government, he felt, was to protect society from foreign invasion, control crime, and provide some public services. Smith believed that government involvement in economic matters restrained the natural human self-interest and desire to profit. Because free competition on the market is based on that self-interest, Smith argued, nations become wealthy when they allow self-interest to take its course in the marketplace. The hands-off policy of the government was called laissez-faire, an economic doctrine that opposes government regulation of commerce and industry beyond the minimum necessary.

New industry

The Civil War slowed the overall advances of industrialism somewhat, but some of the large northeastern industries were thrust into large-scale production by war needs. For example, the textile, ready-made clothing, and shoe industries provided Union soldiers with their uniforms and the gun industry armed them. Many of these industries maintained the large-scale production methods they developed for the war after it was over, and served as an example that other industries followed. Some new industries in the western territories, such as mining, lumber, and range cattle, were also stimulated into growth by war demands.

In the eastern states new industries were emerging that would have significant effects after the war. In 1859 a successful effort to drill for oil in Pennsylvania sparked the creation of the oil industry. In the mid-1860s steel production dramatically increased as new technologies allowed manufacturers to produce higher-quality grades of steel. Blessed with abundant iron ore fields in the Great Lakes region, the United States stood ready to become the world's leading steel producer.

Capital

Many key factors of industrial expansion were in place in 1860, including advanced technology, abundant natural resources, a large labor force, and a friendly government. But industrialism on a national scale required massive amounts of capital—much more than even the largest of the earlier enterprises like the canals or steamboats had needed. The national corporations had to meet the high costs of building and maintaining plants, machinery, new technologies, and large workforces. It took many millions of dollars to establish a large industrial company, and several million more to maintain it.

By the postwar years, the major U.S. industrialists no longer viewed their roles as those of entrepreneurs (people who organize and manage new businesses) who were responsible for running their companies and providing an adequate life for their employees. Instead they saw themselves as money-movers, or capitalists. Capitalism is an economic system in which wealth is put to use in order to create more capital. In a capitalist system, the means of production (labor, land, and factories) and distribution (trains and ships) are privately owned by individuals or groups and competition for business establishes the price of goods as well as workers' wages. Profit is the key consideration when making economic decisions.

The renowned capitalists of the postwar years made tremendous personal profits as they built large industries. Though praised by some for expanding and modernizing the capitalist system, these businessmen were also viewed by many as greedy, dishonest, and unethical. These business tycoons included banker and financier J. P. Morgan (1837–1913); oil industrialist John D. Rockefeller (1839–1937); steel mogul Andrew Carnegie (1835–1919); financiers James J. Hill (1838–1916), James Fisk (1834–1872), and Jay Gould (1836–1892); and railroad magnates Cornelius Vanderbilt (1794–1877) and Collis Huntington (1821–1900).

The new, larger, factory-based manufacturers used some underhanded methods to suppress their competition, and they were greatly aided by the government's laissez-faire system. The monopolies (exclusive possession or right to produce a particular good or service) led to a concentration of capital in just a few huge corporations, especially in transportation and other large industries. They enabled the businessmen to eliminate potential competitors, raise prices, and subsequently realize huge profits that were pumped back into their businesses. Many businessmen converted their business skills into political might, buying the favors of elected officials and ensuring limited regulation of their activities and few taxes on their profits. Their monopolies dominated the American economy for several decades after the Civil War.

The New York Stock Exchange

As big businesses began to dominate the economy, the United States developed new ways of investing. One of the ways to invest included the stock market, a system for trade in companies, ventures, and other investments through the buying and selling of stocks (shares of part ownership in the company), bonds, mutual funds, limited partnerships, and other securities. The New York Stock Exchange (NYSE) was the first stock market established in the United States. It began operations on a very minor scale in New York in 1792. In 1825 the NYSE opened its new headquarters at 11 Wall Street in New York City. In these early years most shares traded were in canal, turnpike, mining, and gaslight companies. As the U.S. economy expanded in the nineteenth century, businesses found it harder to fund ambitious new undertakings like railroad construction by relying only on their own resources or loans from banks. To raise the needed capital, companies turned to the stock market, where they sold stock to the

A 1792 meeting of the New York Stock Exchange.
(© Bettmann/Corbis.)

public. After the Civil War, industries began to dominate the NYSE trading floor as the nation became increasingly oriented toward manufacturing.

The changing nation

Many Americans reaped the benefits of the new industrial economy. Along with the very wealthy class of industrialists and money professionals, a large new middle class arose. The standard of living in the United States was higher than it had ever been. American industry provided consumers with a wide array of products and, in the first years after the war, jobs were plentiful.

While many Americans were content to leave business and industry to the forces of the market, others were not so sure. A long list of grievances arose, beginning with the plight of

Black Friday

During the post–Civil War years, many people were driven to get rich quick during the nation's booming but largely unregulated expansion. Two notorious Wall Street speculators, James Fisk (1834–1872) and Jay Gould (1836–1892), developed a scheme to dominate the market on gold by buying up most of the gold available on the U.S. market. Buying so much gold would drive up its price by creating the appearance of increased demand in the market. Before this false rise in gold prices could collapse, Fisk and Gould intended to sell their gold to other speculators and make a substantial profit. They found a valuable ally in this scheme in New York financier Abel R. Corbin, the brother-in-law of President Ulysses S. Grant (1822–1885;

served 1869–77). In the summer of 1869 the unsuspecting Grant mentioned to Corbin that he was planning to decrease government sales of gold. Corbin informed Fisk and Gould and the three began buying up as much gold as they could. This drove the price of gold from $140 to $162 per ounce. By summer's end Grant began to suspect the conspiracy. Fisk and Gould learned of Grant's suspicions and, before he could take action, began to sell huge quantities of gold to investors at the top price. On Friday, September 24, 1869, the president instructed the secretary of the treasury to sell $5 million of gold. After the government's sale, gold fell to $135 an ounce. Fisk and Gould made huge fortunes, but the rapid fall in the value of gold wiped out the speculators who had bought gold from them and caused many banks and businesses to fail. For this reason the day was referred to as "Black Friday."

working people who suffered long hours of labor at low pay and the fate of American farmers who were being destroyed by low crop prices and high transportation costs. Moreover, many citizens were concerned that the new industrial economy was not compatible with American beliefs in democracy and equality. Their concern grew as the stories of excess and dishonest practices in railroad construction were reported in the postwar years. It was clear that the United States was changing and taking a new direction over which the majority of Americans had no control. In his 1869 article "A Chapter of Erie," writer and railroad executive Charles Francis Adams (1835–1915) summed up the nation's fears of a government controlled by big business: "It is a new power, for which our language contains no name. We know what aristocracy, autocracy, democracy are; but we have no word to express government by moneyed corporations."

From the Civil War years to the turn of the twentieth century, the United States transformed from an agricultural to an industrial economy, and from a rural to an urban society. The number of industrial workers jumped from 1.3 million to 5.3 million. By 1900 the United States was no longer primarily a farming nation and the country was producing manufactured goods worth twice as much as its agricultural goods. Whether the remarkable advances in industry were due to the greed of dishonest businessmen or to an ideal combination of abundant resources, a large labor force, advanced technology, and sophisticated systems of business management, the United States rapidly became the richest and most powerful industrial nation in the world. But the struggling groups of Americans did not all share in the wealth of industrialism, and many of the problems, as well as the successes, that originated in the Gilded Age remain with the nation today.

For More Information

Books

Brogan, Hugh. *The Penguin History of the USA*. 2nd ed. London and New York: Penguin Books, 2001.

DeSantis, Vincent P. *The Shaping of Modern America: 1877–1916*. Boston, MA: Allyn and Bacon, 1973.

Murphy, Richard R. *The Nation Reunited: War's Aftermath*. Alexandria, VA: Time-Life Books, 1987.

Porter, Glenn. "Industrialization and the Rise of Big Business." In *The Gilded Age: Essays on the Origins of Modern America*. Edited by Charles W. Calhoun. Wilmington, DE: Scholarly Resources, 1996.

Smith, Page. *The Rise of Industrial America: A People's History of the Post-Reconstruction Era*. Vol. 6. New York: McGraw-Hill, 1984.

Web Sites

Adams, Charles Francis. "A Chapter of Erie." *Chapters of Erie and Other Essays*. Boston, MA: James R. Osgood and Co., 1871. http://yamaguchy.netfirms.com/adams/erie_01.html (accessed on June 30, 2005).

Smith, Adam. *An Inquiry into the Nature and Causes of the Wealth of Nations*. Published 1776. http://www.wsu.edu:8080/~wldciv/world_civ_reader/world_civ_reader_2/adam_smith.html (accessed on June 30, 2005).

Railroads: The First Big Business

An increase in railroad construction between 1860 and 1900 changed the United States, helping make it the industrial nation it is today. As the chief system of transportation of goods and people, railroads were essential to American industry. Where railroads went, towns and cities with bustling new commerce arose, all dependent on the railways for shipments of food and goods. The construction of the railroads spawned huge new industries in steel, iron, and coal. No other business so dramatically stimulated and embodied the industrialization process. In *The Rise of Industrial America: A People's History of the Post-Reconstruction Era* author Page Smith comments: "In retrospect it appeared it had been the lack of adequate transportation, above all else, that had kept civilization moving at a mere camel's pace, or a mule's or ox's pace, prior to the railroad era ... the railroads accelerated the process to a degree that the mind could hardly comprehend."

The race to build railroads in the last four decades of the nineteenth century was dramatic but not graceful. Early railroad magnates (powerful and influential people in the

The completion of the transcontinental railroad. *(Getty Images. Reproduced by permission.)*

Words to Know

bankruptcy: A state of financial ruin in which an individual or corporation cannot pay its debts.

bond: A certificate of debt issued by a government or corporation that guarantees repayment of the original investment with interest by a specified date.

capital: Accumulated wealth or goods devoted to the production of other goods.

gauge: Distance between the rails of a railroad track.

grant: A transfer or property by deed or writing.

magnate: A powerful and influential person in an industry.

monopoly: The exclusive possession or right to produce a particular good or service.

patent: A legal document issued by a government granting exclusive authority to an inventor for making, using, and selling an invention.

transcontinental railroad: A railroad that spans a continent, from coast to coast.

industry) found many opportunities to get very rich. Some methods were legitimate, others questionable, and many were downright illegal. The railroad tycoons engaged in destructive competition with each other and exploited their laborers. Still, even though the government did offer some help, the tremendous expansion of the railroads in the second half of the nineteenth century was accomplished mainly through the active private enterprise of the railroad magnates.

The transcontinental railroad

By the 1850s most Americans recognized that westward expansion and industrial growth depended on a transcontinental railroad—one that spanned the continent from the East Coast to the West Coast. Many thought building such a railroad was impossible because of the great distance to be covered and the engineering obstacles to be overcome, especially the tremendous amount of money required for the project. The transcontinental railroad was clearly going to cost more than any previous American businesses, and by 1850 most people agreed that the federal government should provide aid to railroad companies to start the process. That year Congress authorized its first federal grant (a transfer or property by deed or writing), which consisted of public land to help promote and finance railroad construction. More land grants to the railroads occurred throughout the decade, but the greatest land grants were the result of the Pacific Railroad acts of 1862 and 1864.

Pacific Railroad Act

The Pacific Railroad Act of 1862 called for building a transcontinental railroad from Omaha, Nebraska, to Sacramento, California. Under the act, two companies, the Central Pacific and the Union Pacific, were to build the railroad. Construction on the Central Pacific lines was to begin in Sacramento and work its way east. The Central Pacific Company had been organized in California by railroad engineer Theodore Dehone Judah (1826–1863), who had long dreamed of building a railroad that would cross California's Sierra Nevada Mountains and travel eastward. To handle the business end of the Central Pacific, he brought together a group of California men who came to be known as the Big Four: store owner Collis P. Huntington (1821–1900), one-term California governor Leland Stanford (1824–1893), businessman Mark Hopkins (1813–1878), and store owner Charles Crocker (1822–1888). Judah died before the work was fully underway, but the Big Four went on to oversee the building of the Central Pacific Railroad.

The other railroad created by the 1862 act was the Union Pacific Railroad Company. It was to build its tracks from Nebraska west to meet the ongoing construction of the Central Pacific. Investor Thomas C. Durant (1820–1885), the railroad's vice president, was largely in control of Union Pacific from the start.

The Pacific Railroad Act granted public land to the railroads in alternating 200-foot and 10-mile sections along the lines. The railroads used the extra land surrounding the railways as backing for loans or sold it to raise money for construction. The government agreed to loan the railroad companies $16,000 a mile for construction in level country, $32,000 in the foothills (low hills at the base of a mountain), and $48,000 in the mountains. To expand the amount of public land available to the railway companies, the act also authorized the United States to renege on (fail to carry out) government treaties it had signed with Native Americans granting the same land for their use.

The government gave railroad companies a total of about 130 million acres of land, with the states adding another 50 million acres of land grants. Though the government aid stimulated railroad construction, only 18,738 miles of railroad line—8 percent of the total railroad mileage built in the United States between 1860 and 1920—were built as a direct result of federal land grants and loans. Most of the railroads were funded through private enterprise.

Building the first transcontinental railroad

The Union Pacific and the Central Pacific Railroads began construction in 1863. From the start both companies viewed the project as a race, each trying to obtain as much land and money from the government as possible before the two lines met.

Construction of the Union Pacific

The construction of the Union Pacific began in Omaha in December 1863 with great fanfare, but enthusiasm died quickly when work slowed due to a lack of laborers. With most healthy males fighting in the American Civil War (1861–65; a war between the Union [the North], who were opposed to slavery, and the Confederacy [the South], who were in favor of slavery), the Union Pacific could build only forty miles of line between 1864 and 1865. When the war ended, returning soldiers turned to the railroads for work, and the Union Pacific also recruited large numbers of recently arrived Irish immigrants from the eastern cities.

After the slow start, former Union army Brigadier General Jack Casement (1829–1909) was hired to oversee the Union Pacific work crews. Casement carefully divided the construction work into specialized tasks, creating a simple, repetitive routine. One group brought in the rail tracks on horse-drawn carts. Another group unloaded the carts and laid out the rails. The next, called gaugers, measured the rails to make sure they were the right gauge, or distance, apart. The rails were then joined together by the bolters. Finally a group of workers hammered spikes (very large nails) into the railroad ties to secure the rail to the bed, the surface of the earth prepared with gravel or broken stones to serve as the foundation for the rail. The process was repeated over and over and the tracks grew about two miles a day. The workers lived in a mobile tent city. As the railroad expanded from one location to the next, the whole town was transported on flat cars to the point where new railway construction ended.

Construction of the Central Pacific

When Leland Stanford, one of the associates of the Central Pacific, was elected governor of California in 1862, anti-Asian sentiments were strong due to prejudice. The Chinese who had immigrated to California looked different than other settlers there, with their long queues, or braids, and different style of clothing. They spoke a different language and practiced a different religion. Many Californians viewed them as immoral slaves and drug users. Leland promised to "protect" the state from Chinese immigrants. But as the construction of the Central Pacific got underway, Leland's partner, Charles Crocker, could not find enough laborers willing to do the difficult and dangerous work. He tried using Chinese workers and they proved so satisfactory that more than twelve thousand Chinese laborers were employed to build the Central Pacific, making up about 80 percent of its workforce. They were disciplined workers whose customs differed greatly from European American workers. They did not drink alcohol, they ate fresh vegetables and drank boiled tea, and they bathed regularly. Consequently, they remained far healthier than their European American counterparts. They were also willing to work for less money. The Central Pacific paid Irish workers $35 a day, with meals; they paid Chinese laborers $27 a day, without meals.

Central Pacific laborers faced nearly impossible obstacles: brutal mountain winters, desert heat, and the prospect of blasting tunnels through the steep, 7,000-foot-high peaks of the Sierra Nevada Mountains. The Chinese workers were first organized into gangs of twenty men under a supervisor, but later, as the work became more difficult, the gangs grew larger. The work of these crews was intense and physically demanding. They cut through solid rock, mainly using pickaxes, and often while perched in precarious positions on the mountain peaks. Then the heavy loads of rock and dirt had to be carried away on the workers' backs. Powerful snowstorms and multiple accidents killed several laborers. Gradually, the crews fulfilled Judah's vision by laying track through the nearly impassible canyons and peaks of the Sierra Nevadas.

In the spring of 1869 Union Pacific and Central Pacific construction crews came within sight of each other. Promontory Point in Utah was chosen as the junction of the two lines. The Union Pacific had laid 1,086 miles of track and the Central Pacific had laid 689 miles. When the new 1,775 miles of tracks running from the Missouri River to the West Coast was added to existing railway starting from the East Coast, the nation was connected by 3,500 miles of transcontinental railroad from New York to California. Traveling across the American continent had previously taken several months, but with the transcontinental railroad it took about six days. At the ceremony celebrating the connection of the rails, Thomas Durant and Leland Stanford hammered the last spike, made of gold for the occasion, into the railroad tie. Then the engines of the two railroads met nose to nose on the track as whistles blew, bells rang, and the crowd cheered. People throughout the nation celebrated this milestone in history.

The Erie War

The opportunities offered by the new transportation systems of the nineteenth century attracted daring pioneers, ruthless businessmen, and greedy crooks, and sometimes they fought bitter feuds, each trying to take property and profits from their competitors. Daniel Drew (1797–1879), Jay Gould (1836–1892), and James Fisk (1834–1872) were among the most notorious criminals of the day. Drew began his business career buying cattle and sheep in New England and the Midwest and selling them to butchers in New York City. While his cattle were on the way to market he often deprived them of water and then gave them salt and let them drink heavily just prior to their sale. His cattle, swollen with water to a higher weight and a beefier appearance, brought in more money than they were worth. This practice was the origin of the term "watered-down stock," which would soon be applied to company stocks that were overvalued by dishonest executives like Drew.

THE GREAT RACE FOR THE WESTERN STAKES 1870

In this political cartoon of the Erie War, Cornelius Vanderbilt and James Fisk race for control of the Erie Railroad. *(© Bettmann/Corbis.)*

In the 1860s Drew, Fisk, and Gould started buying great quantities of Erie Railroad stock and thus became controlling directors of the New York railroad. The three soon ran into a tough opponent, Cornelius Vanderbilt (1794–1877), and the resulting business feud became known as the "Erie War." Vanderbilt had made his vast fortune in steamboat services. He was known to be a ruthless businessman who drove his competition off the playing field. At the age of seventy, Vanderbilt decided railroads were the wave of the future. In 1857 he purchased a controlling interest in the Harlem Railroad, followed by the Hudson River Railroad in 1865 and the New York Central in 1867. He then merged his holdings into one system that extended from New York City to Buffalo, New York.

In 1867 Vanderbilt faced one last competitor in the region, the Erie Railroad. In his usual pattern, he lowered the rates on his railroad services drastically to take away the Erie's business. Rather than lowering Erie rates in response, Fisk bought a herd of cattle and shipped it at the reduced rate on Vanderbilt's railroad, costing Vanderbilt dearly. A disgusted Vanderbilt then decided to buy out the Erie altogether and proceeded to purchase all available shares of the railroad company. Drew, Gould, and Fisk promptly issued one hundred thousand worthless stock certificates for the Erie. Vanderbilt bought the worthless certificates and then realized he had been cheated. He called for the arrest of Fisk, Gould, and Drew, but they had fled to New Jersey to escape New York law. They were able to bribe several New York legislators to pass a law that made their dealings legal and got away with their swindle, keeping possession of the Erie Railroad, which they then drove into bankruptcy. Though Vanderbilt lost the Erie Railroad, he went on to extend his railway service to Chicago, Illinois. He was reportedly the richest man in the United States when he died.

Jay Cooke and the panic of 1873

After the completion of the first transcontinental railroad, construction continued at a feverish pace. Between 1865 and 1873 railroad mileage doubled, increasing by some thirty thousand miles. This increase was well beyond the immediate needs of the country. In the West, where the sparse population did not justify the operation of so many trains, the returns on railroad investment were very poor.

In 1869 Jay Cooke (1821–1905), owner of a large private bank and promoter of government bonds during the Civil War (see Chapter 5), became the banker and agent for the Northern Pacific Railway Company. The line was projected to link Lake Superior in Minnesota with the Puget Sound on the coast of Washington, which made it the largest railroad construction project in American history. Though the land it covered was sparsely populated, many believed that with railroad service Minnesota and the Pacific Northwest would soon become booming territories. The anticipated new traffic of the region was expected to pay for construction and operations. This plan proved too optimistic, however. There was no new traffic and Cooke could not raise sufficient funds from the investors to complete the construction. Therefore, in 1871 Cooke decided to sell $100 million in Northern Pacific bonds to the public. Bonds are certificates of debt issued by a government or corporation that guarantees repayment of the original investment with interest by a specified date. Cooke sent his sales agents all over the nation and spent hundreds of thousands of dollars advertising the bonds. Still, the public was not buying.

The Northern Pacific was struggling while Cooke pursued the bond sales. The railroad repeatedly overdrew its account at Cooke's bank. The overextension became so large that in 1873 Cooke's entire banking company collapsed. The failure of the leading private bank in the United States caused a national panic. Stocks fell so severely that on September 20, 1873, the New York Stock Exchange closed for ten days. Throughout the nation banks were forced to close. Businesses failed. The panic of 1873 was the worst depression the nation had experienced to that point. It was not until 1879 that there was any sign of a business revival.

Railroad company management

Railroads were too big to be run effectively by existing business practices. The day-to-day management of these corporations was highly complex. By 1890 there were an estimated 749,000 American railroad workers nationwide, and the railroads were the largest employer in the United States. Managing a nationwide workforce, keeping the accounts, setting the fares, making the schedules, incorporating new inventions, maintaining machines, and accomplishing the thousands of other complicated tasks needed coordination. In an 1874 *Harper's Monthly* article, Lyman Abbott described the complex operations of the Erie Railroad, noting that it employed fifteen thousand people and that its operations were continual. Abbott said, "The administration of such a force of men, the management of such a system of railroad trains, without clashing or collision, requires executive ability of the very highest order."

After the panic of 1873, railroad executives tried to minimize waste and tighten up their operations. Strong hierarchies (ranks) of management developed, often imitating the ranks of the military. Railroads were usually run by a board of

Important Innovations and Updates

Steel versus iron rails. In 1856 British engineer Henry Bessemer (1813–1898) developed a new process for making steel cheaply by blasting preheated air through molten iron. Two years later the Siemens-Martin open-hearth method of producing steel was introduced. These processes greatly reduced the cost of producing steel. The first Bessemer converter in the United States was built in 1864, and the first open-hearth furnace, which was better suited to American iron ore, was built in 1868. Both increased steel production in the United States. This meant that the railroad companies could begin to lay steel rails rather than the troublesome iron ones, which tended to warp. By 1873 the United States was producing nearly 115,000 tons of steel rail, accounting for approximately one-eighth of all U.S. steel production. As the price of steel continued to drop, steel rails completely replaced iron rails.

Uniform gauges. As competing railroad companies built their tracks, they used many different gauges, or distances between the two rails. Because of this, competing lines could not connect with each other, causing delays and accidents. It was not until 1880 that some of the railroads of the East and Midwest began to adopt standard gauges of 4 feet 8.5 inches. By 1890 this gauge was uniform to all regions.

Air brakes. Accidents on the railroads were common and cost thousands of lives. The braking systems were often responsible. To stop the early railroad cars the engineer sent out whistle signals to brakemen stationed along the length of a train. The brakemen then turned hand brakes on each car. Inventor George Westinghouse (1846–1916) created a train brake that consisted of an air pump powered by the train's engine. It was controlled by the engineer or brakeman. The air brake system ran the length of the train, with mechanical devices installed on each car to activate the brakes. By 1900, 75 percent of all trains were equipped with air brakes, making them much safer.

directors. The top managers were hired, promoted, and fired based on their performance, which hinged on the success of the railroad they managed. Specialized lower-level managers carried out their instructions. Due largely to the efforts of the managers, railroad companies were leaders in business innovation.

Railroads faced some major problems as they modernized their operations. In order to coordinate schedules and employees and to avoid collisions, the railroads were first in the nation to adopt a system of standard time. (Previously the country had run on a system of solar time, in which the local time was determined by the position of the Sun. When the Sun was directly overhead, the clocks were set at noon. However, noon in one town was several minutes apart from noon in a town miles away.) They also set up a system of railroad telegraphers to relay information about train arrivals or delays to distant stations. Prior to the widespread use of telegraphs in railroads, tight scheduling was nearly impossible and railroad collisions were frequent and deadly.

The railroad strike of 1877

After the panic of 1873, many railroads were nearly bankrupt. Bankruptcy is a state of financial ruin in which an individual or corporation cannot pay its debts. In 1877, in order to improve their finances, the Pennsylvania, New York Central, and Baltimore and Ohio Railroads began reducing wages. When they announced another 10 percent reduction, the railroad firemen (the men who feed the train's fires) of the Baltimore and Ohio line at Martinsburg, West Virginia, walked off the job in protest, preventing some six hundred trains from moving. The governor of the state called out the state militia, or army, but the militiamen had friends and relatives among the strikers and would not take strong action. About four hundred federal troops finally dispersed the protesters and put an end to the strike in Martinsburg.

Within a week railroad workers in Pittsburgh went on strike and prevented the movement of all trains. Fires broke out, destroying five hundred freight cars, one hundred locomotives, and thirty-nine buildings. The state militia was again sympathetic to the strikers, so federal troops were called in. The strike spread to New York City, St. Louis, Missouri, Chicago, Illinois, and as far west as San Francisco, California. The workers were not organized, and thus within a couple of weeks the strike had been broken and train traffic was back to normal.

In those few weeks, about ten thousand railroad workers had gone on strike. More than one hundred were killed by federal troops and about one thousand were jailed. Afterward, railroad owners and managers began to fear the potential power of the labor movement. In many large cities, state national guards were given special arms

One of the Baltimore & Ohio Railroad strikes of 1877. *(© Bettmann/Corbis.)*

and training to combat labor violence. Railroads and other corporations began to make use of Pinkerton detectives (security agents for hire) as private armies to protect their property. Companies also attempted to discover, and fire, all union members.

Competition in the railroad business

The cost of running railroads was high. Between track and engine maintenance and salaries for thousands of workers, it cost nearly as much money to run empty trains as it did to run full ones. No railroad could afford to halt operations. Therefore when a railroad faced competition for traffic, it was usually forced to cut its rates, either directly or by offering large shippers rebates (return of part of the payment) to keep its business. This competition had destructive results for the railroad industry.

George Pullman

In 1851 contractor George Pullman (1831–1897) took his first overnight train ride from Boston to Westfield, Massachusetts. At that time overnight passengers who wished to sleep were given cots or mattresses. Many sat up all night on stiff benches in smoky cars. Due to the growing number of businessmen traveling between cities, Pullman realized there was a market for comfort. Under a contract with the Chicago and Alton Railroad, he designed two oversized coach cars, dividing the space into ten sleeper sections with curtains. He hinged the upper berths so they could be opened at night and did the same with the chairs, so that both could swing up out of the way. Pullman paid enormous attention to details, outfitting the cars with cherrywood berths, plush upholstered seats, and soft, glowing oil lamps.

Pullman's next luxury car, the *Pioneer,* was patented (granted exclusive authority by the government for making, using, and selling an invention for a period of time) in 1864. The sleeper was huge at 54 feet long and 10 feet wide, with accommodations for fifty passengers. Each car contained thick carpeting, heavy curtains, French plate mirrors, black walnut woodwork, oil chandeliers, and fine linens that were changed daily. Porters carried baggage and attended to the riders' needs. The luxury cars cost four times more to build than other sleepers. But

Internior of a Pullman car. *(© Bettmann/Corbis.)*

the $2 fare for an overnighter in Pullman's *Pioneer* was only fifty cents more than conventional sleepers, and travelers loved them. In 1865 the *Pioneer* was chosen to transport the body of assassinated president Abraham Lincoln (1809–1865; served 1861–65) back to Springfield, Illinois, for his funeral.

Pullman went on to add new elements of luxury to train cars. In 1868 he unveiled the first dining car, known as the *Delmonico.* In 1875 the first parlor car was introduced and featured upholstered swivel reclining seats. Within ten years of starting his business, Pullman held a virtual monopoly on luxury train travel in the United States.

Throughout the 1880s, new railroad construction occurred at a frantic pace. Approximately 71,000 miles of track were laid during the decade. The railroad network became overbuilt. Competing lines were racing to put down track in order to lay claim to the best sites, whether railroad service was needed there or not. Many of the powerful businessmen were out for personal profit and did not care how long or well their company operated. The reckless expansion of the railroad companies set off a financial panic in 1893 in which hundreds of railroads collapsed. By 1895 one-third of the nation's railroad mileage was in bankruptcy.

By 1890 wealthy financier J. P. Morgan (1837–1913) began to consolidate and reorganize the nation's railroads, adopting a strategy that became known as "Morganization." Morgan acquired bankrupted railroads, infused them with enough new capital (accumulated wealth or goods devoted to the production of other goods) to survive, implemented strict cost cuts, and oversaw agreements with competing lines to reduce unnecessary competition. By the turn of the twentieth century, he owned some five thousand miles of railroad. Although he made a great fortune, his intention was to benefit the troubled industry. His reorganization of the railroads created a more stable environment, bringing the rocky era of warring railroad magnates to a close.

For More Information

Books

Brogan, Hugh. *The Penguin History of the USA.* 2nd ed. New York and London: Penguin Books, 1999.

Cashman, Sean Dennis. *America in the Gilded Age.* New York and London: New York University Press, 1984.

Smith, Page. *The Rise of Industrial America.* Vol. 6. New York: McGraw-Hill, 1984.

Web Sites

Abbott, Lyman. "The American Railroad." *Harper's New Monthly Magazine,* 1874. *Cornell University Library.* http://cdl.library.cornell.edu/cgi-bin/moa/moa-cgi?notisid=ABK4014-0049-48 (accessed on June 30, 2005).

Dunbar, Willis F. "Railroad History Story: RR Operations before the Telegraph." *RRHX: Internet Railroad History Museum of Michigan.*

http://www.michiganrailroads.com/RRHX/Stories/OperationsBeforeThe Telegraph.htm (accessed on June 30, 2005).

"The Pullman Era." *Chicago Historical Society.* http://www.chicagohs. org/ history/pullman.html (accessed on June 30, 2005).

"Transcontinental Railroad." *American Experience: PBS.* http:// www.pbs.org/wgbh/amex/tcrr/peopleevents/index.html (accessed on June 30, 2005).

The Robber Barons

During the period of the Industrial Revolution known as the Gilded Age (an era lasting roughly from the early 1860s to the turn of the century), shrewd businessmen from humble backgrounds became multimillionaires by seizing opportunities in the country's new industries. Their fortunes quickly became legendary, inspiring many young men to leave their family farms and head for the city with hopes of becoming rich. In this era the very act of making money was idealized in the arts and media, and even in church sermons. The "rags-to-riches" story, in which an impoverished young man rises to wealth and prominence through his own hard work and determination, spread throughout the popular culture.

The inspiration for rags-to-riches dreams of this period came from a relatively small number of American businessmen who created gigantic industries unlike anything known before. They became enormously wealthy and held great influence over the economy and even over the government. Some Americans viewed them as "robber barons," a ruthless and greedy bunch that would stop at nothing in pursuit of their own fortunes. Others viewed them as captains of industry and credited them for making the United States the richest industrial nation of the world.

The robber barons came into power around the close of the American Civil War (1861–65; a war between the Union [the North], who were opposed to slavery, and the Confederacy [the South], who were in favor of slavery), at a time when all the pieces were in place for tremendous expansion. The country was rich in natural resources such as iron, coal, and oil. Technological advances had greatly improved manufacturing processes. Population growth, fed by the arrival of immigrants, provided a steady labor force that worked for low wages. The country was connected for the first time by a national railway system. Although Congress had imposed income and estate taxes on individuals to support the Civil War in 1862, these taxes were unpopular and ceased in 1872. (There were no personal or corporate income taxes again—except for one brief period in 1894–95—until 1913, when the 16th Amendment to the Constitution made the income tax a permanent feature of the U.S. tax system.) In general during the Gilded Age the nation's policies were extremely favorable for big business, as the government maintained a laissez-faire (hands-off) attitude and did not regulate or oversee the businesses. The robber barons turned these factors to their advantage, building great industrial empires. Whether they benefited or took advantage of the U.S. economy—or both—is an issue still being argued today.

The trouble with free competition

Until the Civil War there had been little competition among manufacturers. Most companies served the market in their own region, and new companies simply went where they were needed. But after the war the large new industries sold their products across the nation, creating true business competition for the first time in American history. This competition caused some major problems. When several manufacturers tried to sell the same product to the same market (population of buyers), the result was often a flooding of the market with more goods than consumers could buy. With too much product on the market, manufacturers lowered their prices to draw customers away from competitors. Sometimes they were

Words to Know

capital: Accumulated wealth or goods devoted to the production of other goods.

capitalism: An economic system in which the means of production and distribution are privately owned by individuals or groups and competition for business establishes the price of goods and services.

consolidation: A process in which companies purchase other companies and fold them into one large corporation.

evolution: Evolution is the process by which all plant and animal species change over time because of variations that are passed from one generation to the next. The theory of evolution was first proposed by naturalist Charles Darwin (1809–1882).

horizontal expansion: Growth occurring when a company purchases rival companies in the same industry in an effort to eliminate competition.

industrialism: The social system that results from an economy based on large-scale industries.

industry: A distinct group of profit-making enterprises that produces a certain product, such as the textile or steel industry.

interstate commerce: Trade that crosses the borders between states.

laissez-faire An economic doctrine that opposes government regulation of commerce and industry beyond the minimum necessary.

monopoly: The exclusive possession or right to produce a particular good or service.

muckrakers: Journalists who search for and expose corruption in public affairs.

philanthropy: The desire or effort to help humankind, as by making charitable donations.

pools: Agreements among rival companies to share their profits or divide up territories to avoid destructive competition and maintain higher prices.

refinery: A building in which a raw material is processed to free it from impurities.

strike: A work stoppage by employees to protest conditions or make demands of their employer.

trusts: A group of companies, joined for the purpose of reducing competition and controlling prices.

vertical expansion: Growth that occurs when a primary company purchases other companies that provide services or products needed for the company's business, in order to avoid paying competitive prices.

forced to drop their prices below the cost of producing the goods. Unlike large companies that had strong financial backing, small companies could not survive a period with meager earnings and collapsed when prices fell too low.

Although free competition on the market fit American ideals, overproduction and price wars made an unstable economic environment for many businesses. The U.S. government did not have rules and regulations that extended to national businesses at the time, so the industrialists of the Gilded Age took it into their own hands to establish a more stable market for their products.

Pools and trusts

During the late 1860s, rival companies in some industries got together to form pools—agreements among rivals to share their profits or divide up territories in order to avoid destructive competition and maintain higher prices. U.S. salt producers were among the first to create a successful pool, when competition had created a chaotic price war. After the formation of the Michigan Salt Association in 1869, the salt companies agreed to divide up their territories and were immediately able to double the price of salt. Other industries soon formed similar pools. While this stabilized the market for the companies, the lack of competition in the market hurt consumers, who had to pay higher prices.

Pool agreements were informal agreements among businesses and not legal contracts; therefore they could not be enforced and some companies did not live up to their word. This caused new price wars. From the 1870s on, the largest trend in business was toward consolidation, a process in which companies purchased other companies and folded them into one large corporation. There were two general ways to consolidate. One was horizontal expansion, in which the primary company purchased as many of its rival companies as possible. The end result, if the primary company was successful, would be a monopoly, or ownership of all companies in the industry. The other way to consolidate was vertical expansion, in which the primary company bought up companies that provided the services it needed, thus avoiding having to pay competitive prices for equipment, transportation, and manufacturing.

Some new big businesses began to form trusts, or groups of companies joined together to reduce competition and control prices. A trust was formed when several companies in the same industry transferred their properties and stocks to a board of

The Meat Industry and Gustavus Swift

Gustavus Swift (1839–1903) moved his meatpacking business to Chicago in 1875 and began shipping beef to consumers in the Northeast. In those days only live cattle were shipped and it was a costly process. The cattle had to be fed along the way, some died in transit, and the railroads charged per pound. A 1,000-pound steer yielded only about 600 pounds of beef and the rest was a loss for the company. Swift wanted to butcher the cattle first and then ship the beef, so he explored ways to keep the meat from spoiling during transport. He successfully sent one carload of beef during the coldest part of winter in 1877, but railroad-car refrigeration technology was inadequate for shipping during the rest of the year. Swift hired an engineer to perfect a refrigeration car that used circulating fresh air cooled by ice. He contracted ice harvesters in Wisconsin to produce enough ice for the cars and established icing stations along the railroad routes heading east. After finding partners in the railroad industry, he built functioning refrigerated railroad cars for his business.

However, many obstacles remained. Consumers in eastern cities did not feel safe eating meat slaughtered elsewhere, as they feared it might spoil before it reached them. Railroads preferred the larger freight profits from shipping live cattle, and they joined together against Swift, charging high prices for his packaged meats. Undaunted, Swift mounted large-scale advertising campaigns to win public confidence and made partnerships allowing him to sell through local butchers. For transport, he negotiated good rates with the Grand Trunk Railway, which had never made much profit shipping cattle. Swift's success continued and after fifteen years his company was worth $25 million.

trustees who then ran all the companies. As the trusts got bigger and stronger, they were able to buy out more and more of their competition. Capital (accumulated wealth or goods devoted to the production of other goods) became concentrated in just a few huge corporations, especially in transportation and heavy industry. The pioneer and best example of the gigantic trusts of the Gilded Age was the Standard Oil Company Trust, formed by John D. Rockefeller (1839–1937).

Rockefeller and Standard Oil

Prior to the 1850s people usually lit their lamps with whale oil. As the supply of whales diminished, oil producers had to look for oil elsewhere. Crude oil (liquid petroleum in its natural state) could be refined into flammable oil called kerosene for lighting lamps, but it was obtained by a difficult process of skimming it off the tops of ponds of water. The first modern oil well was drilled in 1859, and crude oil was suddenly available in large quantities. In 1861 the first petroleum refinery (a building in which a raw material is processed to free it from impurities) opened in the United States, churning out mostly kerosene. Four years later, Rockefeller, co-owner of a very successful wholesale grocery business in Cleveland, Ohio, expanded into oil refining as a side business. Though few thought there was much of a future in it, his interest had been captivated. In 1865 he shifted his focus exclusively to refining oil. By the end of the year, his oil refinery was producing at least twice as much as any other refinery in Cleveland.

Since Standard Oil was not close to the oil wells in Pennsylvania or many of its consumers, the company shipped massive quantities of oil on a regular basis. Low shipping rates were essential to maintaining competitive prices and high profits. Railroads at the time commonly gave favored shippers rebates, or partial refunds, on their publicly stated rates. The larger the shipper, the higher the rebate. Rockefeller manipulated the railroads to get the lowest rates possible, offering large and consistent business in return. This allowed him to sell for a lower price than his competitors.

Rockefeller invested in the top machinery and consistently rearranged his manufacturing processes in order to save a few cents per step. Standard Oil began making its own barrels to ship oil. Since the company needed wood for the barrels, Rockefeller bought his own timber tracts, or wooded areas purchased for logging. He owned his own warehouses, bought his own tank cars, and, to the extent possible, owned or produced the raw materials and transportation he needed to operate.

South Improvement Company and the Cleveland Massacre

In 1870 Standard Oil joined the South Improvement Company, a secret partnership among important railroad lines and a few of the largest oil refiners. Participating companies formed a pact (agreement) that the railroads would post their shipping rates at a high level, but they would pay rebates to the refiners who were members of the South Improvement

Company. In addition, the railroads would pay drawbacks, or duties, to the members for all shipments made by nonmembers. Thus, oil refiners who were not in the pact would end up paying a great deal more for shipping than the members. In the end their losses would drive them out of business. When news of the pact leaked, the public was infuriated. The South Improvement Company was shut down before it made a single transaction and Rockefeller's reputation was badly tarnished.

Rockefeller was nevertheless convinced that the health of the refinery business depended on getting rid of destructive competition. Indeed, the petroleum industry was chaotic. Unregulated drilling and oil strikes produced irregular floods of oil. It cost no more to build a small refinery than to open a hardware store, so when oil prices rose, several newcomers built refineries in an attempt to seize quick profits. Their production would flood the market with oil, causing prices to fall and destroying small companies. Only the large companies with vast reserves could hold out until prices rose again. Rockefeller believed that these alternative waves of boom and bust could be abolished by combining the refineries under the leadership of Standard Oil, placing the entire refining industry in the hands of what was essentially a federation of its strongest units.

During the commotion over the South Improvement Company, Rockefeller had been carrying out a scheme of horizontal expansion that came to be called the Cleveland Massacre. Early in 1872 he offered to buy out most of the twenty-six Cleveland oil refineries. Owners could accept either a cash offer or Standard Oil stock, or risk being driven out of business and losing everything. Twenty-one refiners sold out within three months. Some claimed they had been pressured into selling at prices less than their businesses were worth. Others felt threatened by the looming South Improvement Company agreement. Standard Oil was suddenly one of the industrial giants of the time.

By the end of 1872 Rockefeller and his associates controlled all the major refineries in Cleveland, New York City, Pittsburgh, Pennsylvania, and Philadelphia, Pennsylvania. Over the next decade, the Standard Oil Company developed a pipeline system, purchased new oil-bearing lands, acquired extensive oil shipping facilities, and constructed an elaborate and efficient marketing system. By 1879 Standard Oil Company controlled between 90 and 95 percent of the American refining capacity, dominating the American petroleum industry.

Creation of the Standard Oil Trust

In buying up its competition, Standard Oil acquired stock in other companies, which was illegal in Ohio. To get around the law, the stocks were simply purchased in the names of various stockholders acting as trustees. For years the trustee system allowed the company to expand well beyond the borders of Ohio. However, there was no provision for the death or resignation of a trustee. A more formal arrangement was needed, so in 1882 the Standard Oil Trust was formed by an agreement that placed all properties owned or controlled by the Standard Oil Company in the hands of nine trustees, including Rockefeller. The trust included fourteen companies that it owned outright and twenty-six more that it owned in part. The trustees exercised general supervision over them all. Rockefeller retired from active leadership in 1897.

Carnegie and U.S. steel

In the 1850s industrial demand for iron, particularly for the railroads, stimulated major expansion in the U.S. iron industry. After 1865, however, steel slowly began to replace iron in popularity. Steel is an alloy (a compound made up of two or more metals) of carbon and iron that is harder and stronger than iron. It had previously been too expensive to produce in quantity in the United States, but in 1856 British inventor Henry Bessemer (1813–1898) invented a converter that could efficiently remove carbon from pig iron (processed crude iron) in amounts necessary for mass production of steel. In the early 1870s, thirty-six-year-old Scottish American businessman Andrew Carnegie (1835–1919) was visiting England and witnessed the Bessemer steel-making process. Upon returning to the United States, he built the largest steel mill in the country using the Bessemer process.

Carnegie, who had raised himself out of poverty, learned a great deal about business working for the Pennsylvania Railroad. He was knowledgeable about the future of railroads and understood the value of steel rails. By keeping costs down, technology updated, and always hiring the most talented managers, he produced steel more efficiently than his rivals and sold his steel rails at the lowest prices on the market. His company was an immediate success. In 1881 he combined his company with several others, naming it the Carnegie Steel Company. By the 1890s Carnegie's mills had introduced the Siemens-Martin process, an advanced and more efficient open-hearth furnace process that is still used in steel making today. (The process is named after English engineer Charles William Siemens [1823–1883], who designed an improved regenerative furnace for steel production, and French engineer Pierre Émile Martin [1824–1915], who created a variation of Siemens's design.)

Carnegie expanded vertically to keep costs low and competition at bay. He purchased a large coke (a form of coal used as fuel) company and vast acres of coalfields and iron-ore deposits that furnished the raw materials needed for steel making. Then he purchased the ships and railroads needed to transport these supplies to the mills. Carnegie was able to defeat his competitors by always having the lowest prices and the highest profits. By the end of the nineteenth century, the Carnegie Steel Company controlled all the elements it used in the steel production process and was producing one quarter of the nation's steel.

The Homestead Strike of 1892

Homestead, Pennsylvania, was the center of Andrew Carnegie's enormous steel empire, the Carnegie Steel Company, which produced fully one-quarter of the nation's steel by 1892. Most of the steelworkers belonged to the Amalgamated Association of Iron and Steel Workers, a strong union with 24,000 members. In the past, Carnegie had publicly supported the right of workers to form unions, but by 1892 he opposed the union in his plants. He believed they interfered with good management of the company and he was also aware that a strike (work stoppage) could cripple his steel empire.

In 1892, as Carnegie's contract with the union was about to expire, he instructed his general manager, Henry Clay Frick (1849–1919), to announce that the steel mill would now employ nonunion workers and pay lower wages. Carnegie then left for Europe, leaving management to Frick, whose opposition to unions was well known. The Homestead workers went on strike on July 1. Frick employed 300 company guards

The Carnegie Company's Homestead Steel Works plant in Pennsylvania.
(Courtesy of The Library of Congress.)

hired through Pinkerton's National Detective Agency to seize the millworks from the strikers. When the guards attacked on the night of July 5, the strikers had been alerted and were waiting. The eight-hour battle that followed resulted in 35 deaths and about 60 seriously wounded men.

An unsuccessful assassination attempt on Frick's life by a Russian radical soon after the confrontation turned public opinion against the union. The state of Pennsylvania sent 4,000 soldiers to occupy the factory, which was soon turned over to management. Nonunion workers were hired and the millwork resumed normal operations. Four months later, the Amalgamated voted to end the strike, but the organization was now crushed, effectively ending unionism in the steel industry (see Chapter 10).

Robber Barons and Philanthropy

Quite a few of the great industrialists of the Gilded Age believed it was their responsibility to use part of their large fortunes to promote the public good. Their philanthropy resulted in the creation of some of the nation's great institutions of learning, science, and culture.

John D. Rockefeller virtually created the University of Chicago with gifts totaling $80.6 million. He created the Rockefeller Institute for Medical Research in 1901 and the General Education Board in 1902. In 1913 he formed the giant Rockefeller Foundation. Rockefeller's gifts to the public totaled more than a half billion dollars.

Andrew Carnegie funded 2,509 public libraries, built Carnegie Hall in New York City, and founded the Carnegie Institute of Technology, which later became Carnegie-Mellon University. In 1905 he established the Carnegie Foundation for the Advancement of Teaching, and in 1910 the Carnegie Endowment for International Peace. In 1911 he founded the Carnegie Corporation of New York. Throughout his lifetime Carnegie distributed some $350 million towards the public good.

J. P. Morgan was a trustee of the American Museum of Natural History for more than forty years from its founding in 1869. He purchased and donated many of its great collections. He was also a trustee of the Metropolitan Museum of Art and through his contributions was responsible for making it an extremely successful and respected museum.

Cornelius Vanderbilt gave $1 million to Vanderbilt University (previously Central University) at Nashville, Tennessee, and is regarded as the school's founder.

Philip Danforth Armour founded the Armour Mission and the Armour Institute of Technology. He contributed large sums of money for the construction of low-cost housing for his workers.

Gustavus Swift was one of the founders and chief supporters of St. James Methodist Episcopal Church in Chicago and was a generous donor to the University of Chicago, Northwestern University, the Young Men's Christian Association (YMCA), and other causes.

The gospel of wealth

Carnegie believed society benefited from the concentration of industry in the hands of a few, but only so long as the rich industrialists used their extra wealth for the common benefit. In his essay "Wealth," which originally appeared in the 1889 *North American Review,* Carnegie declared, "The man of wealth [becomes] the mere trustee and agent for his poorer brethren, bringing to their service his superior wisdom, experience, and ability to administer, doing for them better than they would or could do for themselves." Carnegie practiced extensive philanthropy, or the desire or effort to help humankind, as by making charitable donations.

J. P. Morgan and U.S. Steel

Wealthy financier J. P. Morgan (1837–1913) created his first business monopolies by purchasing most of the railroad industry in the eastern United States in the 1890s (see Chapter 6). By the turn of the twentieth century, Morgan's attention had shifted to steel. He purchased two major steel producers, Federal Steel and National Steel, and then sought to buy Carnegie Steel. Carnegie did not like bankers and would not sell. The powerful Morgan was able to make Carnegie's customers cancel their contracts and his competitors lower their rates. Carnegie fought back as long as he could, but in January 1901 Morgan bought him out, paying $492 million for Carnegie Steel. Morgan's United States Steel Corporation was the nation's first billion-dollar enterprise. No rival could hope to compete against such a monopoly.

English philosopher Herbert Spencer first developed the theory of social Darwinism. *(© Michael Nicholson/Corbis.)*

Social Darwinism: The survival of the fittest

Many robber barons shared a popular viewpoint about their wealth called social Darwinism. The theory was established by English philosopher Herbert Spencer (1820–1903) and refers to biologist Charles Darwin (1809–1882) and his theory of evolution. Evolution is the process by which all plant and animal species change over time because of variations that are passed from one generation to the next. Spencer believed that the human social world is in a constant evolutionary process. He coined the phrase "the survival of the fittest," arguing that the wealthy and powerful took their place at the top of society because they were the best adapted

Journalist Henry Demarest Lloyd is considered one of the first muckrakers. *(Courtesy of The Library of Congress.)*

to the environment, while those who did not compete well became poor and eventually died out. (It is worth noting that Darwin did not agree with this social theory.)

In the United States the most eloquent spokesperson for social Darwinism was Yale professor William Graham Sumner (1840–1910). He argued that human beings struggle against one another by nature. To Sumner, the economy was part of the instinctive struggle between humans and a part of the evolution of society. Sumner believed that governments had no business interfering with the economy, and also held that trade unions, charities, and other forms of social welfare were obstacles to the natural course of things.

Some ministers of the era held similar views, claiming that the making of money was the proper work of a Christian. In his popular "Acres of Diamonds" sermon, Baptist minister Russell H. Conwell (1843–1925) preached pure capitalism (an economic system in which the means of production and distribution are privately owned by individuals or groups and competition for business establishes the price of goods and services): "I have come to tell you . . . you ought to be rich and it is your duty to get rich." He concluded the lecture by saying that "to make money is to preach the gospel." Conwell was careful to distinguish between making money for its own sake, of which he did not approve, and seeking wealth to do good.

Early response to the monopolies

The American public was not convinced by social Darwinism. An early voice against the robber barons was journalist Henry Demarest Lloyd (1847–1903), who began a campaign in 1881 with his *Atlantic Monthly* article "Story of a Great Monopoly," which exposed the methods of the railroads and the Standard Oil Company. Lloyd saw the dangers of the rising monopolies and became a tireless champion of the independent competitor, the consumer, and the worker. He is considered to be one of the first muckrakers, a group of journalists who search for and expose corruption in public affairs. Lloyd's most important book, *Wealth Against Commonwealth* (1894), was a strong criticism of monopolies, especially the Standard Oil Company.

Members of the clergy, led by Congregational minister Washington Gladden (1836–1918), started a new movement known as the social gospel to secure social justice for the poor. The movement paved the way for the Christian religion to be linked with reform and for future progressives to take action against the power of the robber barons. But true reform would not be accomplished for many years.

Washington Gladden, founder of the social gospel movement. *(Courtesy of The Library of Congress.)*

The Interstate Commerce Act

By the 1880s large and powerful trusts controlled many industries, including those producing sugar, meat, lead, natural gas, cotton oil, linseed oil, and whiskey. But it was the railroads that sparked the most public anger. By favoring large customers such as Standard Oil, the railroads hurt and even destroyed some small businesses and farms. Public displeasure with the railways led state legislatures, especially those in the Midwest, to create commissions to oversee the railroad business. But as railway networks continued expanding across state lines, it was soon beyond the power of any one state to regulate railroads. By the late 1880s it was clear that interstate commerce, or trade that crosses the borders between states, could only be regulated by the federal government.

The government had maintained its laissez-faire position for most of the nineteenth century, but in 1886 the Supreme Court proclaimed that only the U.S. Congress had the right to regulate interstate commerce. In 1887 Congress passed the Interstate Commerce Act, the first regulatory act designed to establish government supervision over a major industry. The Interstate Commerce Commission (ICC), the nation's first regulatory agency, was given the daunting mission of trying to regulate railroad rates and stop unfair practices.

Sherman Antitrust Act

By the 1890s, after hundreds of mergers and consolidations, there were only six mammoth railroad systems left, and J. P. Morgan owned four of them. The railroad, steel, and other monopolies, like Standard Oil, were so powerful that no government commission could regulate them, and public resentment grew. In 1889 Kansas enacted the first state antitrust legislation, and the effort soon spread across the South and the West. By 1900 twenty-seven states had created laws prohibiting or regulating trusts.

Many trusts were simply too big to be controlled by the laws of any one state. For example, when the state of Ohio moved against the Standard Oil Company in 1892, the trust simply reformed under the more business-friendly laws of New Jersey. Most trusts and monopolies were interstate in scope. Once again, pressure mounted for the federal government to take action. Unfortunately, the federal government was in no hurry to respond. The business trusts donated heavily to political campaigns, bribed legislators, and were in a position to make or break many politicians.

Finally, in 1888, Senator John Sherman (1823–1900) of Ohio introduced an antitrust measure in the U.S. Senate. Two years later Congress passed the act after considerable revision. The Sherman Antitrust Act barred any "contract, combination in the form of trust or otherwise, or conspiracy, in restraint of trade" and made it a federal crime "to monopolize or attempt to monopolize, or combine or conspire...to monopolize any part of the trade or commerce among the several states."

Unlike the Interstate Commerce Act, which established a commission to investigate violations of the law, the Sherman Act left enforcement up to the U.S. attorney general, the chief law officer of the nation. Most attorneys general at that time did not think it necessary to move against trusts. The presidential administrations of Grover Cleveland (1837–1908; served 1885–89 and 1893–97), Benjamin Harrison (1833–1901; served 1889–93), and William McKinley (1843–1901; served 1897–1901) filed a total of only eighteen antitrust suits, and four of them were against labor unions. In fact, more combinations and trusts were formed between 1897 and 1901 than at any other time in American history.

For More Information

Books

Brogan, Hugh. *The Penguin History of the USA.* 2nd ed. London and New York: Penguin, 1999.

Cashman, Sean Dennis. *America in the Gilded Age: From the Death of Lincoln to the Rise of Theodore Roosevelt.* New York and London: New York University Press, 1984.

Chernow, Ron. *Titan: The Life of John D. Rockefeller, Sr.* New York: Vintage Books, 1998.

Sinclair, Upton. *The Jungle.* New York: Doubleday, Page & Co., 1906.

Smith, Page. *The Rise of Industrial America: A People's History of the Post-Reconstruction Era.* Vol. 6. New York: McGraw-Hill, 1984.

Web Sites

Carnegie, Andrew. "Wealth." *North American Review,* June 1889. http://www.swarthmore.edu/SocSci/rbannis1/AIH19th/Carnegie.html (accessed on June 30, 2005).

Rockefeller Foundation. http://www.rockfound.org/display.asp?context=2&SectionTypeId=32&Preview=0&ARCurrent=1 (accessed on June 30, 2005).

Urbanization

A major result of industrialization in the United States was the transformation of the rural, agricultural nation to an urban one. At the time of the American Revolution (1775–83), when the American colonists fought England to win their independence, 95 percent of the U.S. population lived in rural areas, and most Americans were farmers. This was slowly changing by the time of the American Civil War (1861–65; a war between the Union [the North], who were opposed to slavery, and the Confederacy [the South], who were in favor of slavery), when about 20 percent of the American population, or 6.2 million people, lived in urban communities, or towns with populations of 2,500 or more. Despite this there were still fewer than four hundred communities with populations of 2,500 or more in the entire nation, and in 1850 only seven cities had populations over 100,000. After the Civil War, the population of the country as a whole increased very rapidly, doubling by the turn of the century. By 1900 the population in urban areas comprised about 40 percent of the population, or about 30 million people. At that time there were 1,737 communities with populations of 2,500 or

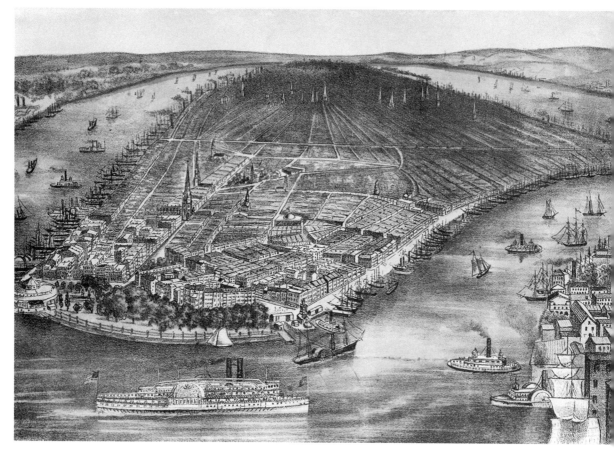

The first large U.S. cities, like New York, were eastern seaports.
(© Bettmann/Corbis.)

more, and thirty-eight U.S. cities had populations over 100,000. The trend toward urbanization never ceased. In 1920, for the first time, more people lived in the city than in the country in the United States, and in the early twenty-first century about 75 percent of the U.S. population was urban.

In the post–Civil War years, the rise of big industries, the expansion of railroads, and a tremendous inflow of immigrants led to the rapid growth of cities. As industries grew within a city, the number of laborers they needed rose beyond the supply of labor available locally. The promise of employment drew people from distant places. For example,

Words to Know

assimilation: The social process of being absorbed, or blending into the dominant culture.

capitalist: A person who invests his or her wealth in business and industry.

infant mortality: The percentage of babies born in a year that die before they reach the age of one.

omnibus: A horse-drawn coach for hire.

settlement houses: Places established and run by educated, and often wealthy, reformers to provide social and educational services to the residents of poor urban immigrant communities.

slums: Severely overcrowded urban areas characterized by the most extreme conditions of poverty, run-down housing, and crime.

tenement: Urban dwellings rented by impoverished families that barely meet or fail to meet the minimum standards of safety, sanitation, and comfort.

in 1850 Chicago's population was only 29,963. The first railroad reached the city that year, and a dozen more connected to the city within the decade. By the 1870s Chicago was a center of railroad operations and railroad construction, and it was also a leader in the meatpacking industry and the home of agricultural machine manufacturing. Industries in the city employed hundreds of thousands of laborers. Some workers came from American farms, but the majority of new workers were immigrants from European countries, mainly Germany and Ireland, who had traveled great distances to find jobs. By 1900 Chicago was the nation's second-largest city with a population of 1,698,575.

The urbanization of the United States did not occur at the same rate among the nation's regions. The first large U.S. cities were all eastern seaports, such as Boston, Massachusetts; Baltimore, Maryland; New York, New York; New Orleans, Louisiana; and Philadelphia, Pennsylvania. In 1860 about one-third of the population in the Northeast was urban, and it remained the most urbanized region of the nation into the twentieth century. The South, on the other hand, remained a largely rural area, though it did have some growing cities. Urban development began between 1820 and 1850 in the Midwest, as new towns and industries arose first on the accessible water routes and later along the paths of the expanding railroads that networked across the nation. The railroads made cities possible in areas where there was no water access, and were responsible for a great deal of the urbanization in the Midwest. Farther west, in the Rocky Mountain area and along the West Coast, most urban development did not begin until the 1880s. Many western cities were once part of Mexico; others were Indian communities. U.S. businesses eventually moved into the West, however, establishing industrialized agriculture, mining, and cattle ranching. As fresh populations moved in, earlier cultures were often enclosed in the new urban society.

The cities of the nineteenth century were as diverse as the people of the nation. New York City, the largest city and the financial capital of the nation, served as the port for nearly 70 percent of the nation's imports and 61 percent of its exports. Nearly half of the nation's largest industries had their headquarters in New York City. A vast garment industry and many smaller manufacturing businesses were located there as well. Pittsburgh, Pennsylvania, had its steel mills; New Haven and Hartford, Connecticut, produced firearms; and Lynn, Massachusetts, made shoes. Some cities became known for certain products and companies. Hershey, Pennsylvania, became famous for its chocolate. Dayton, Ohio, housed the headquarters of the National Cash Register Company. Corning, New York, became known for its glass kitchenware. Memphis, Tennessee, produced cotton seed oil, and Milwaukee, Wisconsin, gained recognition as the home of a number of famous German breweries.

The early cities

Before 1850 all large cities—those with populations over 100,000—were ports on the Atlantic Ocean. In these cities the harbor formed the hub of economic activity. Until the mid-nineteenth century there was little urban public transportation, so cities tended to be very compact. For example, about 85 percent of New York City's population lived within two miles of the city's center. In most early U.S. cities, residential and business districts mingled. Two-story factories, looking more like barns than industrial buildings, stood beside offices, stores, churches, and houses. The upper,

A horse-drawn street railcar. *(© Corbis.)*

middle, and lower social classes usually lived in the same neighborhoods.

By 1870 transportation by horse-drawn street railcars allowed residents to live farther away from their work. Cities spread out and divided into districts. As key financial institutions, retail shops, and entertainment facilities moved away from the residential and industrial areas, early business districts, with their clusters of tall buildings, began to emerge. Continued industrial growth and rapid population increases led to the crowding of laborers into congested areas surrounding the factories. Those who could afford it moved away from the industrial areas. A classic American urban pattern appeared. The heart of each city was its central business district. The business district was immediately surrounded by slums and working-class residential areas. Slums are severely overcrowded urban areas characterized by the most extreme conditions of poverty, run-down housing, and crime. Suburbs serving as residences for the wealthy were found farther away from the center. Many downtown residential areas fragmented into a series of neighborhoods divided by class and nationality or ethnic origin.

Immigration

Even by the 1850s, it was clear to industrialists and railroad managers that the United States needed more laborers to build its railways and operate its factories. Many companies actively recruited for workers in Europe, promising land and jobs in the United States. Large numbers of Europeans and some Asian immigrants heeded the call. In the period between 1866 and 1900, over 13 million immigrants entered the United States. The majority of the earlier arrivals were from the western European nations of Germany, Ireland, Britain, and Scandinavia. These were called the "old immigrants," because they were the first wave. Immigration from Italy, Greece, Poland, Austria-Hungary, the Balkans, and Russia became prominent by the 1890s, and these people were called the "new immigrants." Most immigrants left their homes seeking jobs and better financial opportunities in the United States. Some, like the Jews in Russia and Poland, left because of religious or political oppression. Most arrived with little money and no professional skills. Many immigrants were young males who intended to stay in the country only long enough to earn some money and then return home—and, in fact, many did return. Others settled permanently in the United States and saved money to pay for their loved ones to join them.

Although many immigrants came to the United States hoping to establish farms, the majority settled in the large cities of the Northeast and Midwest. In 1870 people of foreign birth made up about 33 percent of the populations of U.S. cities with populations of 25,000 or more, even though they only made up about 14 percent of the nation's population as a whole. Foreign-born people made up 40 percent or more of the populations of New York City; Chicago, Illinois; San Francisco, California; Cleveland, Ohio; Detroit, Michigan; Milwaukee, Wisconsin; Scranton, Pennsylvania; and Lawrence and Fall River, Massachusetts.

Not all immigrants came from Europe. In 1900 there were about ninety thousand people of Chinese ancestry in the

United States, most of them men. Many young Chinese males had made the seven-thousand-mile trip to California to seek their fortunes in the Gold Rush of 1848, but few found much reward in the mines. (In early 1848 gold was discovered in California. By the end of the year about 6,000 miners had arrived there and obtained ten million dollars' worth of gold.) Though they intended to return to China, many stayed in the United States. A crew of more than twelve thousand Chinese laborers worked on the construction of the Central Pacific Railroad in the 1860s, building tracks across the treacherous Sierra Nevada Mountains in California. In 1882 anti-Asian sentiments (due to prejudice and fears of job competition) in the United States spurred the country's first major immigration restriction, the Chinese Immigration Act, which prevented Chinese workers from entering the country for six decades. The act made it impossible for the male Chinese immigrants to bring wives or families to their new home. The men formed what became known as a "bachelor society" and Chinese urban neighborhoods called Chinatowns sprang up along the West Coast, with the largest neighborhood located in San Francisco. Most Chinatowns began with a temple, a cluster of stores, and gambling rooms for the entertainment of the single men.

The Chinese faced some of the worst discrimination as immigrants, but almost every group was met with hostility, suspicion, and prejudice. Assimilation (the social process of being absorbed, or blending into the dominant culture) was not easy for them. These immigrants had their own languages, religions, and histories, and they often lived in racial and ethnic ghettos in the cities where they could practice their own familiar traditions and preserve the cultures they had left behind in their native country. Their native customs would contribute to the diversity of culture in American cities in the years ahead.

Migrating from farm to city

Immigrants were not alone in moving into U.S. cities. In the post–Civil War years, millions of native-born European Americans moved from family farms to small towns, then to larger towns, and finally to the big industrial cities. Some relocated out of financial need. Economic depressions, often referred to at the time as panics, occurred during the 1870s and

Streetcars Shape the Cities

The earliest urban transportation was the omnibus, or horse-drawn coach for hire, that bumped across the cobblestone streets of large eastern cities such as New York, Philadelphia, and Boston beginning around 1830. By 1852 these streetcars were pulled along grooved rail tracks that lay flush with the pavement. This improvement increased speed and capacity, and decreased interference with other coach and wagon traffic. By the mid-1880s, hundreds of horse-car companies carried millions of passengers in many U.S. cities.

In San Francisco in 1874 a cable car railway system was introduced in which underground cables powered by steam engines were clamped to the trolley cars. Many cities followed suit and installed cable cars. Then, in the mid-1880s, the electric streetcar with an overhead electric wire was introduced. It could travel up to twenty miles per hour. Electric streetcars ran along street tracks like cable cars, but they were cleaner and cheaper to operate. By 1903 twenty-nine thousand miles of electric streetcar tracks carried 98 percent of the nation's urban passengers. As city streets became congested, large urban centers undertook expensive public works projects to build elevated tracks to run elevated streetcars or to dig tunnels to run subways. Boston opened the first American subway in 1897; New York's first subway line opened in 1904.

1890s, causing many railroad companies to collapse. Without the railroads farmers were unable to get their crops to market, and many small farms failed. Additionally, people living on farms tended to have large families. As machinery reduced the need for labor, some farms could no longer support all of the family members. Young people from farming communities often left home to seek adventure, captivated by the stories they heard about the bright lights and prosperity of the big cities.

From 1861 to 1865 the American Civil War was fought between the Union (the North) and the Confederacy (the South). One of the main issues of the war was slavery; the North opposed slavery, while the South favored it. The South lost the war and all slaves were set free. For the most part, freed African American slaves in the South remained in the region for several decades after the Civil War, but a very slow northward migration was in its early stages. In 1870 about 68,000 southern blacks had migrated to northern cities. By the first decade of the twentieth century, that number had grown to about 194,000. African Americans faced prejudice in the northern cities and usually were forced to live in segregated (separate) neighborhoods. Many African Americans seeking urban opportunities tended to migrate to southern cities such as Savannah or Atlanta, Georgia, or Nashville, Tennessee.

The gap between rich and poor

During the period of the Industrial Revolution known as the Gilded Age (the era of industrialization from the early 1860s to the turn of the century in which a few wealthy individuals gained tremendous power and influence; see Chapter 5), large cities became centers of American high society. In New York the wealthy and powerful resided in elegant brownstone homes or fancy new mansions in uptown areas such as Fifth Avenue or Washington Square. People like Caroline Webster Schermerhorn Astor (1830–1908), the "queen of New York society," and the Vanderbilts (heirs to railroad magnate Cornelius Vanderbilt) lived in extreme luxury, with beautiful mansions fully staffed by uniformed servants. They wore the finest hand-tailored clothing and costly jewelry, and they hosted extravagant costume balls with lavish dinners and highly restricted guest lists.

The cities of America reflected the nation's economy in general, wherein the wealth was highly concentrated in the hands of a very small segment. In 1860, 2 percent of the U.S. population owned one-third of the nation's wealth, and fully three-quarters of that fortune was owned by the richest 10 percent. The workers, who labored long hours in the industries that made the capitalists (people who invest their wealth into business and industry) rich, owned practically nothing. They lived under miserable conditions, crowded into unhealthy tenements (run-down apartment buildings built for the poor) in the growing slums of the cities. At the turn of the twentieth century, 1.2 million people, or about 75 percent of New York City's population, lived in 37,000 overcrowded tenement buildings without adequate water, air, sewage, or garbage removal.

Indeed most large American cities during the late nineteenth century were overcrowded and dirty. Tenement buildings were hastily thrown together to house the exploding population of

Many working-class people lived in unhealthy tenements. *(© Bettmann/Corbis.)*

the working class. They were usually between four and seven stories high with several apartments on each floor, and most had cramped, dark, poorly ventilated rooms. In the absence of any garbage services, airshafts in the center of many tenements served as garbage dumps, creating a foul odor that spread throughout the building. Despite these conditions, rent in the tenements was high and tenants often found it necessary to rent part of their cramped quarters to other families.

Health and safety were in short supply in large cities. The streets in the slums were filthy as a result of inadequate drains and old sewers. Drinking water was often contaminated

City Political Machines

Post–Civil-War city politics were among the most corrupt in U.S. history. Many American cities were run by political machines, power structures identified with political parties that were led by a boss and his associates. The political machines often had tremendous power over elected officials in the city and the state. Political machines ruled the city neighborhood by neighborhood. Each neighborhood was overseen by a ward captain, or heeler, who could deliver the votes of his district to the political boss. In turn he could win favors for the neighborhood's people, such as jobs, licenses, and contracts. Because they manipulated the voting system by granting favors, political machines were engaged in illegal practices, with some resorting to threats and intimidation, and others cheating government agencies out of a great deal of money. The extent of criminal activity varied.

Political bosses often had a better understanding of the needs of cities' immigrant populations than did social workers and reformers. Urban political machines provided many services, such as feeding hungry families, posting bail, giving families hams and turkeys at holiday time, and fighting to protect native customs. Many historians believe some city bosses played a vital role in developing city governments and services.

New York City was one of the most corrupt cities in the nation. In the 1860s its political machine, Tammany Hall, was led by William Marcy "Boss" Tweed (1823–1878). Tweed made sure that the governor and state legislature of New York were under his control. Tweed stole an estimated $100 million from

and epidemics of the deadly diseases typhoid and cholera killed thousands. Infant mortality (the percentage of babies that die each year before they reach the age of one) was very high. As many as one-third of all babies born in certain city neighborhoods died soon after their birth. Crime was rampant, and the murder rate soared in the large cities. Gangs forced slum residents and business owners to pay them for "protection" using thinly veiled threats of violence. (If the resident paid the gangs a certain amount of money on a regular basis the gangs promised to protect them against violence from other crime groups taking over the neighborhood, but basically this was just a way for the gangs to demand money.) Children in the crowded slums learned to steal at a very early age.

William Marcy "Boss" Tweed. *(© Bettmann/Corbis.)*

New York, mainly by instructing all the city's contract workers to pad their bills, charging more than a particular service was worth. The surplus, or padding, was then turned over to Tweed and his gang. For example, in May 1870 a city commission authorized more than $6 million as payment for the building of a new county courthouse. Of this sum only about 10 percent went to the actual construction. When New Yorkers protested, Tweed is reported to have replied, "What are you going to do about it?" Eventually the elected governments recovered power. For Boss Tweed, the end came in 1872 when he was jailed on corruption charges. He escaped and fled to Spain, but Spain returned him to the United States and prison in 1876. Hoping that he might secure release from jail in return for his testimony, he supplied considerable information to the state, testifying frankly about many of his crooked transactions. He died in jail in 1878 before the court ruled on his case.

City reform

Social Darwinist theories promoted the idea that the gap between the classes was the unavoidable outcome of natural human competition (see Chapter 7). Social Darwinists believed it was wrong to help the poor, as it might upset the natural course of things. But as the century drew to a close, significant reform movements developed.

Jacob Riis

Danish-born journalist Jacob Riis (1849–1914) was responsible for forcing many upper-class New Yorkers to open their eyes to the misery of the working poor in their city. Appalled by conditions in the slums of New York, he began to photograph the poor and write about their problems. In his 1890 book *How the Other Half Lives,* Riis depicted dreadful living conditions and called for reform. He wrote newspaper articles that probed every aspect of city life for the poor: sanitary conditions, family life, and the fate of women and children. His pictures showed filthy children dressed in rags, overcrowded apartments crawling with rats and insects, and alleys full of garbage.

Jane Addams and the settlement movement

In 1884 a group of English social reformers established the first settlement house, Toynbee Hall, in London. The idea behind settlement houses was for well-educated reformers to live in the neighborhoods of the poor so that they could truly understand their needs. Settlement houses were centers of education for working people to provide knowledge to help them fight against their harsh living conditions. After visiting Toynbee Hall in 1888, American Jane Addams (1860–1935) decided to establish her own settlement house, Hull House, in Chicago.

Hull House residents and volunteers provided programs to help their immigrant neighbors. Educational programs included kindergarten classes, adult education classes, lectures, concerts, a nursery, a museum that emphasized the ethnic traditions of immigrants' homelands, and courses in cooking and housekeeping. There were also classes to teach recent immigrants to speak, read, and write English. Settlement residents also worked with their immigrant neighbors to seek solutions to the difficult social and economic problems. Hull House residents fought for and achieved many of their goals, which included building parks and playgrounds for children, providing clean and well-lit streets, improved health care, and better working conditions. The settlement house movement was the seed from which grew child labor laws, urban sanitation, juvenile courts, and public education. By 1900 there were more than one hundred settlement houses nationwide.

Improvements in the cities

It was not until the years between 1880 and 1899 that many middle- and upper-class homes were connected to city services supplying water, heat, light, and sewage systems. During the 1870s hauling fresh water into the house and carrying wastewater out was a daily chore for many women and children. By 1880 most cities of more than ten thousand people had some sort of municipal water supply for certain neighborhoods. People in tenements might get water from street hydrants or water taps in hallways. Most urban dwellers prior to 1870 heated their homes with stoves fueled with coal. By the end of the nineteenth century, middle-class Americans had begun to install central, coal-burning furnaces in their cellars that provided heat through a system of ducts and vents to the entire house. Working-class families generally continued to heat with stoves, being unable to afford the installation of a new heating system.

Light and electricity

After the Civil War, some homes were still lit by candles and oil lamps, but most used kerosene lamps that provided much better light. During the 1880s and 1890s, gas and electrical lighting replaced kerosene lamps. Most Americans first experienced gaslights at mid-century in public places such as city streets, department stores, schools, hospitals, and government buildings. If the homeowner could afford it and lived close to a gas supply, gas lighting offered a welcome alternative to the dirt and odor of the kerosene lamp.

In 1879 inventor Thomas Edison (1847–1939) and his colleagues at his laboratories in Menlo Park, New Jersey, demonstrated an incandescent lamp—an artificial light produced by passing electric current through a thin wire filament—that burned for thirteen-and-a-half hours. The lamp gave only a feeble reddish glow, but it was the first lamp that could be used economically for lighting homes. Edison used his new invention to light the town of Menlo Park, causing such a sensation that special trains ran from New York City so that people could view the spectacle at night. While Edison's early experimental lamps used electricity from batteries, he soon developed a generator capable of sustaining a large electrical system. He then began work on an underground electric-wire system for a generating station in the Pearl Street district of lower Manhattan. On September 4, 1882, the Pearl Street electrical station came on line, supplying power to four hundred incandescent light bulbs owned by eighty-five customers. In 1893 about five hundred households and one thousand businesses in the city had electricity. By 1907 about 8 percent of households nationwide had electric lighting.

Thomas Edison with a replica of his first incandescent lamp. *(© Bettmann/ Corbis.)*

Bathrooms and sewers

For most Americans during the Gilded Age the toilet was a privy (outdoor toilet) or a chamber pot tucked under a bed. People washed using a bowl and pitcher in a bedroom and took baths in a portable tub. Before 1880 drainage was managed by open ditches. Some cities began building sewage systems during the 1880s, but they were mostly for draining storm water, not wastewater. The result was that unpaved areas were likely to be muddy and dotted with foul-smelling and unhealthy puddles. It took decades before sewers were built to carry waste from individual homes. Even then it was difficult to convince landlords to install indoor plumbing and sewer connections. Indoor bathrooms with toilets did not come into general use until after the development of sewage systems and were not widespread in American cities until after 1910.

The cities blossom

Though their growth was too sudden to be graceful, American cities gradually improved in some respects. Libraries, parks, museums, churches, and a variety of shops became available to the public. Theatrical and dance performances, musical concerts, and art galleries were available to those who could pay the price of admission. Consumers were able to find a huge assortment of goods at the new department stores like Macy's in New York and Marshall Field's in Chicago. By the turn of the century, many cities had developed effective fire and police departments. Most of the nation's great institutions—universities, hospitals, and social programs—were located in the growing cities, drawing celebrated thinkers, activists, artists, and professionals from all over the world.

Chicago had an unfortunate, but unique, opportunity to redefine itself after 1871, when a fire destroyed much of the city. There had been very little rain that summer, so the wooden buildings of the city were vulnerable. When a fire started in a barn behind a DeKoven Street home, the surrounding buildings soon caught fire, as well, and the fire spread a distance of over three miles. The fire burned for two days, destroying thousands of homes and the entire business district. As Chicago prepared to rebuild itself from the ground up, architects from around the country arrived to participate. These architects concentrated mainly on office buildings, warehouses, department stores, and other commercial structures. Consequently, the style they developed came to be called the Commercial Style. They instituted major technological changes, including the widespread use of the elevator and central heating, which helped make tall buildings possible.

The rebuilding of Chicago led to a new age of skyscrapers. The father of Chicago's tall buildings was William Le Baron Jenney (1832–1907). His Home Insurance Building, built in 1885, is often regarded as the first true skyscraper. Jenney was the first architect to use steel framing and the curtain wall, a sheet of masonry that covered the frame instead of bearing the building's weight. Louis Sullivan (1856–1924) was the most influential of the Chicago school of architects. His modern skyscrapers set the stage for Chicago's soaring urban skyline. Though other cities did not have to start from scratch as Chicago did, they soon followed its example. The twentieth-century American city, with its towering steel and glass buildings, was born.

For More Information

Books

Barrows, Robert G. "Urbanizing America." In *The Gilded Age: Essays on the Origins of Modern America.* Edited by Charles W. Calhoun. Wilmington, DE: Scholarly Resources, 1996.

Brogan, Hugh. *The Penguin History of the USA.* 2nd ed. London and New York: Penguin, 1999.

Cashman, Sean Dennis. *America in the Gilded Age: From the Death of Lincoln to the Rise of Theodore Roosevelt.* New York and London: New York University Press, 1984.

Daniels, Roger. "The Immigrant Experience in the Gilded Age." In *The Gilded Age: Essays on the Origins of Modern America.* Edited by Charles W. Calhoun. Wilmington, DE: Scholarly Resources, 1996.

Smith, Page. *The Rise of Industrial America: A People's History of the Post–Reconstruction Era.* Vol. 6. New York: McGraw-Hill, 1984.

Web Sites

"Urban Experience in Chicago: Hull House and Its Neighbors, 1889–1963." *Jane Addams Hull House Museum, University of Illinois at Chicago.* http://www.uic.edu/jaddams/hull/urbanexp/contents.htm (accessed on June 30, 2005).

9

Workers in the Industrial Age

During the last three decades of the nineteenth century, the majority of Americans became wage earners, people who worked for someone other than themselves. This was a first in U.S. history, as self-employed farmers had previously made up the majority of the population. Unlike farmers, industrial workers labored under the complete control of their employer. Though their grueling efforts led to great profits for the manufacturing companies, this rarely resulted in pay increases or lighter loads for the workers. In fact, keeping workers' wages as low as possible and their production high were key to the profitability of the industries. Workers were extremely vulnerable to their employers' demands because the nineteenth-century workplace was not regulated by the government. Many laborers were forced to work long hours in unsafe and unhealthy conditions. Benefits, such as health insurance or retirement plans, were almost unheard of, and the wages of many industrial workers were so low that they were forced to live in poverty. The prosperity of the golden age of industrialism did not extend to a large portion of its workers.

A young girl operates a spinning machine. *(© Bettman/Corbis. Reproduced by permission.)*

Words to Know

compulsory attendance: Mandatory obligation to go to school.

labor union: An organization of workers formed to protect and further their mutual interests by bargaining as a group with their employers over wages, working conditions, and benefits.

laissez-faire An economic doctrine that opposes government regulation of commerce and industry beyond the minimum necessary.

mass production: The manufacture of goods in quantity by using machines and standardized designs and parts.

sweatshop: A factory in which workers work long hours in poor conditions for very low wages.

tenement: Urban dwellings rented by impoverished families that barely meet or fail to meet the minimum standards of safety, sanitation, and comfort.

ventilation: Air circulation or access to fresh air.

The workforce hierarchy

Industry created a tremendous demand for labor. In 1865 there were around 1.3 million people working in manufacturing companies. By 1900 that number had increased to 4.5 million and ten years later it was estimated at about 8 million. Many workers migrated to the industrial towns from the farmlands of the nation, but even more were emigrating from other countries in Europe and Asia.

Industrial work varied in aspects such as the sizes of the factories or mills and the types of work that laborers performed. However, there were often many similarities. For instance, machines tended by human operators did most of the work. Processes were divided so that each worker performed only one small part of the whole and therefore required little training. Professional managers supervised the work. In most large manufacturing companies, the owners were investors who were not present at the work sites. A board of directors was appointed to determine company policy and hire the management.

Not all workers were treated alike. Skilled craftsmen—the machine builders, carpenters, glassblowers, and others—made significantly more money than their unskilled counterparts, and many lived in relative comfort. Skilled laborers were generally white males of English, Scottish, Irish, German, or Scandinavian descent—the first wave of immigrants from western Europe called "old immigrants." Eventually, the principles of mass production (manufacturing goods in quantity by using machines and standardized designs and parts) transformed the jobs of many of the skilled craftsmen, replacing them with more repetitive, unskilled tasks.

Unskilled labor was performed by those willing to take the lowest wages: women, children, and the "new immigrants" from southern and eastern Europe and Asia. "New immigrants" were those who had come from Italy, Greece, Poland, Austria-Hungary, the Balkans, and Russia in the 1890s. While the pay rate for skilled labor was usually enough to live on, the rate for unskilled labor was often well under the poverty level. Men earned 75 percent more than women and 250 percent more than children for doing the same work.

Factory conditions

People who were new to industrial labor found the discipline of factory work to be very different from other types of work. The job was often monotonous because laborers performed one task over and over. It was also strictly regulated. The average workweek was about sixty hours, at ten hours a day and six days a week, but some worked far longer hours. For men and women from agricultural backgrounds these new conditions proved to be a challenge because farm work tended to be more flexible and offered a variety of tasks. Factory work was also foreign to skilled artisans, who had once handcrafted goods according to their own schedules.

Factory jobs were unsteady. Company profits rose and fell with the market. In bad times manufacturers tended to lay off (suspend or dismiss employees, usually due to lack of work) a significant portion of their unskilled labor. People barely making enough to scrape by suddenly found themselves without work. Families went hungry as they searched for a means of survival. It was common to see groups of homeless people traveling from town to town looking for work or handouts.

Without government regulation of business in the nineteenth and early twentieth centuries, there were no building codes or fire inspections. There was no limit on the number of hours a person could be required to work. Child labor laws were nonexistent. More industrial accidents occurred in the United States than in any other industrial country. Employers were not under any obligation to compensate a family if a worker was hurt or killed on the job, and most companies did not offer help. By 1900 industrial accidents killed thirty-five thousand workers each year and disabled five hundred thousand others. Occasionally the general public became concerned with industrial accidents, especially when scores of workers were killed in a single widely reported incident, such as coal mine disasters or the Triangle Shirtwaist Company fire in 1911, but the staggering number of deaths that occurred on a regular basis often escaped public notice (see section entitled "The Triangle Shirtwaist Factory fire" in this chapter).

Industrial workers received little support from their employers, the government, or other agencies. Arrangements for the care of orphaned, neglected, or delinquent children were inadequate or nonexistent. The death or desertion of the family wage earner, usually the male head of household, spelled tragedy for mothers without insurance, widows' benefits, or government support. Bereaved mothers who had to work outside the home were often forced to leave a child as young as eight or nine to care for even younger children.

Child labor

The number of children employed in factories rose steadily over the last three decades of the nineteenth century. By 1900 roughly 1.7 million children under the age of sixteen worked in factories; less than half that many children had been employed thirty years before. Large numbers of children labored in textile mills, mines, glass factories, and canneries. Factory managers preferred to hire children because they worked for the lowest wages. Other urban youths worked as newsboys, messengers, bootblacks, and peddlers. In rural settings they were likely to work on farms.

Many young lives were lost in industrial labor. Working children were often exposed to toxic substances. Some were poisoned when their bodies absorbed dyes in textile mills or phosphorus used in making matches. Others inhaled varnish used in furniture manufacturing or fumes from rubber making. Many suffered from lung diseases like bronchitis and

Some child laborers worked in canneries. *(© Horact Bristol/Corbis.)*

tuberculosis due to poor ventilation, or air circulation. Some children were shipped from state to state, following seasonal work in agriculture or canning. In southern cotton mills, children who operated looms (cloth-weaving devices) throughout the night had cold water thrown in their faces to keep them awake. Long working hours for children also meant that accidents were more likely to occur. Even in the best of conditions, working children were denied their right to an education. If they made it to adulthood, they had little alternative but to continue working in unskilled industrial work.

Child labor reform

During the period of the Industrial Revolution known as the Gilded Age (the era of industrialization from the early 1860s to the turn of the century in which a few wealthy individuals gained tremendous power and influence; see Chapter 5) the United States practiced a laissez-faire approach to the economy, following an economic doctrine that opposes government regulation of commerce and industry beyond the minimum necessary.

Because child labor became increasingly important to the industries that were advancing the wealth of the nation, people tended to ignore the suffering of working children. Some even went so far as to say it was good for these children, as it taught them their lot in life as part of the working class at an early age.

The earliest protests were voiced by workers' associations that opposed child labor because it kept wages low and compromised job security for adults. But others felt children should be defended and protected for their own sake. In 1842 the Massachusetts legislature passed a law that limited children under twelve to working no more than ten hours a day. Many other states passed legislation that restricted child labor, but the laws were difficult to enforce (with employers frequently hiding their child workers during inspections) and some state inspection agencies were lax about enforcing them. The number of children in the workplace continued to expand.

In 1893 reformers Florence Kelley (1859–1932) and Jane Addams (1860–1935) were instrumental in the passage of the Illinois Factory Act regulating hours and the minimum age for working children. Kelley also helped to establish free medical examination centers for some child laborers and recommended legislation related to controlling dangerous machinery in the workplace. The Illinois Supreme Court, however, adhering to laissez-faire policies and listening to the powerful Illinois business advocates, declared the Factory Act unconstitutional. Illinois did not pass an effective child labor law until 1903.

Interest in improving the legislation that affected children and the enforcement of these laws resulted in the formation in 1904 of the National Child Labor Committee. This committee investigated conditions in a number of states. In the end it was not effective because each state feared that adopting restrictive child-labor legislation could give other states a competitive advantage in recruiting industry. In 1907 a federal law against child labor was introduced to Congress, but it was defeated. In 1910 there were still an estimated two million children employed in industry.

In 1908 the National Child Labor Committee hired Lewis Hine (1874–1940), a teacher, to research child labor. Hine traveled around the country photographing children at work. When his pictures were published, the American public was horrified to see young boys and girls laboring in harsh

Public Education

Children who worked in the mills had little chance of a future outside industrial labor. Without a mandatory educational system in the country, there seemed little hope for breaking the cycle of poverty. Reformer Horace Mann (1796–1859), who was appointed secretary of the Massachusetts State Board of Education in 1837, championed the idea of a state-supervised and -supported public school system. He urged that each school offer the same curriculum and conduct classes over a continuous ten-month term. He also argued for carefully designed school buildings and state schools to train professional teachers. He sought to extend educational opportunities to farm families and the children of poor laborers in the growing manufacturing towns. One of Mann's more controversial proposals was mandatory full-time schooling for all children up to the age of sixteen.

In the Northeast the public was largely in favor of public schools and provided the necessary funding. Many farming families in the Midwest depended on their children's labor and preferred voluntary intermittent schooling that could coincide with agricultural work. Nevertheless, free public education was established in Indiana in 1852, Ohio in 1854, and Illinois in 1855, and other states soon followed. From 1861 to 1865 the Union (the North) and the Confederacy (the South) fought a civil war, in part over the issue of slavery, which the South favored and the North opposed. The South lost the war and all slaves were set free. While the war had a mostly positive effect on the economy of the North, stimulating manufacture of army supplies, the Southern economy declined. Crops and railroads had been destroyed during the war and major cities were in ruins. In the devastated post–Civil War South, public schools were established, but the funds to operate them were lacking. Only one pupil out of ten who enrolled in school reached the fifth grade and only one in seventy reached the eighth grade. In the late 1890s the economy improved, but the South still entered the twentieth century with public school systems far inferior to those in the rest of the United States.

Children in the workforce usually did not have the opportunity to attend school, and generally there was no tradition of education in their family background. In order to get children into the public school system, Massachusetts put a compulsory-attendance law (mandatory obligation to go to school) into effect in 1852. Over the next thirty years, sixteen more states enacted similar laws, but most were not well enforced, if enforced at all. By 1918 all states had compulsory-attendance laws.

conditions in the factories and mines. Public outcry resulted in the establishment in 1912 of the Children's Bureau, an agency of the Department of Commerce and Labor. Its mandate was to investigate matters involving the welfare of children, including child labor. The Children's Bureau was led by social reformer Julia C. Lathrop (1858–1932), the first woman to head a federal agency. Progress remained slow, however. Effective federal legislation against child labor was not passed until 1938 with the Fair Labor Standards Act.

Women workers

By 1920 women composed 23.6 percent of the labor force, and 8.3 million women over the age of fifteen worked outside the home. Women had been working in industry since the first textile factories opened early in the nineteenth century (see Chapter 4). Factory jobs had lured young women in earlier times with promises of independence and education, but by the 1850s few women had any illusions about working conditions in factories. Women who desperately needed money to feed themselves and their families, however, often had little choice but to accept the unsafe and exhausting work.

Women were attractive to employers because they could be paid less for doing the same jobs as men. In fact, women's wages were so far below men's that most women did not earn enough to live on. Some women were paid as little as $5 or $6 per week, while a man received more than $9 per week. Most female laborers performed unskilled or semi-skilled machine work, but some were employed in industries that demanded heavy labor. Some women, for instance, worked on railroads, while others were machinists. Male workers often tried to discourage females from working in mills and factories, fearing that because women would work for lower wages, it might bring down the general wage.

Employers who hired women thinking they were less likely to protest poor working conditions than men were sadly mistaken. Women voiced their complaints, particularly about long working hours, in many arenas. They were often not accepted by their male co-workers, however, which made their protests ineffective. Efforts to improve working conditions for women were consistently undermined by society's uncertain attitude about combining the roles of wife and mother with those of worker and professional. The Women's Bureau, a new federal agency approved by Congress in June 1920, was charged with reporting the conditions of women in industry and promoting the welfare of working women. The Women's Trade Union League (WTUL) also fought to improve women's labor conditions. Both the Women's Bureau and WTUL fought for shorter workdays, and by the early 1920s all but five states upheld the ten-hour day/fifty-hour weekwork schedule.

Immigrant labor

Between 1830 and 1880 about nine million people entered the United States, mainly coming from Ireland and Germany, but also from Great Britain and Scandinavia. Then, during the late 1880s, increasing numbers of immigrants from eastern and southern Europe began arriving. The new immigrants were overwhelmingly non-Protestant and few spoke English. Between 1880 and 1914 about twenty-five million people entered the United States.

Most left their countries of origin because they were poor and hoped to better their lives. They arrived in American cities with dreams of economic security and better living conditions for their children. Italians, who numbered almost five million between 1880 and 1930, were the largest group of new immigrants. Jews from Poland, Russia, and Romania constituted the second largest group. Large numbers of Slavs—such as Ukrainians, Poles, Croatians, Czechs, and Serbs—as well as Greeks and Portuguese also arrived.

The vast majority of the new immigrants settled in the big industrial cities and usually had to take the least desirable jobs available. Workers were frequently introduced to employers by relatives or friends from their homelands, and as a result certain ethnic groups dominated specific industries. For instance, Slavs worked in steel factories, meatpacking, and other heavy industries. Greeks opened small businesses selling fruit, flowers, ice cream, and food. Italians worked construction. Mexicans worked at agricultural jobs in the West. Many Jews settled in New York City, where large numbers of them entered the growing garment industry.

Many first-generation immigrants had very difficult lives in their new country. They lived in crowded, unsanitary tenements (urban dwellings for the poor), sometimes sleeping four or five people to a room. To help pay the rent, many families took in boarders, which made their apartments still more cramped. Many men and women, old and young, worked at home making paper flowers, wrapping cigars, or sewing garments, laboring long hours in a crowded living space. Children worked alongside parents or grandparents at these jobs.

Sweatshops

The term sweatshop is defined as a factory in which workers work long hours in poor conditions for very low wages. During the last decades of the nineteenth century, the ready-made garment industries in New York City and Chicago operated mainly through sweatshops. Many were located in the employers' tenement apartments, which were packed with foot-operated sewing machines. Impoverished immigrant women and children, mainly Jewish and Italian, worked in the sweatshops for extremely low pay. Working long hours in poorly ventilated rooms, these women often fell victim to epidemics of smallpox and typhoid that swept through their crowded neighborhoods. Sweatshops became notorious for spreading these diseases to consumers on the garments they purchased.

The Triangle Shirtwaist Factory fire

The Triangle Shirtwaist Company was a large sweatshop in New York City. Located in the top three stories of a ten-story building near Washington Square in Greenwich Village, the company had become highly successful making tailored blouses for the growing population of female clerical workers. Triangle employed one thousand workers, mostly recent Italian and Russian Jewish immigrants between sixteen and twenty-three years of age, with some girls even younger. They worked long hours for pennies a day, jammed elbow-to-elbow and back-to-back at rows of tables.

Like many makeshift factories of the time, Triangle was a firetrap. Scraps of the highly flammable fabric were scattered on the floor. Cutting machines were fueled by gasoline. Smoking was prohibited, but workers commonly ignored the rule while supervisors looked the other way. Water barrels with buckets for putting out fires were not filled regularly. There was one rotting fire hose, attached to a rusted valve. In general, conditions were ideal for a fire to break out and spread at any time. Escape in case of fire was difficult or impossible. The only interior exit from the

Firefighters try to put out the fire at the Triangle Shirtwaist Factory. *(© Underwood and Underwood/Corbis. Reproduced by permission.)*

workroom was down a hall so narrow that people had to walk single file. There were four elevators, but usually only one was functional. The stairway was as narrow as the hall. Of the two doors leading from the building, one was permanently locked from the outside by management in order to minimize the workers' breaks and to ensure no one stole lace or cloth from the factory. The other opened inward.

On Saturday, March 25, 1911, the offices below the factory were closed for the weekend. About half of the Triangle workforce, or five hundred people, were in the factory. No one knows how it started, but a fire broke out. The flames spread far too quickly to be stopped by the meager water supply in the barrels, and the fire hose did not work. In the stampede to get down the narrow passages and stairways to the doors, people were trampled. Some tried to break through the locked door. Others surged to the other door only to be crushed as they tried to pull it inward. As people crowded into the elevators, others tried to ride down on the tops of the cars, hanging onto the cables. Soon there were so many bodies in the shafts that the one functioning elevator could no longer be used. Those trapped in the workroom threw themselves out of the windows and fell to their deaths. Others tried to use the fire escape. Already too flimsy to hold much weight, it soon melted in the heat and twisted into wreckage.

When it was over, the death toll was 146: 133 women and 13 men. Many others were severely hurt. The company owners were indicted on charges of criminal negligence but were acquitted eight months later in a jury trial and only had to pay a small fine. They later received $65,000 in insurance payments for property damage.

Though work-related deaths and accidents were commonplace, to date none had been so large and so appalling to the American public. Outrage fueled legislation on factory safety. The New York state legislature appointed investigative commissions to examine factories statewide, and thirty laws in New York City were enacted to enforce fire prevention measures. Significant labor reform for garment workers took longer to achieve.

At a memorial service held at New York's Metropolitan Opera House, Rose Schneiderman (1882–1972), an influential member of the WTUL and later its president, gave a scathing speech, calling on the crowd of workers, public officials, and interested citizens of all classes to join a working-class movement for reform. Tens of thousands of New Yorkers marched in tribute to those killed in the Triangle fire.

Coal mining

There were many other industrial jobs besides those in the factories or workshops. One such example was coal mining. As canals and railroads reached into Pennsylvania, Virginia, West Virginia, Kentucky, and Ohio, substantial supplies of coal became available to the nation's expanding mills, forges, factories, and railways. The coal mines supplied American manufacturers and railroads with inexpensive fuel for steam power, and with plentiful supplies of domestic iron. Coal supplies were essential to famous industrialist Andrew Carnegie's (1835–1919) steel mills and later to electric power plants.

Miners dug deep into the earth to extract coal. By the 1860s some anthracite (hard) coal mines in northeastern Pennsylvania reached down as far as 1,500 feet. The miners worked in narrow shafts and tunnels supported by heavy wood beams. They performed physically exhausting labor with sledgehammers and pickaxes in damp, cramped, and airless spaces. They inhaled coal dust all day and many came down with a deadly lung disease called black lung. Many children were employed in the mines. Boys, some as young as nine or ten, were hired to separate rock from coal. Nicknamed "breaker boys," they crouched for ten- to fifteen-hour shifts picking slate from coal chutes, breathing clouds of coal dust. Many boys were required to transport

Breaker boys separating rock from coal. *(© Corbis.)*

coal on their backs, leading to spinal problems and even paralysis. Accidents such as crushed hands and cut fingers were common. All too often boys were pulled into machinery and mangled to death.

Coal mining was unsafe as well as unhealthy. Deep in the mines, rocks fell and tunnels caved in. Because the mines reached so far underground, water accumulated in them and had to be pumped out. There was always a risk of flooding. Lack of air in the mines was also a problem. Early miners built furnaces in the depths of the mines to cause drafts that would ventilate them. Unfortunately, the furnaces could ignite terrible, deadly fires. In order to keep costs down, coal mine owners often sacrificed the safety of their workers. Tens of thousands of men and boys had died in mine accidents by the turn of the century.

Avondale mining disaster

In 1869 sparks from the ventilating furnace of the Avondale coal mine in Pennsylvania started a fire within the mine. The fire spread to the shaft that served as the only exit from the mine. The fire soon roared aboveground, alerting the miners' families of trouble. They realized in horror that the men working below were trapped. The townspeople poured water into the mine for several hours before sending down rescuers, but it was apparent that there was no hope. At about 6:30 that evening, deep in the mine a room was discovered in which sixty-seven of the miners had gathered to try to escape the fire. They had died there together. Others who had perished were found throughout the mine. In all, 108 men and boys had suffocated. Had there been a second exit from the mines, it is possible that many would have survived. Though the Avondale mining disaster was the worst up to that point, many similar disasters would occur before the century ended.

Questioning laissez-faire policies

By the turn of the twentieth century, many workers, reformers, and much of the American public believed the government was too closely adhering to its laissez-faire policies. Men, women, and children were dying or trapped in miserable lives as large, impersonal companies tended to profits and productivity. The public would voice their dissatisfaction in many arenas in the first quarter of the twentieth century. First, though, the industrial workers would confront their oppressors through organized labor unions, or an association of employees that bargain with employers over the terms and conditions of employment.

For More Information

Books

Cashman, Sean Dennis. *America in the Gilded Age: From the Death of Lincoln to the Rise of Theodore Roosevelt.* New York and London: New York University Press, 1984.

Cordery, Stacy A. "Women in Industrializing America." In *The Gilded Age: Essays on the Origins of Modern America.* Edited by Charles W. Calhoun. Wilmington, DE: Scholarly Resources, 1996.

Smith, Page. *The Rise of Industrial America: A People's History of the Post-Reconstruction Era.* Vol. 6. New York: McGraw-Hill, 1984.

Summers, Mark Wahlgren. *The Gilded Age, or, the Hazard of New Functions.* Upper Saddle River, NJ: Prentice-Hall, 1997.

Web Sites

"Child Labor in America, 1908–1912. Photographs of Lewis W. Hine." *The History Place.* http://www.historyplace.com/unitedstates/childlabor (accessed on June 30, 2005).

"The Triangle Factory Fire." *The Kheel Center, Catherwood Library, School of Industrial and Labor Relations, Cornell University.* http://www.ilr.cornell.edu/trianglefire/ (accessed on June 30, 2005).

10

The American Labor Movement

The rise of the huge and powerful railroads and other giant industries during and after the American Civil War (1861–65) signaled a loss of voice for workers. In the small, employer-owned businesses of earlier times, the worker and employer usually came to terms with each other as individuals, settling their differences and agreeing on wages, hours, and other issues through face-to-face discussions. This changed drastically in post–Civil War industry, when the owners hired professional managers to streamline the work. In the new era of mass production, in which goods are produced on a large scale, getting the most work from laborers at the lowest possible wages was a matter of company policy. With machines taking over many jobs, more labor became unskilled. Less value was placed upon the skills of the craftsmen, and workers were easily replaced. Large national labor unions arose to play an essential part in the fight for the rights and dignity of the workers. Labor unions are associations of workers formed to protect their common interests, particularly with respect to wages and working conditions.

An Industrial Workers of the World (IWW) demonstration. *(© Bettmann/Corbis.)*

The history of U.S. labor unions dates back to colonial times. Workers in certain trades, such as carpenters, shoemakers, typesetters, cabinetmakers, machinists, and tailors, began to create associations to obtain better wages and to keep inferior, untrained workmen who worked for lower wages out of their industries. In the 1830s some of the local unions began to unite and join other similar unions within their city. Unions began to unite nationwide in 1852, when the International Typographical Union joined local unions across

Words to Know

anarchist: An individual who advocates the use of force to overthrow all government.

aristocracy: A government controlled by a wealthy, privileged social class.

bankruptcy: A state of financial ruin in which an individual or corporation cannot pay its debts.

boycott: Consumer refusal to buy a company's goods in order to express disapproval.

capitalism: An economic system in which the means of production and distribution are privately owned by individuals or groups and competition for business establishes the price of goods and services.

feudalism: A system in which most people live and work on farms owned by a noble who grants it to them in exchange for their loyalty.

intellectual: A person devoted to study, analysis, and reflection, using rational intellect rather than emotions in pursuit of enlightenment.

labor union: An organization of workers formed to protect and further their mutual interests by bargaining as a group with their employers over wages, working conditions, and benefits.

mass production: The manufacture of goods in quantity by using machines and standardized designs and parts.

socialism: An economic system in which the means of production and distribution is owned collectively by all the workers and there is no private property or social classes.

solidarity: Unity based on common interests.

strike: A work stoppage by employees to protest conditions or make demands of their employer.

workers' compensation: Payments made to an employee who is injured at work.

the United States and Canada. All of the early trade unions were comprised of skilled workers or craftsmen. Before 1861 unskilled industrial workers, for the most part, were not organized.

Unions were slow to grow in the United States in the late 1860s. Part of the problem was that millions of immigrants were arriving in the country willing to take jobs at very low wages. The diversity of the workforce, which resulted in different cultures and languages among the workers, made it difficult for workers to communicate and unite for common issues and goals. Additionally, industry owners were determined to keep their workforces from organizing and sometimes resorted to drastic means, including violence and intimidation, to eliminate labor unions or to keep them from being established. Many workers were forced to sign contracts in which they pledged never to join a union or participate in a strike. Most laws and law enforcers backed the employers.

Eight-hour day and the National Labor Union

Around 1863 workers nationwide began to unite with a central demand for a labor law limiting the workday to eight hours. The eight-hour day slogan—"eight hours for work, eight hours for rest, eight hours for what we will"—quickly became the rallying cry of the labor movement and remained so for decades. A large portion of the American public found the idea of an eight-hour day law too extreme. Many feared the measure would result in higher prices and believed that industry owners had the sole right to dictate the terms of their business. A common argument was that the eight-hour day legislation would deprive workers of their rights by limiting them to eight hours of work per day when some might wish to work longer.

In 1866 delegates from many unions nationwide formed the National Labor Union (NLU) to promote the eight-hour day. William Sylvis (1828–1869), president of the Molders Union, was elected president of the NLU. Under his able leadership the organization grew rapidly, claiming 600,000 members by 1872. The NLU extended its aid to skilled and unskilled workers, including women and African Americans. For a short time the National Labor Union successfully served as a voice and center for working people. After Sylvis died in 1869, his successors tried to transform the union into a political party. The effort eventually failed, causing the fall of the NLU in 1874.

Knights of Labor, 1869–79

Another major effort at a national union began in Philadelphia in 1869. Under the leadership of garment maker Uriah S. Stephens (1821–1882), the Noble Order of the Knights of Labor was founded. Its platform called for the eight-hour day and workers' compensation, or insurance that ensures that workers who are injured on the job are paid. Stephens emphasized the fraternal solidarity (brotherly unity based on common interests) of labor. He advocated admission to the Knights of all workers, regardless of religion, political affiliation, gender, or race. Stephens devised a secret ceremony for the Knights, insisting that the union keep even its name secret from nonmembers to maintain stability.

The Knights of Labor grew slowly under these conditions, its membership reaching about nine thousand nationwide in 1878. Stephens viewed the Knights of Labor not simply as a trade union, but as a foundation for a new economic system in which wage labor was replaced by cooperative efforts between workers and industrialists. Stephens advocated education as the proper means for workers to achieve their goals. He believed workers could use boycotts (consumer refusal to buy a company's goods in order to express disapproval) rather than the strike as an economic weapon, though several strikes did occur.

Strikes are work stoppages planned by workers to help them bargain as a group with the company management or to protest company policies. Most strikes occur only after all other avenues of bargaining have been exhausted. They usually result in damage to the employer's business and loss of pay for employees. Some strikes are small and involve only one company while others are nationwide and involve many different companies and industries.

Depression of 1873

In 1873 the nation experienced a grave economic depression—the worst in the nation's history up to that point. It began when many railroads went bankrupt (were financially ruined). The steel mills were hit hard by the failure of the railroads, which were their largest customers. In turn the coal mines that supplied the steel mills were forced to slow their production. Banks closed and businesses failed. Layoffs (job losses, often on a temporary basis) of laborers occurred in huge numbers, and soon an estimated three million unemployed industrial workers took to the roads seeking any means of survival available. Homelessness and starvation were common. Even workers with jobs went hungry as companies reduced their wages repeatedly. Frustrated, some workers resorted to violence.

A meeting of the Molly Maguires. *(Courtesy of The Library of Congress.)*

The most notorious of the radical worker groups at the time was the Molly Maguires, a small group of Irish miners in the eastern Pennsylvania coal mines. Coal miners labored under miserable and dangerous conditions. Many were forced to work sixteen-hour shifts digging deep below the earth's surface and did not see the light of day for weeks at a time. Thousands of miners were killed each year and thousands more were seriously injured in mine explosions, fires, floods, and collapses. They were paid poorly and irregularly for their efforts. Mine owners did everything they could to stop the miners from forming unions. Some resorted to intimidation and violence and most had the local police on their side. The Molly Maguires formed secretly to fight back. They burned and destroyed property and used physical threats to intimidate the mine owners. On several occasions the Molly Maguires resorted to severe beatings and murder. In 1875 the Molly

Maguires managed to incite a coal miners' strike, but it was quickly broken by the arrest of the group's leaders. A Pinkerton guard (a hired security agent from the Pinkerton Agency) named James McParlan (1844–1919) had been hired by the Philadelphia and Reading Coal and Iron Company to pretend to be a miner and participate in the Molly Maguires' meetings as a spy. He revealed the identities of gunmen responsible for the deaths of nine mine company foremen, and they were convicted and hanged in 1877. The American public read about the Molly Maguires with fear and revulsion, but to some of the mine workers the group seemed to be the only force looking out for them.

The Great Strikes of 1877

In the spring of 1877, the fourth year of the depression, the Pennsylvania Railroad cut wages by 10 percent. In June it announced another 10 percent cut. At the same time the Baltimore and Ohio Railroad announced plans to reduce wages by 10 percent and to cut back the workweek, giving each worker only two or three days of work. Although most railroad workers were not organized in a union, they decided to strike.

The strike started on July 16 when a group of train firemen in Baltimore, Maryland, walked off the job. Brakemen followed them and the strikers proceeded to halt all freight traffic. As news of the strike spread throughout the city, workers in many industries walked off their jobs in sympathy. Workers around the nation learned of the strike and prepared to participate. Large populations of workers in West Virginia and later Illinois, Indiana, Kentucky, Missouri, Pennsylvania, and California joined the strike. Within days, over half of all American railway lines were closed. Violence broke out in several cities, and President Rutherford B. Hayes (1822–1893; served 1877–81) sent federal troops to subdue unruly crowds. The worst violence took place in Pittsburgh, Pennsylvania, where troops fired into a crowd, killing twenty people, including three young children. Enraged, the crowd attacked the federal troops, driving them from the city. The angry mob then began destroying railroad property and looting and burning businesses. Federal troops continued to provide assistance to other states that were unprepared to deal with the strikers and

their unexpectedly large group of sympathizers. It is estimated that more than one hundred people were killed in the confrontations. The strikes lasted only a couple of weeks, but they convinced many laborers of the need to organize to avoid the chaos and bloodshed that had occurred in 1877.

Powderly leads the Knights of Labor

In 1879 Terence Powderly (1849–1924) became head of the Knights of Labor. Powderly, appalled at the violence of the Great Strikes, wanted the union to become a mediator, able to intervene peacefully between labor and employers and help solve disputes. He believed that with one great union serving all the needs of the nation's labor, the economic system could be transformed. Like other early labor leaders, Powderly hoped to eliminate the capitalist wage system altogether and to replace it with a cooperative system in which employers and workers profited more equally from their efforts. As head of the Knights, Powderly sought to lead laborers collectively towards this goal. He preferred to negotiate labor matters in a nonconfrontational manner rather than to strike.

Terence Powderly became head of the Knights of Labor in 1879. *(© Bettmann/Corbis.)*

Under Powderly the Knights of Labor's membership grew dramatically from fewer than 9,000 members to 730,000 members by 1886. Recruiting women, African Americans, and immigrants, as well as unskilled and semiskilled workers, the Knights of Labor began working for reforms, including better wages, hours, and working conditions. Despite Powderly's influence, the Knights of Labor became involved in numerous strikes from the late 1870s to the mid-1880s, and some were quite successful. For several years the Knights of Labor organized many diverse groups with widely varying goals. By 1886, however, differences over whether or not to engage in strikes as well as diverse political goals began to divide the organization.

The Federation of Organized Trades and Labor Unions

In November 1881 delegates representing carpenters, cigar makers, printers, merchant seamen, and steelworkers gathered in Pittsburgh to form a new organization called the Federation of Organized Trades and Labor Unions. They were interested in combining the existing craft unions into a national federation that would be able to lobby for legislation in Washington and the state capitals. The new organization would allow its members complete freedom to govern their own operations. The union leaders were not interested in idealistic political goals; they wanted to secure immediate "bread-and-butter" goals—visible benefits in terms of wages and working conditions.

In 1884 the federation had adopted a resolution asserting that after May 1, 1886, eight hours should constitute a working day, and it strongly promoted a one-day nationwide strike on May 1, 1886, to secure this goal. Though it was a popular idea, the Knights of Labor did not endorse the strike. This caused a rift between the federation and the Knights of Labor.

Haymarket riots

On May 1, 1886, more than 190,000 American workers nationwide went on strike for the eight-hour day. Railroads and factories stopped. By the end of the day 150,000 workers had earned a guarantee of shorter working hours—a great victory for organized labor. But disaster followed in the city of Chicago, where earlier that year the McCormick Harvester Company had locked out (not allowed to enter the workplace or be paid) fourteen hundred strikers and then brought in nonunion workers to take the strikers' jobs. Two days after the successful nationwide May Day strike, the McCormick strikers clashed with these replacement workers. Police fired into the crowd, killing one protester and seriously wounding six others.

The angry strikers called a mass meeting for the evening of May 4 in Haymarket Square to protest the killing. Around 10:00 PM, after a peaceful rally, hundreds of police appeared. Someone from the rally threw a bomb into their ranks, instantly killing a policeman. The police fired on the crowd,

Someone threw a bomb at the police during the Haymarket Square Riot.
(© Corbis.)

killing ten people and wounding about fifty others. They then arrested several hundred labor leaders. The state pressed charges against eight leaders of the strike, although only one of them had even been at the rally when the bomb exploded. (The individual who had reportedly thrown the bomb fled to his native country of Germany immediately after the incident.) Several of the arrested leaders were known to be anarchists, or individuals who advocate the use of force to overthrow all government. Most historians agree that the trial that followed made a mockery of the justice system because no one even tried to prove that the accused were guilty of the bombing; in the heightened emotions after the violence, it was enough for the prosecution simply to prove their radical political beliefs. Seven of the eight accused were convicted and sentenced to be hanged.

Marx and Engels on the Struggle between Capital and Labor

In the early 1840s young German philosopher Karl Marx (1818–1883) perceived the changes happening in his country. With the rise of industrialism, people moved to cities and worked in factories or mills using increasingly advanced machinery. The factories and large businesses were owned and operated by private citizens who made profits from the work of others. This economic system is called capitalism.

Marx thought capitalism divided people and demeaned the lives of the workers. Marx and German philosopher Friedrich Engels (1820–1895), who shared many of Marx's beliefs, developed a theory called historical materialism. They agreed that history had been shaped by struggles between social classes, and that new economic systems were formed by these struggles. Capitalism pitted the wealthy upper class in a struggle against the workers. Marx and Engels predicted that this struggle would result in a system known as socialism, in which the means of production and distribution—the farms, factories, ships, railroads, and stores—would be collectively owned by all the laborers. All people would be workers in a cooperative effort, and there would be no private property and no social classes. Marx and Engels wrote about their concept of historical materialism in *The Communist Manifesto* (1848), which became one of the most widely read works in history.

In the United States socialist and Marxist groups were fairly small. Though some preached violent revolution, there was little support for it. The Socialist Party of America (SPA) was formed in 1901. The party included a diverse combination of workers and intellectuals, paupers and millionaires, recent immigrants and native-born Americans. The SPA did not, however, welcome most women or African American members. The Socialist Party generally won reforms through political action. Candidates from the party ran for local offices and sometimes won. Between 1901 and 1917, the SPA's victories in elections and in passing reform legislations led to what has become known as the "golden age of American socialism." After 1912 the organization's membership fell dramatically. Workers were more interested in the issues of wages and working conditions than in idealism, political reform, or revolution.

The Knights of Labor threatened to expel any affiliate union that supported the move for clemency (mercy) for the accused, hoping to distance itself from the small anarchist movement. It was not a popular stand among workers. Soon after the Haymarket incident in 1886, several factions of the Knights of Labor withdrew from the organization. Much diminished, the Knights of Labor remained intact for three more decades before it officially dissolved in 1917.

The Federation becomes the AFL

After the Haymarket event, the Federation of Organized Trades and Labor Unions re-formed, becoming the American Federation of Labor (AFL). Samuel Gompers (1850–1924) was elected its president and the union was structured according to his wishes. Gompers insisted that the organization represent skilled workers only, that it be built as a federation of independently operated trade unions, and that it stay out of politics while striving for attainable goals such as the eight-hour day, child labor legislation, workplace safety, immigration restriction, and workers' compensation.

The AFL grew slowly at first. In 1890 it claimed only 100,000 members, but by 1900 membership had risen to 548,000, and by 1914 it was approaching two million. Along the way the AFL attracted some very large unions such as the United Mine Workers (UMW, founded in 1890). But there were other sizable organizations that did not affiliate. Most notable among these were the Railroad Brotherhoods, including the Engineers, who formed in 1863, and the Firemen, formed six years later.

The Pullman strike

Between 1861 and 1865, George Pullman (1831–1897) created a manufacturing industry with his distinctive line of luxury sleeper and dining cars. In the 1880s he decided to build a state-of-the-art factory about fifteen miles outside of Chicago, and he also built a town there for the workers to live in. Pullman envisioned his town as a model of efficiency and healthfulness. In 1884 workers and their families began moving into the row house rentals provided for them in Pullman, Illinois.

A depression seized the economy in the winter of 1893, causing a drop in orders of Pullman cars. Pullman laid off more than half the workers in his town and cut the wages of the rest by more than 25 percent. He did not, however, reduce the high rent he charged on the workers' row houses or lessen charges in other facilities of the town. The Pullman employees began striking on May 11, 1894. A popular new union, the American Railway Union (ARU), which had been created by young labor leader Eugene Debs (1855–1926), voted to support the Pullman strike. Within a week, 125,000 railroad workers

The History of Labor Day

The first Labor Day celebration and parade was sponsored by the Knights of Labor and took place on September 5, 1882, in New York City. Ten thousand workers took an unpaid day off from work and marched from city hall to Union Square to honor the nation's workers and to voice complaints about their lot. Two years later the Federation of Organized Trades and Labor Unions (later the American Federation of Labor) supported the idea of an annual Labor Day scheduled on the first Monday in September. On that day most northeastern cities sponsored parades of workers.

Several states adopted Labor Day, but the federal government consistently resisted the call to make it a federal holiday. In the months after the Pullman strike, many Americans questioned the harshness with which President Grover Cleveland (1837–1908; served 1893–97) had handled the strike. In 1894, two years before he was up for reelection, Cleveland pushed the Labor Day bill through, hoping to mend fences with the nation's workers. Cleveland was not reelected, but the United States had a new federal holiday.

The first Labor Day parade, held in 1882.
(© Bettman/Corbis. Reproduced by permission.)

nationwide refused to work on a train carrying a Pullman sleeper, shutting down rail traffic in the West and Midwest. Debs was insistent that there was to be no violence, no stopping of trains, and no destruction of railway property.

Pitted against the workers was the General Managers' Association (GMA), an organization that represented the twenty-six railroads in their battles against the unions. The GMA urged the federal government to attach mail cars to trains carrying Pullman cars. This allowed President Grover Cleveland (1837–1908; served 1893–97) to call out the U.S.

Army by arguing that the strike was interfering with the federal mail system. When troops marched into ARU headquarters in Chicago on July 4, a violent conflict resulted in thirteen deaths. Resistance spread outward from Chicago; skirmishes between strikers and federal troops and state militia flared in twenty-six states, stretching from Maine to California. Thirty-four people were killed.

Debs could see that the ARU was fighting a losing battle. The American Federation of Labor and the Railroad Brotherhoods refused to cooperate. The final straw occurred when the government secured an injunction (court order or formal command) against the strike leaders that forbade them from doing their jobs in the strike. Debs and the other leaders ignored it and they were arrested on July 17.

The Pullman strike quickly collapsed. After the strike the ARU was disbanded and the employees at Pullman were persuaded to sign pledges that they would never form or participate in another union. Debs was sentenced to six months in prison for his part in the strike. Noting that presidents from both parties had sided with the employers against the workers during the strike, Deb turned to the Socialist Party, believing it was the only party that would carry out the struggle for the rights and dignity of working people.

The Homestead Strike

One of the most violent business-labor clashes of this turbulent period involved a company that typified the new industrial economy: Carnegie Steel, which by 1892 had become the nation's largest steel maker. At first, founder Andrew Carnegie (1835–1919) had endorsed workers' rights to form unions and had been relatively generous in settling earlier disputes with his workers, most of whom were members of the Amalgamated Association of Iron and Steel Workers (AAISW). But Carnegie's view changed and he opposed the unionization of the workers in his plants, believing that unions interfered with good company management.

Trouble began in 1889, when Carnegie Steel announced a 25 percent reduction in wages for steelworkers. The AAISW called for a work stoppage and threatened violence. One of the company's directors signed a three-year contract in which the union agreed to accept the new pay scale, but under the new contract the AAISW became the sole bargaining agent in the mill and required that no steelworkers could be hired or fired without union approval. Carnegie was not happy with this arrangement and he quickly chose his partner Henry Clay Frick (1849–1919) to manage the Homestead mills. Previously an operator of coal mines, Frick had established a reputation not only as a shrewd manager, but also as a tough union buster who had violently suppressed strikes at his coalfields.

By 1892, both Carnegie and Frick wanted to lower wages even further and to eliminate the union as the exclusive bargaining agent in the mill. Just before the contract of 1889 expired, Frick announced the terms of a new contract, cutting wages and the power of the union. Carnegie left for an extended trip to Europe, leaving Frick in complete control. Frick knew there would be a strike, so he fortified the mill, erecting a massive stockade around it equipped with watchtowers, gun slits, and barbed wire. He then arranged with the Pinkerton Detective Agency to send 300 security guards into the plant as soon as the workers went on strike.

The strike began on July 1, 1892, and the Pinkertons arrived five days later. They were spotted by union lookouts as they came upriver from Pittsburgh on barges, and when they attacked in the night at the Homestead plant, the strikers were waiting. A battle began, one of the most famous in American labor history. By late afternoon of July 6, the Pinkertons surrendered. As they were being escorted out of the town, an angry mob of workers attacked them, killing several and severely beating others. The workers held the plant for several days, until the governor called out the state militia to restore order on July 12. Even with the state in control of the plant, operations could not take place without the skilled steelworkers, and the strike continued. Nine days later a Russian immigrant with no connection to the mill attempted to assassinate Frick in his office. Frick was wounded but survived, and the news shifted the nation's sympathy, which had been with the strikers, over to management.

Innovations in steel industry technology became available just months after the strike began, providing new machines for making steel that did not require skilled operatives. Frick reopened the Homestead plant with 700 immigrant strikebreakers.

The union was defeated and on November 20 the strike was officially called off. AAISW membership fell from a peak of 24,000 in 1891 to 10,000 in 1894. By 1903 no steel mill in the country was unionized, a condition that remained unchanged until the 1930s.

In the first decade of the twentieth century there were three times as many strikes as in the 1890s, and they resulted in more violence than in previous years. Many Americans felt threatened by this violence and sided with the businesses. Government had clearly shown its support for the employers, using court injunctions and armed troops to put down strikes and break unions. In the 1890s the federal government used the Sherman Antitrust Act, which had been designed to regulate big industries, against unions more often than against businesses.

The Industrial Workers of the World

Founded in 1905 by the leaders of forty-three labor organizations, the Industrial Workers of the World (IWW) was a radical labor union. The IWW's long-term goal was to overthrow capitalism and rebuild society based on socialist principles. Though small in numbers because of its extremist views and tactics (its membership probably never exceeded 100,000), the IWW and its members, called "Wobblies," attracted national attention. Socialist Party leader Eugene Debs endorsed the organization's anticapitalist agenda and became one of its leaders.

Founded and led by miner William "Big Bill" Haywood (1869–1928) and agitator Mary "Mother" Jones (1830–1930), the IWW aimed to unite all workers in a camp, mine, or factory and prepare them for an eventual takeover of their employer's industrial facility. The union organized strikes in lumber and mining camps in the West, in the steel mills of Pennsylvania, and in the textile mills of New England. The leadership advocated the use of violence to achieve its revolutionary goals and opposed most forms of negotiation. During World War I (1914–18), IWW-led strikes were suppressed by the federal government. The organization's leaders were arrested and the organization dissolved. Haywood was convicted of sedition (inciting resistance to lawful authority) but managed to flee to the Soviet Union.

African American labor unions

Most unions of the nineteenth and early twentieth centuries were largely hostile or indifferent to African Americans. As a result, black workers in many cities organized their own unions or associations to represent their members' interests. Isaac Myers (1835–1891), a caulker in Baltimore, Maryland, was one of the early activists in the black labor movement. Black caulkers in Baltimore had been organized since at least 1838, and they had successfully bargained with shipyard owners on wages and working conditions. The increase in immigration from Europe, however, brought an inflow of workers who competed with African Americans for jobs. The resulting tension between the two groups led to a series of riots directed against African Americans in 1858. In 1865 white shipyard workers went on strike to protest the presence of black workers. As a result, many black longshoremen and caulkers lost their jobs.

In 1869 Myers was one of nine African American delegates to attend the National Labor Union convention with the intention of establishing a parallel union devoted to handling the specific problems of black workers. The Colored National Union was formed with the full support of the National Labor Union, and Myers was placed at its head. Black-white unity between the NLU and Colored National Union quickly broke down, however, and by 1871 this attempt to organize black workers had failed. The Knights of Labor and later the IWW recruited African American workers. The dominant national union, though, the AFL, left policies up to the individual unions. Black workers were usually excluded.

In the late nineteenth century, black workers tended to organize separately from their white counterparts. All-black and all-white local unions formed, sometimes competing for jobs and benefits, sometimes cooperating. For example, on the docks of New Orleans in the 1880s, and again from 1901 to 1923, black and white longshoremen and cotton yardmen belonged to separate unions, but they agreed to divide available work equally between blacks and whites, to abide by identical rules and accept the same wages, and to present a united front in all union-management negotiations. Similarly, in the coalfields of Alabama in the 1880s and 1890s, black and white locals of the Knights of Labor and the United Mine Workers jointly represented miners of both races.

The World War I era witnessed several large-scale strikes by black workers. During this period associations of African American railroad workers—including porters, dining car workers, locomotive firemen, brakemen, and yard switchmen—lodged thousands of protests with managers and federal officials, calling for an end to race-based differences in pay, promotion, and job assignment. In 1925 the Brotherhood of Sleeping Car Porters (BSCP) was founded. The union was composed entirely of the African American porters and maids who worked on the railway trains that traversed the nation. The BSCP was organized in Harlem, New York City, in 1925 by Asa Philip Randolph (1889–1979), a newspaper publisher and member of the Socialist Party who believed that unions provided the best opportunity for black workers to secure a fair wage and to defend their rights.

Rise and fall of unions in the twentieth century

In 1902 labor unions scored a major victory when President Theodore Roosevelt (1887–1934; served 1902–9) intervened in the United Mine Workers strike. Federal troops were called in to support the workers rather than the employers for the first time in U.S. history. It was a sign of change in public opinion. Reforms in work hours and conditions, child labor, benefits, and workers' compensation gradually followed. After World War I, however, labor unions lost their force and did not regain momentum until after 1941. Unions then remained fairly strong through the 1960s and 1970s, but support for them dropped again in the 1980s.

For More Information

Books

Arnesen, Eric. "American Workers and the Labor Movement in the Late Nineteenth Century." In *The Gilded Age: Essays on the Origins of Modern America*. Edited by Charles W. Calhoun. Wilmington, DE: Scholarly Resources, 1996.

Aronowitz, Stanley. *From the Ashes of the Old: American Labor and America's Future*. Boston, MA: Houghton Mifflin Company, 1998.

Cashman, Sean Dennis. *America in the Gilded Age: From the Death of Lincoln to the Rise of Theodore Roosevelt*. New York and London: New York University Press, 1984.

Smith, Page. *The Rise of Industrial America: A People's History of the Post-Reconstruction Era.* Vol. 6. New York: McGraw-Hill, 1984.

Summers, Mark Wahlgren. *The Gilded Age, or, the Hazard of New Functions.* Upper Saddle River, NJ: Prentice-Hall, 1997.

Web Sites

"The Haymarket Tragedy." *The Illinois Labor History Society.* http://www.kentlaw.edu/ilhs/haymarket.htm (accessed on June 30, 2005).

"The Pullman Strike." *Illinois Periodicals Online (IPO), Northern Illinois University Libraries.* http://www.lib.niu.edu/ipo/ihy941208.html (accessed on June 30, 2005).

11

The New South

I n the period before the American Civil War (1861–65; a war between the Union [the North], who were opposed to slavery, and the Confederacy [the South], who were in favor of slavery), the South had remained a largely rural society, reliant for the most part on one crop, cotton, which was by far the nation's largest export. Southern plantations and farms supplied three-fourths of the world's cotton to textile manufacturers in both the United States and Great Britain. Attempts to diversify (give variety to) the Southern economy had nearly ceased in the decade before the war because cotton prices rose more than 50 percent, stimulating even more new cultivation. Not surprisingly, the Southern economy remained overwhelmingly agricultural. Southern capitalists (people who invest their money into businesses) invested much more money in cotton than in factories or even land. More precisely, they purchased slaves who provided the necessary labor for the cotton business. In 1860 the average slave owner had invested almost two-thirds of his wealth in the purchase of slaves.

SCENE ON A COTTON PLANTATION. GATHERING COTTON.

Workers picking cotton on a Southern plantation. *(© Bettmann/Corbis.)*

The pre–Civil War economy

The outcome of the Civil War was heavily influenced by the advantages the North gained from its industry. In 1859 the North had about 21,900 miles of railroads compared to the South's 6,600. In the North, railroads connected the farming and manufacturing centers, but in the South railroads lacked direct connections between major cities. During the war the Southerners had problems getting supplies where they were needed and failed to get needed food to the armies in the field. The North had 90 percent of the nation's industrial capacity. By 1860 northeastern states such as Massachusetts and Pennsylvania had nearly $100 million each invested in

Words to Know

capital: Accumulated wealth or goods devoted to the production of other goods.

capitalism: An economic system in which the means of production and distribution are privately owned by individuals or groups and competition for business establishes the price of goods and services.

Confederate states: The eleven Southern states that withdrew from the United States in 1860 and 1861.

hydroelectric power plants: Plants that produce electricity from waterpower.

industrialization: The development of industry.

magnate: A powerful and influential person in an industry.

philanthropy: The desire or effort to help humankind, as by making charitable donations.

sharecropper: A tenant farmer who works the land for an agreed share of the value of the crop, minus the deductions taken out of his share for his rent, supplies, and living costs.

tenant farmer: Someone who farms land owned by someone else and pays rent or a share of the crop for the use of the land.

Yankee: A Southern word for Northerners.

manufacturing enterprises. Virginia, the most industrialized of the Southern states, had invested less than $20 million in manufacturing, and other Southern states had invested less than $5 million apiece in industry. The South's lack of manufacturing industries made it nearly impossible to provide its army with sufficient arms and ammunition.

Before the war there were no significant financial institutions in the Confederate states (the Southern states that withdrew from the United States in 1860 and 1861). Most cotton farmers had to borrow money annually to prepare their crops, and they were forced to borrow it from Northern bankers at high interest rates. Processing and shipping cotton were handled by Northern industries. Even the slave trade was controlled mainly by Northern merchants. The South's agricultural economy made it difficult to raise large sums of money. During the war the Confederate government ran out of cash and finally resorted to printing paper money, but the currency came to have so little value that people eventually turned to the practice of bartering, or trading goods. In the end the South was unable to raise the capital (accumulated wealth or goods devoted to the production of other goods) it needed to support the war effort. This inability to raise capital continued long after the war was over.

The plantation system of the South resulted in a very different type of economy than the industrial economy developing in the North. Large plantation owners had sizable workforces on their estates and often produced their own goods and services on site. Since the plantations were in some ways self-sufficient communities, there were few towns in the pre-war South. Most Southern plantation owners wanted it that way. They strongly preferred their rural, agricultural society to the commercialism, industry, and wage labor of the Northerners, whom they called Yankees.

Large cotton plantations with slave workforces created a great deal of the South's wealth, but they were not the norm. Nearly three-fourths of families in the South were small farmers who did not own slaves. Still, most slaves lived on plantations, and the bulk of the cotton crop came from plantations worked by twenty or more slaves.

After the Civil War

The South was economically devastated by the Civil War. Its major cities, such as Richmond, Virginia, and Charleston, South Carolina, had been badly damaged. Its banks had failed, its currency was worthless, the transportation systems were unreliable, and many plantations and farms lay idle. About 258,000 Southern men had died and many who survived were maimed for life and incapable of supporting themselves. Farmers in the South lost much of their livestock and farm tools. The largest financial shock to the South was the loss of its slave labor force. The Southern slave owners had invested most of their capital in the purchase of slaves. An estimated $4 billion had been invested—more than the value of all the land in the South.

During the Reconstruction Era, the period from the end of the war until 1877, the Confederate Southern states were reorganized as free (nonslave holding) states and brought back into the United States. During Reconstruction federal troops were stationed throughout the South to ensure that blacks were allowed to participate in the political system. The former

Journalist Henry W. Grady supported Southern industrialization. *(© Bettmann/Corbis.)*

Southern elite did not accept the new laws imposed by the federal government. Most were hostile to the civil rights of the African Americans to vote and participate in government. Although President Rutherford B. Hayes (1822–1893; served 1877–81) withdrew the last federal troops from the South in 1877, the attempt to make a smooth transition for the freed slaves into the Southern economy and society failed. Soon the Southern states instituted racial codes that discriminated against African Americans in the South for many years to come. The experience of the Reconstruction Era left both Northerners and Southerners bitter and hostile toward one another.

The economy in the South was still in poor shape in 1880. According to Sean Dennis Cashman in *America in the Gilded Age,* the average per capita (per person) wealth in the United States outside the South in 1880 was $1,086. In the South it was only $376. Some Southerners began to talk about industrialization (the development of industry) as a means to recover, and foremost among them was journalist Henry W. Grady (1850–1889), the editor of the weekly newspaper *Atlanta Constitution.* In his column and in speeches made throughout the country, Grady preached the virtues of a "New South," calling for the development of local resources, the diversification of crops, and, most importantly, the development of manufacturing. Grady urged embittered Southerners to seek reconciliation with the North and to strive for new relations with African Americans. Southerners had long cultivated the image of being too easy-going and refined to compete in the business world. Grady and other advocates of the New South urged Southern businessmen to emulate the Yankees and create new industries that would provide much-needed jobs and wealth in the South.

The new industries

The South had a lot of unclaimed federal land in the late 1870s that was reserved for people who were willing to settle there and farm it. Several states changed their laws so they could distribute federal lands to speculators who could invest in extracting the South's great natural resources, particularly lumber, iron, and coal. Millions of acres fell into the hands of Northern and European capitalists who rushed in to dig mines and strip the hills and valleys in order to ship the resources to the factories in the North.

By the 1880s the South was experiencing a boom in railroad construction. From 1880 to 1890 the number of railroad track miles jumped from 16,605 to 39,108. Small competing railroad lines successfully combined with each other. In the 1890s wealthy financier J. P. Morgan (1837–1913), with his millions of dollars of investment capital, reorganized railroads nationwide through a strategy that became known as "Morganization." Morgan acquired bankrupted railroads, funded them with enough new capital to survive, cut costs, and negotiated agreements between competing lines to reduce unnecessary competition. In this way Morgan built up the Southern railway system, opening the way for more industrial expansion in the region.

Manufacturing increased significantly in the South in the 1880s and 1890s. New enterprises included cotton mills, iron forges, and commercial fertilizer manufacturing plants (by 1877 South Carolina alone was shipping more than 100,000 tons of fertilizer to foreign markets). The number of cotton mills rose from 161 in 1880 to 400 in 1900. Cottonseed oil also became a major Southern industry. Southern iron makers began to run modernized coal mines, coke (a hard, dry carbon substance produced by heating coal to a very high temperature in the absence of air) ovens, and blast furnaces. The town of Birmingham, Alabama, became a major industrial center during this period, boasting substantial ironworks that eventually became steelworks.

James Buchanan Duke and the tobacco industry

In 1874 Washington Duke (1820–1905), a former tobacco farmer, set up a tobacco factory in Durham, North Carolina. His son, James Buchanan Duke (1856–1925), soon joined him and began transforming the business. In 1884 James Duke

James Buchanan Duke. *(© Bettman/Corbis. Reproduced by permission.)*

acquired the Bonsack cigarette-rolling machine, which allowed mechanized mass production of cigarettes. Once he had firmly established the production system, he opened a company office in New York City and began a series of marketing strategies. He offered free samples of his cigarettes to new immigrants, hoping they would come back for more as paying customers. He advertised on billboards and in newspapers and magazines. He used the company name to support sporting events and included coupons inside packets of his cigarettes. Duke's aggressive marketing techniques were highly unusual in his day and proved hugely successful. By 1889 W. Duke, Sons and Company, produced 45 percent of all cigarettes sold in the United States. That year the company merged with four other major tobacco manufacturers. With Duke as its president, the new American Tobacco Company controlled 90 percent of all tobacco sales in the United States.

Duke followed in the path of the notorious Northern industrialists, such as John D. Rockefeller (1839–1937), who founded the Standard Oil Trust. First he cut costs by closing less efficient factories, discontinuing unpopular cigarette brands, and hiring nonunion labor at low wages. Then he undercut the prices of his competition. He also signed a contract with the Bonsack Company to restrict the sales of its automatic cigarette-making machine to any company other than the American Tobacco Company. By 1898 the American Tobacco Company had almost eliminated its competition. The U.S. government watched the company's business practices and in 1907 began to file lawsuits alleging violations of antitrust regulations (laws enacted to protect trade from monopolies and other unfair business practices). In 1911 the U.S. Supreme Court ordered the American Tobacco Company to break into four smaller firms: the American Tobacco Company, Liggett and Myers, P. Lorillard, and R. J. Reynolds.

Duke's attention by that time had turned to other industries. He invested in hydroelectric power plants (plants that produce electricity from waterpower), founding the Southern Power System in 1905, and then used the power from them to run family-owned textile mills producing cotton and wool. Eventually the Southern Power Company supplied electricity to more than three hundred cotton mills, as well as cities, towns, and factories in North and South Carolina. The company came to be known as the Duke Power Company and is still operating today. In his later years Duke, like Rockefeller, devoted a large portion of his fortune to philanthropy (efforts to promote human welfare, often by giving money), notably providing critical funding to Trinity College in Durham, North Carolina, which today is called Duke University.

Sharecropping and tenant farming

The most radical economic change brought about by the Civil War was the elimination of slavery. Suddenly hundreds of thousands of freed people needed homes and jobs. In the first Reconstruction initiatives, the Union army confiscated (took) land from the Confederate landowners and gave them to former slaves in 40-acre parcels along with a mule. But by the end of the Reconstruction Era, the confiscated land had been returned to its former owners. Gradually the hopes of the freed people for the "forty acres and a mule" promised to them disappeared and they sought other ways to maintain themselves. Most of the former plantation owners had neither the resources nor the equipment to continue the plantation system that had supported the South before the war. Some tried to adjust to the new era by paying wages to their workforce, but most were unable to do this because the war had seriously depleted stocks of money in the South. The planters, unable to hire farm labor, resorted to breaking their estates into small farms and contracting with farmers in two different arrangements: sharecropping and tenancy.

In the sharecropping system, the landowner furnished the farmer and his family with a house and a plot of land, along with seed, fertilizer, and other necessary supplies and equipment to start a crop. The sharecropper and his family did the cultivating, planting, tending, and harvesting. After the harvested crop was sold, the costs of the supplies provided by the owner were subtracted from the proceeds, and the remainder was divided between the owner and the farmer. Frequently the entire crop was insufficient to meet the farmer's obligations to the owner, and the sharecropper fell into debt that was difficult or impossible to repay.

Tenant farmers owned everything necessary for farm production except the land. In exchange for the use of the land, they paid the landowner with cash or part of their crops. Tenant farmers had more independence in the operation of their farms than sharecroppers, but there were traps in that system as well. When tenant farmers did not have the money to buy necessary supplies to run the farm, they usually applied to a local storekeeper or merchant for a loan secured by the future crop. Throughout the year the farmer would buy groceries, clothing, seed, fertilizer, and other supplies on credit. After the crop was harvested the storekeeper/merchant would sell the crop and pay up the farmer's account. If there was anything left the farmer received it in a cash payment or in additional credit. Often the crop did not bring in enough to meet the bills, and the farmer consequently found himself in constant debt.

Tenant farmers and sharecroppers almost always grew cotton because it brought in the cash that Southern landowners desperately needed. With most farms producing cotton and little else, more cotton began to hit the market than was needed. This resulted in a fall in cotton prices. In 1866 cotton sold for 43 cents a pound. Between 1882 and 1902, it never went above 10 cents a pound, and in 1894 it fell to 4.6 cents a pound.

Sharecropping and tenant farming resulted in an increase in the number of farms in the South and a reduction in their size. In 1860 there were 672,313 farms in the South. In 1910 there were 3,097,547. The average size of farms during this time fell from 335 acres to 114 acres, and many were less than 50 acres. Tenant-operated farms in the South grew from about 36 percent of all farms in 1880 to between 60 and 70 percent in 1910. About 80 percent of African American farmers and 40 percent of white farmers were either sharecroppers or tenant farmers struggling to survive the system.

Booker T. Washington and the Tuskegee Institute

For many African Americans in the South, the end of slavery led to lowly work, debt, and dire poverty. There were few avenues through which they could improve their circumstances. Southern education systems suffered from lack of funding, yet it was clear to many black leaders that education was vital to improving the lives of the former slaves. The leaders, however, did not always agree on the type of education that was needed.

Educator Booker T. Washington (1856–1915) had been born of a slave mother and a white father on a Virginia farm. After experiencing many hardships in his early life, he entered Hampton Normal and Agricultural Institute, one of the early Negro vocational schools in Virginia. General Samuel Chapman Armstrong (1839–1893), who headed Hampton, believed that blacks should do without liberal education (arts and humanities) and not strive for political and civil rights until they had improved their own economic status. Hampton was there to provide its students with what Armstrong called "industrial education," practical learning that would help them enter a trade like carpentry or stonemasonry. Students were expected to support themselves while attending Hampton.

In 1881 Washington was selected to be the principal of a new school to be founded at Tuskegee, Alabama. When he arrived on the site of the campus, however, he found only an abandoned plantation—the school had not been built yet. Over the next few years, Washington supervised the planting of crops and the making of bricks. By 1888 the buildings of the Tuskegee Normal and Industrial Institute (now Tuskegee University) spread out over 550 acres. Over four hundred students were enrolled in such trade programs as farming, carpentry, printing, shoemaking, tinsmithing, and cooking. Washington emphasized manual and industrial education, as well as practical trades such as carpentry, farming, mechanics, and teaching. He also emphasized discipline and cleanliness to his students, seeking to pass on a philosophy of African American self-sufficiency. By 1915 the school had fifteen hundred students and more financial donations than any other black institution.

In 1895 the Cotton States and International Exposition was held in Atlanta to exhibit the commercial and industrial growth of the South. Before an all-white audience of

Students in class at the Tuskegee Institute. *(Courtesy of The Library of Congress.)*

about two thousand people, Washington gave a speech that has come to be known as the "Atlanta Compromise," in which he outlined his proposal for racial harmony in the United States. He explained that self-improvement of African Americans in economic and educational matters would make them more law-abiding and less resentful toward white Americans. Washington spoke out against the public protests of African Americans occurring at that time; he believed economic advancement was a more effective solution for African Americans than political demonstrations. Ultimately, he accepted racial segregation (separation) in exchange for economic opportunities. As he said in the speech: "In all things that are purely social we [blacks and whites] can be as separate as the fingers, yet one as the hand in all things essential to mutual progress."

The African American Migration North

At the end of the Civil War, approximately 92 percent of all African Americans lived in the South, and, despite the harsh circumstances in the years following the war and Reconstruction, few left the region for the remainder of the century. One exception was a migration between 1879 and 1881, when about sixty thousand African Americans moved to Kansas and the Oklahoma Indian Territories. European immigration may be one explanation for the slow start of the migration of African Americans from the South to the North. A great many of the urban factory jobs were filled first by Irish and German laborers and later by immigrants from southern and eastern Europe, so black Southerners had no assurance of getting jobs in the North. It is also likely that some Northerners, displaying their own racism, did not welcome blacks or make it easy for them to obtain jobs.

A large migration of African Americans from the South to Northern industrial cities began in the first decade of the new century. Between 1900 and 1910, 366,880 African Americans migrated to Northern cities from the South. From 1910 to 1920 between five hundred thousand and one million African Americans made the trip north. By 1930 more than one in five blacks resided outside of the South.

By 1930 Chicago's South Side and New York's Harlem had become the capitals of African American life in the North. Chicago drew African Americans because it was the major industrial city of the Midwest and the nation's great railroad hub. Chicago's leading black newspaper, the *Defender,* circulated widely in the South, and the paper's editors urged Southern blacks to come work in Chicago's meatpacking plants and railroad yards. Between 1916 and 1919 about sixty thousand Southern blacks moved to Chicago, and most joined the city's industrial workforce.

A second and even larger migration of Southern blacks occurred between 1940 and the 1960s with a net migration totaling between four million and five million people. The mechanization of Southern agriculture after World War II (1939–45; a war in which Great Britain, France, the United States, and their allies defeated Germany, Italy, and Japan) decreased the demand for low-wage labor and gave further cause for African Americans to leave the South's agricultural areas.

Washington's speech was very popular among white Americans, and he soon developed strong ties with Northern philanthropists such as Andrew Carnegie (1835–1919) and George Eastman (1854–1932), both of whom appreciated Washington's business-like approach to race issues. But the late 1800s were a difficult time for African Americans. Lynchings (killings) increased, Jim Crow laws enforcing racial segregation in public were passed, and whites in the South found ways to stop African Americans from voting. Black intellectuals like W. E. B. DuBois (1868–1963) felt that Washington's educational proposals discouraged African Americans from striving for a higher education and taking their place as equals in American society. He urged talented African Americans to obtain a college education and serve as leaders of the black community so that they could better fight the discrimination that surrounded them.

Southern Alliance

In the end the concept of the industrial New South was more a way of thinking held by a few idealists than a reality. In 1890 only about 10 percent of the Southern population was urban, compared to 26 percent of the population in the North. Agriculture supported the South. Unfortunately, it was not doing a very good job.

Southern farmers were at a disadvantage in securing fair rates with the railroads, grain-elevator owners, and money-lenders. They had no control over the overproduction of cotton or the consequent drop in prices. Southerners were frustrated with prolonged poverty and wanted to do something to better their lot. In the South, as in the American West, they began to organize.

The National Farmers' Alliance emerged in 1875, splitting into two groups: the National Farmers' Alliance (Northern Alliance) in the Midwest and West, and the National Farmers' Alliance & Industrial Union (Southern Alliance) centered in Louisiana, Texas, and Arkansas. By the end of 1887, the Alliance had spread to every Southern state and claimed more than three million members. It appealed to farmers because it was portrayed as a cooperative business venture, that is, one that is jointly owned by all the people who participate. One benefit of cooperatives was that many farmers could join together and buy their farm supplies and equipment in large amounts, thus getting a price break from the manufacturer. They could also band together to try to get better transportation rates.

It seemed that only by joining together in large numbers could the nation's farmers achieve their goals. By the end of the

1880s, there was talk of uniting the Southern Alliance with the Northern, but this never occurred, in large part due to the fact that the Northern Alliance allowed black farmers to join and the Southern Alliance did not. Racial issues also divided another group with similar goals, the Colored Farmers' Alliance. Established in 1886 the Colored Farmers' Alliance was the largest organization of black farmers and farmworkers of its time. By the mid 1890s, it had a membership of over one million farmers and represented every state in the South. At first the Colored Farmers' Alliance advocated cooperation with Southern white farmers, but the Southern Alliance, as well as local authorities, resisted it so fiercely that the Colored Farmers' Alliance became active in its own interest.

In the 1890s Southern farmers, both black and white, did join with others nationwide to establish a third political party, the Populist Party, to fight against the powerful industrialists and railroad magnates (powerful and influential people in the industry) in the interest of the common rural farmer (see Chapter 12).

For More Information

Books

Cashman, Sean Dennis. *America in the Gilded Age: From the Death of Lincoln to the Rise of Theodore Roosevelt.* New York and London: New York University Press, 1984.

Fishel, Leslie H., Jr. "The African-American Experience." In *The Gilded Age: Essays on the Origins of Modern America.* Edited by Charles W. Calhoun. Wilmington, DE: Scholarly Resources, 1996.

Foner, Eric. *Reconstruction: America's Unfinished Revolution, 1863–1877.* New York: Harper & Row, 1988.

Wright, Gavin. *Old South, New South: Revolutions in the Southern Economy Since the Civil War.* New York: Basic Books, 1986.

Web Sites

"America's Reconstruction: People and Politics after the Civil War." *Digital History.* http://www.digitalhistory.uh.edu/reconstruction/ index.html (accessed on June 30, 2005).

12

The Effects of Industrialism on Farming and Ranching in the West

Industrialization took on a variety of forms throughout the United States in the second half of the nineteenth century. While factories and cities developed early in the nineteenth century in the Northeast, rural life and farming remained the rule in most of the rest of the country. In the years after 1865, though, railroads began making their way across the nation, rapidly changing the nature of American farming and ranching in the areas west of the Appalachian Mountains, particularly the Old Northwest (the modern Midwest, including the states of Ohio, Indiana, Illinois, Michigan, and Wisconsin) and the Great Plains (an area of grassland that stretches across the central part of North America eastward from the Rocky Mountains, from Canada in the north down to Texas in the south). New methods of transportation allowed more products to be grown, and new technology for farming and processing foods made it possible for farmers to grow more food. Unfortunately, it would be decades before the country's economic and political systems would adapt to the new capacity of its farms.

Words to Know

foreclosure: A legal process in which a borrower who does not make payments on a mortgage or loan is deprived of the mortgaged property.

grain elevators: Huge storage bins built next to railroad tracks to hold grain until it is loaded into train cars.

grant: A transfer of property by deed or writing.

Great Plains: An area of grassland that stretches across the central part of North America eastward from the Rocky Mountains, from Canada in the north down to Texas in the south.

labor union: An organization of workers formed to protect and further their mutual interests by bargaining as a group with their employers over wages, working conditions, and benefits.

magnate: A powerful and influential person in an industry.

reservations: Land set aside by the U.S. government for use by Native Americans.

slums: Severely overcrowded urban areas characterized by the most extreme conditions of poverty, run-down housing, and crime.

Railroads transform farming in the Old Northwest

Before the 1850s, the lack of transportation in all areas west of the Appalachian Mountains made it nearly impossible for farmers and ranchers to sell large quantities of their products. This is illustrated in an 1852 U.S. Senate report showing that a farmer using wagons on existing dirt roads to ship his crop to a market 330 miles away was likely to spend the entire value of his crop on the cost of transporting it. Transporting by railroad reduced the cost by an estimated 90 percent.

Around the time of the study, two railroad lines, the Michigan Southern and the Michigan Central, first linked Chicago, the most important market for eastern goods, to New York City, the most important Atlantic shipping center. Chicago quickly became the center of the grain trade. Meanwhile, a spreading web of smaller railroad lines began to ship the produce of northern Illinois, Wisconsin, Michigan, Indiana, and Iowa as well. These railroads formed a powerful transportation network with Chicago at its center. By 1850 Chicago was handling as much grain as Saint Louis, the major river port at the foot of the St. Louis River that had

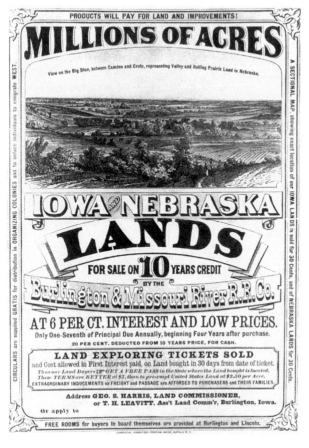

An advertisement for land in Iowa and Nebraska for sale from the Burlington & Missouri River Railroad. *(© Corbis.)*

long been a shipping center. By 1854 more grain was moving along the Great Lakes than through the major port city of New Orleans.

By the early 1860s, grain flowed through the rising cities of the Midwest in railroad cars carrying 325 bushels each. The bushels were sorted and loaded onto steam-powered conveyor belts and borne up into grain elevators, huge storage bins built next to railroad tracks in which the grain was loaded into numbered bins. There it waited to be dropped through chutes into railroad cars and delivered to market.

The grain trade

In the earlier, pre-railroad economic system, the local storekeeper of a given region had been the farmers' key trading partner, receiving produce from them in exchange for food, seed, and manufactured goods such as clothing, farming tools, and medicines. Typically, little cash changed hands in these transactions. More often, the parties bartered (traded goods) or arranged for store credit. After the railroads expanded through the Midwest, a new set of business relations began to form. Farmers getting their crops to market began to deal with agents of the railroad companies at remote offices. Their business grew complicated, involving grain elevators, urban grain merchants, wholesalers and dealers, food processors, and manufacturers. In Chicago a new agency, the Board of Trade, became a central way to coordinate and oversee the buying and selling of grain in bulk. The board, called the Change (or Exchange), graded (evaluated) the grain and then sorted it by grade so that the grains of many farmers could be stored in common bins regardless of who originally sold or owned a given bushel.

The modern farming business transactions were certainly more efficient than the earlier system of bartering with the local store owner. Unfortunately, though farmers began to produce more crops for the market, most were not making more money because of lowering crop prices and high costs of services. Many farmers began to feel they had no control over the process.

Homesteaders in the Great Plains

In 1862 Congress passed the Homestead Act, which made vast areas of the Great Plains available to farmers. It granted to any adult citizen, or to anyone who declared the intention of becoming a citizen, a quarter section (160 acres) of the land owned by the federal government if the occupant agreed to settle and cultivate the land immediately. In order to receive title to the land, the homesteader had to farm it and live on it for five years.

Railroad companies joined the federal government in heavily promoting the settlement of the Great Plains. They sold off large chunks of the land grants (a transfer of property by deed or writing) they had received from the government to homesteaders at low prices, reasoning that settlement in the Plains would generate traffic and lead to a booming railroad business. The Northern Pacific railroad company, for example, had eight hundred agents in Europe to promote immigration. They found Scandinavians particularly open to the idea of moving to the Plains, largely because they wanted inexpensive land to farm. The railroad transported tens of thousands of Norwegians, Swedes, Danes, and Finns into the cool, dry northern plains of Minnesota and the Dakotas.

The railroads lured people to settle in the difficult climate by giving a positive, though not always accurate, description of the region. Settlers who were promised good rains and fertile soil in Minnesota or the Dakotas arrived to find a stark, desert-like climate. Rain was usually very scarce in the plains and there were few natural rivers or streams. There were no trees and only a few hardy grasses grew naturally. The soil was so dry it resisted the farmers' wooden plows. American inventor John Deere (1804–1886) had produced a steel plow in 1837 that could cut deep, clean furrows through the tough sod, but few of the new settlers could afford one (see Chapter 3). After

Extermination of the Buffalo

In the 1860s increasing numbers of white settlers ventured west. Industrial developments such as the expansion of railroads, as well as the discovery of gold and silver and the growing cattle ranching trade accounted for this migration to the region that had long been viewed as the "Great American Desert." At that time the Great Plains—a region of grassland that stretches across the central part of North America eastward from the Rocky Mountains, from Canada in the north down to Texas in the south—was the home of a large number of Indian nations and the center of the Plains Indian culture. (Plains Indians included tribes such as the Sioux, Arapaho, and Cheyenne.) The spread of U.S. industrialization to the West affected the Plains Indian culture in many ways, one of which was the extermination of the buffalo.

In the early nineteenth century, between 50 million and 70 million buffalo, more technically known as the North American bison, roamed the Great Plains. Buffalo were the mainstay of the Plains Indian economy, providing a variety of foods, hides for clothing and shelter, bladders for pouches, gall and blood for paints, bones for utensils, droppings for fuel and heat, and skulls for sacred ceremonies. In the early nineteenth century, white settlers, advancing military troops, and early railroad construction teams killed off buffalo in large numbers, and the population of buffalo on the Plains dropped sharply.

In the 1870s, buffalo robes came into fashion in the East, creating a large demand for buffalo hides. In 1871 a Pennsylvania tannery developed an industrial method to convert buffalo hides into inexpensive commercial leather for harnesses and machine belts. Hides were suddenly worth between $1 and $3 each, and this drew hunters from all over the country to the Plains. The Kansas

arriving on their homesteads, most settlers resorted to hiring teams of men with plows that could break the soil. Once broken, the soil could be more easily plowed in subsequent years, but in the beginning the average farmer was able to cultivate only about forty acres of his homestead. Most homesteaders led a difficult and often poor life on the Plains.

Technology makes bigger crops and larger farms

Improvements in machinery did help the farmers who could afford them. John Deere was manufacturing more than ten thousand plows annually by the early 1860s, and the chilled-steel plow, introduced by James Oliver (1823–1908) in

Pacific and the Santa Fe Railroads, recognizing the profitable new market, carried the hides to eastern markets, and the herds began vanishing rapidly.

As the railroads expanded deeper into the Great Plains in the 1870s, buffalo herds created problems for them. The huge herds sometimes blocked train tracks, creating long delays. They also destroyed sections of tracks as they crossed them. The railroad companies hired hunters to keep the railways clear of buffalo. Some of the railroads that ran through the Great Plains offered hunting specials, allowing their passengers to shoot buffalo from inside the railroad cars. Since buffalo are slow to move away from trouble, the passengers shooting buffalo for sport from their trains managed to kill thousands. The sport became so popular that it increased railroad business, until the stench of rotting carcasses that lined the railroad tracks began to make passengers ill and the railroad companies were forced to stop the practice.

Thrill seekers, hide hunters, and the expanding railroad networks doomed the once massive herds. In 1865 the buffalo population had been an estimated fifteen million buffalo, but it had decreased to seven million by 1872. The herds on the central plains were exterminated by the early 1870s; they were eliminated from the southern plains later in the 1870s; and they vanished from the northern plains in the early 1880s. By the 1890s less than a thousand buffalo remained in scattered areas, mostly on private ranches.

To the Plains Indians the mass killings of buffalo herds was a tragic waste. The Indians had killed buffalo and used every part of their bodies to maintain their daily life, using the meat for food and the hides for clothing and shelter. Without the buffalo, they could not sustain their life on the Plains. Most agreed to move into government reservations (areas of land set aside by the government for Indian tribes), where they were promised food and land to farm.

1868, made breaking tough prairie soil a much easier task, cutting even furrows with little resistance because of its smooth hard face. Mechanical reapers were in widespread use by the 1860s. The first commercially successful reaper had been built in 1831 by inventor Cyrus McCormick (1809–1884). It was pulled by horse and sharply reduced the amount of manual labor required to harvest grain. It had a straight blade linked to a drive wheel. As the drive wheel turned, the blade moved back and forth in a sawing motion, cutting through the stalks of grain, which were held straight by rods. The cut grain stalks then fell onto a platform and were collected with a rake by a worker. The device increased average production from two or three acres a day to ten acres a day. By 1851 McCormick's Chicago factory was making over one thousand mechanical reapers a year, and most of them were being bought and used in the Midwest—one-fourth in northern Illinois alone. (For more information on McCormick's reaper, see Chapter 3.)

By the 1870s farmers had come to depend on mechanical reapers and increasingly sophisticated plows, mowers (machines to cut standing grasses and grains), and spreaders (machines to spread seeds or fertilizer). These innovations stimulated the grand-scale production of wheat. By 1880 wheat had become the chief crop of the Great Plains. Large farms developed, some as vast as twenty-five thousand acres. They used the latest machinery and most planted only wheat.

The cattle industry

The Spanish had introduced cattle ranching to North America in the eighteenth century. By the 1830s a large-scale cattle industry had developed in Texas. The Texans practiced open-range cattle ranching, in which cattle from many different ranches roamed free over vast, unfenced areas. The only way to tell which ranch a cow was from was by its brand, the ranch symbols burned into its hides. Cowboys rounded cattle up every year for slaughter, separating them by their brand. Huge ranches with millions of open-range cattle prospered in Texas until the American Civil War (1861–65; a war between the Union [the North], who were opposed to slavery, and the Confederacy [the South], who were in favor of slavery) interrupted the cattle trade. After the war an estimated five million cattle roamed the Texas plains untended. At that time there was great demand for meat in the rapidly growing cities of the eastern United States, and new railroad lines were available to transport the meat to market. The huge herds of Texas were of little value in Texas, but they would be worth a great deal in the eastern United States.

Illinois livestock merchant Joseph G. McCoy (1837–1915) recognized the potential of a cattle-shipping business and worked out an arrangement among Texas cattlemen, the railroads, and the meatpackers. McCoy formulated a plan of driving the cattle to a shipping point from which they would be transported by train to a market. He chose Abilene, Kansas, on the northern end of the Kansas Pacific Railway, as his shipping point. The cattle would be driven north from Texas stockyards to Abilene, then shipped by railroad to the meatpackers in Chicago.

In the winter of 1867 McCoy sent agents to tell Texas cattlemen of his plan. They sent the first herds on a drive over the Chisholm Trail (the route between southern Texas and Abilene), and they arrived in Abilene in August 1867. By the end of the year, thirty-five thousand cattle had been driven to Abilene, and in 1868 the number rose to seventy-five thousand. In 1871 an estimated 700,000 cattle made the trip to Abilene. Mature animals were shipped eastward for slaughter and processing. Younger stock and breeding cattle were driven farther north and west into the grasslands of the Dakotas, Montana, and Wyoming to increase the size of the herds available for market. America began exporting large quantities of beef to Europe in the mid-1870s. By 1881 the annual beef export total reached 100 million pounds, with most of it going to England. It was the peak time for open-range cattle.

The end of the open range

As they had done for generations in Texas, the herd drivers bringing the cattle up from Texas allowed their cattle to drift over the public domain ranges in western Kansas, Nebraska, the Dakotas, Montana, Wyoming, and Colorado. They considered these lands free for anyone to use. During these years, however, the homesteaders were building their small farms on the range. They objected to having cattle herds driven through their land and towns, and conflicts arose between the cattlemen and the farmers. Due to the lack of trees in the region, farmers on the Great Plains did not have the necessary materials to erect wooden fences, and despite a few violent conflicts, many cattlemen continued to drive the herds through the Plains.

In 1874 American inventor Joseph Glidden (1813–1906) developed barbed wire, fencing consisting of steel wires twisted together to make sharp points resembling thorns. With the advent of barbed wire, farmers were able to fence in their acreage, and by 1890 barbed wire enclosed most private range holdings. The cattlemen found few routes open to their drives and gradually Texas cattlemen stopped sending cattle on drives.

An advertisement for Joseph Glidden's barbed wire. *(© Corbis.)*

Changes in cattle ranching resulted from other factors as well. The environment in the Great Plains is delicate and depends on its surface growth. The tremendous number of cattle crossing the Plains on the drives had resulted in overgrazing of the Plains grasses. By 1885 overgrazing by cattle was seriously damaging the plains by stripping off the surface growth. Grasses and other prairie vegetation were gone and did not come back.

Finally, in the unusually cold and stormy winter of 1886–87, snow and extreme cold wiped out entire cattle herds. The storms, conflicts with the locals, soil erosion, and the widespread use of fencing combined to bring the era of the open range to a close. Additionally, by that time railroads reached into formerly remote locations, eliminating the need for cattle drives. Most of the small cattle ranchers gave up and left the region and only very large, fenced-in cattle ranches remained.

Farmers unite: the Grange

The National Grange of the Patrons of Husbandry (usually called the Grange) was a fraternal society (a group of people organized for a common purpose) founded by agriculturist Oliver Hudson Kelley (1826–1913) in 1867. Its aim was to advance the political, economic, and social interests of the nation's farmers. Kelley, a clerk for the Bureau of Agriculture, had seen the problems faced by U.S. farmers. He resolved to set up an organization to assist farmers by bringing them together to discuss problems and to learn about new agricultural methods. Six of Kelley's associates joined him in forming the group, and the following year he traveled to his native Minnesota to set up the first local Grange (a local lodge providing social and educational facilities as a chapter of the national society). Letters were sent to interested farmers around the country, but response was slight. Before 1870 only a handful of local Granges were established, mostly in Minnesota and Iowa, and in 1871 only scattered chapters could be found in nine states.

In September 1873 a financial panic swept the nation. Banks failed and stock prices fell so severely that the New York Stock Exchange closed for ten days. Thousands of businesses collapsed. Prices on all goods fell dramatically and wages were reduced 10 percent or more. Widespread unemployment led to a reduction in buying power and thus a further fall in prices.

For farmers the financial panic of 1873 was disastrous. The growth in railroad transportation had stimulated an increase in agricultural production—corn yield had increased by 98 percent, wheat by 22 percent, and cotton by 172 percent. Overproduction, the flooding of the market with goods at a time when consumers were unable to afford them, led to a steep plunge in prices for farm products. Most farmers had borrowed money to plant their crops. With the drop in the value of their crops, they could not repay what they owed.

A Grange meeting. *(© Corbis.)*

The panic of 1873 led to a sharp growth in the Grange memberships. While only 132 new Granges were established in 1871, 1,105 were formed in 1872; 8,400 in 1873; and 13,000 in 1874. Most of the Granges were located in the Midwest, but the organization extended into almost every state. Though chartered as social and educational organizations, local chapters of the Grange often became involved in business and politics. By pooling their money and buying supplies, machinery, and equipment in large quantities, the local and state Granges could often make direct deals with manufacturers, who cut prices for large orders. In fact, Montgomery Ward and Company in Chicago was founded with the express purpose of dealing with the Grangers (the members of the local Granges). Some local Granges established factories where farm machinery was produced, eliminating the need to purchase from Eastern industrialists whose large profits came from the high prices of their products.

During the 1870s the Grange claimed a national membership of more than eight hundred thousand. In Illinois, Wisconsin, and other states, Grangers lobbied successfully for state legislation regulating railroad freight and storage charges. These legislations were called the Granger Laws. Despite modest gains, by the end of the 1870s the Granges were in decline due to the mismanagement of their interests and the failure of many of their business initiatives.

The high costs of farming

In the years between 1870 and 1897 many farmers lost their farms, while others struggled to make ends meet. In that period, the prices of crops dropped steadily. Wheat fell from $106 per bushel to $63 per bushel; corn fell from $43 per bushel to $29 per bushel; and cotton fell from fifteen cents a pound to five cents a pound. At the same time the costs of operating a farm remained constant or increased. These costs included shipping rates, interest on loans, and the cost of machinery and other needed commodities. The main reason prices of crops continued to drop was that there was an oversupply of grains on the market, with too many farmers producing too much of the same crops.

Most farmers were not aware of how large the oversupply was. They blamed the railroad companies, the bankers, and the grain elevator operators for the high costs of farming and getting their product to market. Farmers especially despised the railroads, which charged far higher rates in the West than in the East. Railroad executives explained that it was more expensive to run their trains in the West, but the farmers saw the railroad owners getting very rich while they were barely making a living.

Most farmers had to borrow money to keep their farms going, and many were heavily in debt. They were frustrated with the bankers who charged them high interest rates on their loans and foreclosed when the crops failed to bring in enough money for the farmers to pay their debts. (Foreclosure is a legal process in which a bank or other lender takes ownership of a mortgaged property when a borrower fails to make payments on the loan.)

Finally, the railroads did not allow farmers to load their grains directly onto the railroads for shipment. Each train

Urban Industry in the West

As the population of the West increased, dusty trading posts and modest towns became vibrant cities. The railroads and the resources of the West combined to create a network of busy urban centers across the region. Kansas City, Kansas, and Omaha, Nebraska, became major transportation centers for grain and cattle. Denver, Colorado, was a silver town and the administrative and financial center of the Rocky Mountains. Butte, Montana, prospered when copper was discovered nearby. Communities such as Leadville and Virginia City, Nevada, suddenly appeared when gold or silver was discovered nearby, growing rapidly from camps to prosperous towns, only to be abandoned when the mines were emptied.

The new cities of the West suffered from many of the same problems that gripped the older urban areas of the East. Workers and their families often lived in overcrowded, unsanitary slums, urban areas characterized by the most extreme conditions of poverty, run-down housing, and crime. When the economy weakened, jobs became scarce, and life became even harder. Many of those drawn by the lure of jobs were new immigrants from Europe or Asia. They were often treated poorly by the settlers who had been in the country only one generation longer, mainly due to prejudice and cultural differences, but also because some feared competition for work. Many industrial workers in the urban West, as in the East, generally worked very long hours for low pay, often in dangerous or unhealthy conditions. In the 1880s and 1890s, workers in such industries as railroads and mining began to form labor unions, organizations of workers that fought for safer working conditions and better wages.

station had one grain elevator handled by an operator. Farmers were forced to sell their grains to the elevator operators or to pay them a handling fee. Some of the operators took advantage of the situation and cheated the farmers. With costs depleting the value of their crops, farmers often had nothing left to pay their debts and live on.

The Farmers' Alliance

Farmers sought a new organization to help promote their interests after the failure of the Grange in the 1870s. Many joined the Farmers' Alliance, which consisted of a Northern Alliance and a Southern Alliance. The Northern Alliance was founded in Illinois in 1880. Soon other states in the Midwest, especially Nebraska, Kansas, and Iowa, organized their own branches of the organization. By 1882 the Alliance claimed to have 100,000 members. As the 1880s drew to a close, the Southern Alliance had membership in every southern state, and the Northern Alliance had become a force to be reckoned with. Both national Alliances had adopted identical platforms. They called for government regulation or ownership of the railroads, monetary reform that would help farmers, and the abolition of the national banks. In 1890 numerous Alliance politicians were elected to office in states like Kansas, Nebraska, South Dakota, South Carolina, and Georgia. However, there were not enough of them to achieve all their objectives, and farmers continued to struggle with low prices and high costs.

Farm prices continued to fall steadily during the last decades of the century. By the late 1880s, low prices, drought, and crop failures combined to utterly ruin many farmers. Nearly half of all farms in western sections of Kansas and Nebraska were said to have failed—an estimated 100,000 farms altogether.

The People's Party

The economy of the West, like the economy of the nation as a whole, was increasingly dominated by large corporations in the late nineteenth century. Farmers became increasingly dependent on railroads to carry their products to market, and on banks and insurance companies for credit. With crop prices continuing to drop, they could not pay all of their expenses or make a decent living by farming. This led to great discontent. In 1890 representatives from communities across the West and South formed the People's Party, also called the Populists, a political party that combined the farming interests of the South and West with nationwide labor interests. With this force behind it, the Populists aimed to counter the interests of the rich and more politically powerful East. Although by no means confined to the West, the People's Party had its strongest roots in that region.

The platform of the Populists included many reforms that would be put into use in the nation twenty to thirty years later. The Populists demanded that government and economic power be taken out of the hands of a few powerful industrialists and returned to common, hard-working Americans. They called for public ownership of the railroads, an eight-hour workday, and a graduated income tax, which taxes people at low rates for low incomes and at gradually higher rates for higher incomes. They also demanded that the government issue new dollars backed by silver mined in the West. This, it was believed, would increase the money supply and lead to inflation (a rise in the amount of money in circulation in relation to a smaller amount of available goods and products, leading to a rise in prices). Inflation would benefit farmers and other debtors at the expense of the banks and insurance companies that made loans.

The Populist movement gained enough strength to elect numerous candidates to statewide and national offices, and by 1892 the Populists mounted a presidential campaign with General James B. Weaver (1833–1912) of Iowa as their candidate. Their platform called for the government to make an unlimited amount of silver coins and to issue paper money to stimulate inflation and raise crop prices. They also demanded government ownership of the railroads and telegraph system. Weaver won more than one million popular votes and claimed the majority vote in four states, a major accomplishment for a third-party candidate.

By 1896 poor economic times in the farmlands of the Midwest brought new strength to the Populist movement. The Populists and the Democrats both nominated thirty-six-year-old Nebraska lawyer William Jennings Bryan (1860–1925) for president. The Republican candidate was William McKinley (1843–1901). The Populists jumped on the Bryan bandwagon, calling for poor and struggling working Americans to vote for Bryan in order to overthrow the powerful and wealthy industrialists who, according to the Populists, controlled the economy and much of the government as well. The Republicans responded with warnings to American workers that anyone who voted for Bryan could be fired.

It was a very close race, but Bryan lost. His campaign was the last major effort of the farmers of the West and South against the Eastern industrialists. The goals of Populists did not disappear, however. Many of their proposed reforms, such as railroad regulation, the call to grant women the right to vote, and the conservation of public lands, were put into effect in the 1920s.

For More Information

Books

Cashman, Sean Dennis. *America in the Gilded Age: From the Death of Lincoln to the Rise of Theodore Roosevelt.* New York and London: New York University Press, 1984.

Miller, Worth Robert. "Farmers and Third-Party Politics." In *The Gilded Age: Essays on the Origins of Modern America.* Edited by Charles W. Calhoun. Wilmington, DE: Scholarly Resources, 1996.

Smith, Page. *The Rise of Industrial America: A People's History of the Post-Reconstruction Era.* Vol. 6. New York: McGraw-Hill, 1984.

Summers, Mark Wahlgren. *The Gilded Age, or, the Hazard of New Functions.* Upper Saddle River, NJ: Prentice-Hall, 1997.

Web Sites

"Agrarian Distress and the Rise of Populism." *Country Studies: U.S. Department of State.* http://countrystudies.us/united-states/history-81.htm (accessed on June 30, 2005).

"Populism: The Political Crisis of the 1890s." *Digital History: Our Online American History Textbook.* http://www.digitalhistory.uh.edu/database/article_display.cfm?HHID=157 (accessed on June 30, 2005).

13

Reformers Take on Industry: The Progressive Era

Throughout the rapid U.S. industrialization, or development of industry, during the nineteenth century, the government had maintained a laissez-faire, or hands-off, attitude toward the economy, allowing the big corporations to do more or less as they pleased. The top leaders of the nation's industries became so powerful most people felt they controlled the nation's economy and even the state and federal governments. To those who viewed them as crooked manipulators, the top industrial leaders were known as robber barons. To others, who credited them for the nation's prosperity and technological advances, they were the captains of industry. In the last three decades of the nineteenth century, these industrialists had succeeded in creating huge monopolies (the exclusive right to produce a particular product), often by destroying their competition. Economic power was solidly in the hands of trusts—a few large corporations and business firms joined together to reduce competition and control prices. These trusts had formed through the merging of competing companies. Between 1898 and 1904, 5,300 individual companies had combined into just 318 trusts. (For more information on trusts, see Chapter 7.) Most of these large corporations were in the habit of giving gifts,

Words to Know

capital: Accumulated wealth or goods devoted to the production of other goods.

conservation: Planned management of natural resources to prevent their misuse or loss.

depression: A period of drastic decline in the economy.

directorates: Boards of directors of different companies that have at least one director in common.

holding company: A company that is formed to own stocks and bonds in other companies, usually for the purpose of controlling them.

laissez-faire: An economic doctrine that opposes government regulation of commerce and industry beyond the minimum necessary.

mediation: Intervention to help two opposing sides of a dispute reach an agreement.

monopoly: The exclusive possession of, or right to produce, a particular good or service.

muckrakers: Journalists who search for and expose corruption in public affairs.

public domain: Land held by the federal government.

strike: A work stoppage by employees to protest conditions or make demands of their employer.

trusts: A group of companies, joined for the purpose of reducing competition and controlling prices.

Wall Street: Financial district and home of the nation's major stock exchanges in New York, New York.

workers' compensation: Payments made to an employee who is injured at work.

usually of company stock, to key politicians in Washington, D.C., and in state governments. In exchange they expected favorable legislation for business and for the government to look the other way when their business dealings were questionable.

At the end of the nineteenth century the nation was recovering from a severe economic depression, or a period of drastic decline in the economy, that had followed the financial panic of 1893 (see Chapter 12). In its recovery, the nation's productivity increased, mass-produced goods were more widely available, prices went down, and profits went up. Along with new industries there were many fresh job opportunities, increases in educational and leisure activities, and a growing middle class to enjoy it all. But the wealth and income from this economic growth remained unevenly distributed.

For the first time since the beginning of U.S. industrialization people from all walks of life joined together to demand government regulation of business and industry and other moderate political reforms. This was the beginning of the Progressive Era, the period of the Industrial Revolution that spanned roughly from the 1890s to about 1920. These reformers became known as the Progressives. They differed from earlier political reform groups such as the Populists mainly in their inclusive membership. While the Populists had consisted of laborers, small business owners, and the farmers of the West, the Progressives were made up of middle and even the upper class reformers as well as laborers and farmers. (For more information about the Populists, see Chapter 12.) All worked together in the interest of distributing political power and wealth more equally in the United States.

The drive to regulate big business

When the Progressive Era began two measures had already been initiated to regulate the trusts. In 1887 Congress passed the Interstate Commerce Act, which empowered the federal government to oversee the railroads and any organizations that traded in more than one state and established the Interstate Commerce Commission (ICC). In 1890 Congress passed the Sherman Antitrust Act. It barred any "contract, combination in the form of trust or otherwise, or conspiracy, in restraint of trade" and made it a federal crime "to monopolize or attempt to monopolize, or combine or conspire ... to monopolize any part of the trade or commerce among the several states." Neither of these acts made an impact on the railroad companies or the trusts in the decades following their passage. In fact, more combinations and trusts were formed between 1897 and 1901 than at any other time in American history.

The ICC and the courts seemed to favor the interests of the railroads. From 1887 to 1911, the ICC brought railroads to court on only sixteen occasions. The railroads won fifteen out of those sixteen court cases. The Sherman Act placed the nation's attorneys general (chief law officers of the nation) in charge of its execution, and at the end of the century the attorneys general tended to be pro-trust, while the courts were not disposed to rule against private industry. From 1890 to 1901 only eighteen antitrust suits were filed; four of them were actually against labor unions, which were accused of conspiring to thwart free competition.

The muckrakers

As the twentieth century began, the younger generation was more educated and had more access to news and current political thought than their parents. The growing professional class had more time to devote to learning about the economy and social change. Thus, the news media expanded greatly. The number of daily newspapers being published in the nation increased from 1,650 to 2,250 in the twelve-year period from 1892 to 1914. Monthly magazines were especially popular. *Atlantic Monthly, Harper's Weekly,* and *Collier's* published high-quality literature and articles, but these magazines were considered expensive at thirty-five cents an issue. In 1900 a new kind of magazine arose, costing only ten to fifteen cents an issue and full of timely reporting.

The most famous of the cheaper monthlies was *McClure's Magazine,* founded in 1893 by Samuel S. McClure (1857–1949). McClure recruited some of the most talented young journalists of the time, including Ida M. Tarbell (1857–1944) and Lincoln Steffens (1866–1936). *McClure's* established itself at the head of "muckraking" journalism. Muckrakers were journalists who searched for and exposed corruption in public affairs. The term "muckrakers" was coined by President Theodore Roosevelt (1858–1919; served 1901–9) in a speech in 1906, when he referred to a literary character whose job was to rake up dirt and filth and who could look no way but downwards. Roosevelt felt that the muckrakers' investigations emphasized the negative side of things, particularly with regard to big business, while ignoring the positive.

Early in her career, Ida Tarbell's biographies of French emperor Napoleon Bonaparte (1769–1821; ruled 1804–15) and American president Abraham Lincoln (1809–1865; served 1861–65) captivated *McClure's* readers. She went on to write one of the classic muckraking works, *History of the Standard Oil Company,* published in book form in 1904. The book went into great detail about the questionable tactics of the dominant oil-refining company in the country and its owner, John D. Rockefeller (1839–1937). Some critics felt that Tarbell's views were biased (prejudiced), especially since she believed her

Lincoln Steffens was one of the muckracking journalists working for *McClure's* magazine. *(Photo by Hulton Archive/Getty Images.)*

father's oil business had been damaged by Standard Oil's practices. But most agreed that her work was exceptionally well researched and accurate. (For more information on the Standard Oil Company, see Chapter 7.)

In 1900 McClure hired Lincoln Steffens to serve as a reporter and later managing editor of the magazine. For his first project, Steffens conducted a lengthy study of the corruption in the city of St. Louis, Missouri's, political and corporate circles. These reports were published in 1902. He went on to expose the corruption in the Minneapolis, Minnesota, police department. His stories, like those of Tarbell, increased sales of the magazine. Americans were fascinated by the corruption the muckrakers uncovered. As other magazines rushed to imitate *McClure's*, a wave of muckraking journalism energized Progressive reformers across the country.

Novelist Upton Sinclair (1878–1968) joined the Progressive writers when he began a now-famous investigation of the meatpacking business in Chicago, Illinois. In the city he witnessed miserable working conditions, poor wages, crowded immigrant housing, and unsanitary food processing, all of which became the basis of his 1906 novel *The Jungle*. In the novel an immigrant tries to pursue the American dream of acquiring a home and living a comfortable life. He eagerly takes a job in the meatpacking industry, but his optimism soon dissolves under the tough slaughterhouse work. He witnesses the greed and corruption in the industry and the deterioration of the lives of many workers. He is also shocked by the unhealthy handling of the meat. The novel presents graphic descriptions of diseased animals and rotting meat being sold to the American public. *The Jungle* disgusted many readers. Under public pressure, President Theodore Roosevelt appointed a commission to investigate the industry. The book thus played a large role in bringing about the passage of the Pure Food and Drug Act of 1906, which prohibited shipment of impure foods and drugs in interstate commerce and required honest labeling. The Meat Inspection Act was passed in the same year. Government was beginning to take a role in regulating big business.

Theodore Roosevelt's reforms

In September 1901 Republican president William McKinley (1843–1901; served 1897–1901) was assassinated and Vice President Theodore Roosevelt became the nation's new leader. Though Roosevelt supported big business, he quickly identified himself with the reform movement. He was concerned that the govern-

Theodore Roosevelt. *(© Bettmann/Corbis.)*

ment's favoritism toward corporations might push unions and labor parties to extreme actions, hurting business. He therefore believed that the federal government should have the power to control corporations through regulatory boards. Many businessmen agreed with him, believing that such regulation could stabilize the market and stimulate profits.

The Trust-buster

In 1901 James J. Hill (1838–1916), the head of the Great Northern Railroad, and Edward H. Harriman (1848–1909), the head of the Union Pacific Railroad, engaged in a competition to purchase controlling stock in the Northern Pacific Railroad. That railroad company in turn held a controlling interest in the Chicago, Burlington, & Quincy Railroad, the tracks of which provided a highly desirable line into Chicago and ran throughout the northern Midwest region. As Hill and Harriman fought for control of Northern Pacific, the price of its stock soared to $1,000 per share. In their efforts to obtain capital (accumulated wealth or goods devoted to the production of other goods) to purchase Northern Pacific shares, Hill and Harriman dumped other holdings at very low prices. These actions caused stock prices to fluctuate wildly, generally disrupting the stock market, but neither Hill nor Harriman was able to gain a controlling interest in Northern Pacific. They decided to cooperate with each other. They contacted the powerful financier J. P. Morgan (1837–1913), who arranged for the incorporation of the Northern Securities Company, a $400 million holding company (a company that is formed to own stocks and bonds in other companies, usually for the purpose of controlling them) that would, they hoped, bring order and efficiency to the northwestern railroad market by bringing their combined interests—the Great Northern Railroad, the Northern Pacific Railroad, and the Chicago, Burlington, & Quincy Railroad—under the control of one board of directors. The consolidation resulted in one of the largest holding companies formed up to that point.

Morgan was already famous for "Morganization," or buying up small rival railroads and merging them into one big company that then had little or no competition. In the last decades of the century, Morgan had made thousands of miles of railroads throughout the East more efficient by stabilizing prices. To the public and much of the rest of the business world, however, Hill, Harriman, and Morgan were robber barons carrying out disruptive, careless, and crude abuses of power. In March 1902 President Roosevelt instructed the U.S. attorney general to file a lawsuit against the Northern Securities Company. The federal court ruled against the company in 1903, and in 1904 the Supreme Court upheld the decision, ruling that the company should be dissolved in accord with the Sherman Antitrust Act. The decision demonstrated to the business world that the Sherman Antitrust Act could be an effective tool to combat monopolies and trusts that attempted to restrict trade. Roosevelt, who stunned the business world by enforcing the act, became known as the "Trust-buster."

During the Roosevelt administration twenty-four trusts were indicted (formally accused of a crime) under the Sherman Antitrust Act. In a 1905 court decision, the member firms of the giant beef trust were prohibited from engaging in practices designed to restrain competition. This important judicial decision would lead to the dissolution in 1911 of the Standard Oil Company of New Jersey (which at one point controlled more than 90 percent of the oil refinery business) and the American Tobacco Company. In deciding these cases the Supreme Court formulated what became known as the "rule of reason," which stated that only "unreasonable" combinations that unfairly limited competition should be prohibited. Like Roosevelt, the courts seemed to believe that trusts were a permanent fixture in the economic world and that one could differentiate between good and bad trusts.

Roosevelt and labor unions

On May 12, 1902, 150,000 mine workers in Pennsylvania went on strike for better wages and working conditions. A strike is a work stoppage by employees to protest conditions or make demands of their employer. Unlike earlier strikes, this time the

John Mitchell, president of the United Mine Workers.
(© Bettmann/Corbis.)

public sympathized with the strikers. Most Americans had read articles about the terrible conditions in the mines and many believed the workers should be given power to negotiate with the mine owners for better treatment. The media mocked the arrogant mine operators, who seemed intent, one newspaper asserted, upon being "managing directors" of the entire earth, allowing no one to interfere with their business.

Roosevelt was concerned about the strike for another reason. The strike caused the price of coal to increase and as it rose, businesses and schools could no longer afford to buy coal and were forced to close. Public sympathy for the strikers and the looming threat of a winter without coal prompted Roosevelt to try to hasten a compromise. In early October he invited representatives from both sides of the strike to Washington. Roosevelt's plan was to offer both the strikers and mine operators an equal voice in the settlement.

Roosevelt and the Conservation Movement

In 1890 the U.S. Census reported that what had once been the American frontier had become settled. The country had previously seemed so vast that its natural deposits could never be depleted, but tremendous economic development after 1865 had resulted in the reckless misuse of the nation's resources. By the turn of the century, logging was the second largest industry in the country, and vast forest areas had been cleared. The many cattle grazing on the Great Plains had stripped the surface growth on the plains and prairies, severely damaging the ecology (the community of living things and their environment). The buffalo on the Great Plains were nearly extinct. Water shortages affected many western areas.

Roosevelt believed that, through scientific planning, natural resources could be used wisely and would remain available to help the greatest number of people, not only in his time but in future times. (Other conservationists believed that the resources should be left alone, or preserved, rather than being exploited for human use). In 1902 Roosevelt gave his support to the Newlands National Reclamation Act, which provided that proceeds from the sale of public lands in the West be used for large-scale water-use projects, which distributed the nation's water to its users. The construction of the great dams of the West came about as a result of the act.

Roosevelt was responsible for the preservation of vast areas of land. He created five national parks and supported the National Monuments Act of 1906, which allows the president to protect scientifically or historically important areas such as the Grand Canyon. He also created fifty-one wildlife refuges. Not everyone agreed with his environmental plans, particularly the agricultural and lumber industrialists, and Roosevelt fought Congress over this issue. Nevertheless, by some estimates Roosevelt placed about 230 million acres of U.S. land under public protection as national parks, national forests, and game and bird preserves.

In June 1908 Roosevelt established the Federal Commission on the Conservation of Natural Resources, which was headed by the chief force in his conservation crusade, American conservationist and politician Gifford Pinchot (1865–1946). The federal commission had four divisions that oversaw water, forest, land, and mineral resources. Within a year, it was joined by forty-one state conservation commissions.

Roosevelt persuaded the public to become aware of environmental conservation by informing them. He and Pinchot wrote many articles about conservation that were published in popular magazines so the public would have access to the information. Pinchot also designed teaching materials about the environment for schoolchildren.

By the end of Roosevelt's term in office federal agencies oversaw 200 million acres of federal land, and many individual states copied the federal model, establishing state forests, forest services, and conservation boards. Roosevelt's conservation crusade had a tremendous impact on the nation.

John Mitchell (1870–1919), president of the United Mine Workers (UMW), asked the president to appoint a commission to settle the matter. He agreed to accept whatever decision the commission made, as long as the owners also agreed to accept it. But the mine owners refused to negotiate. Their lack of sympathy for the mine workers infuriated Roosevelt. A week after the meeting, the president announced that he intended to send the army in to run the mines, in effect dislodging the owners from their own businesses. The threat worked; the owners agreed to mediation (intervention to help the opposing sides of a dispute reach an agreement), and the strike was called off. Mediation lasted for five months. Though the strikers had initially requested a 20 percent pay raise and an eight-hour day, in the end they accepted a 10 percent pay increase and a nine-hour day.

The Department of Commerce and Labor is established

The mine workers' strike convinced Roosevelt of the need for a federal agency to prevent or help resolve any future national economic crises. In January 1903 he called for the creation of a Department of Commerce and Labor, to include a Bureau of Labor and a Bureau of Corporations. The function of these agencies would be to investigate the operations and conduct of corporations and to provide information about business structure, operations, and working conditions. Roosevelt was able to obtain overwhelming congressional backing for this measure. The Department of Commerce and Labor divided into two separate departments—the Department of Labor and the Department of Commerce—in 1913. These departments filed a few antitrust suits and functioned primarily to help business and commerce in the United States by collecting nationwide data that would help them in their trade.

The election of 1912

Theodore Roosevelt did not seek reelection in 1908. His chosen successor in the Republican Party was William Howard Taft (1857–1930), who won the election. Once in office, however, Taft did not aggressively pursue Roosevelt's policies. Roosevelt decided to run in the election of 1912 but quickly found that he had angered many conservative Republicans.

Woodrow Wilson. *(© Corbis.)*

When they gave the Republican nomination to Taft, Roosevelt formed a new political party, the Progressive Party, named after the popular reform movement with which he was already associated. (After winning the Progressive nomination in the primaries, Roosevelt said he felt like a "bull moose," and so the party was nicknamed the Bull Moose Party).

The Democrats nominated Woodrow Wilson (1856–1924), then governor of New Jersey. Also running in this unusual campaign was the Socialist Party candidate Eugene Debs (1855–1926). In his efforts to reach the progressive reformers, Roosevelt often sounded more like a Socialist than like a Republican. Wilson won with less than 42 percent of the popular vote. Roosevelt ran second with 27 percent, and Taft was third with 23 percent. It was the only time in the twentieth century that a third-party candidate got more votes than a Democratic or Republican nominee.

President Wilson's reforms

Once elected, Wilson, who remained in office until 1921, adopted many Progressive reforms, such as the initiation of the nation's first income tax and the establishment of the Federal Reserve, the government organization that still regulated banking at the beginning of the twenty-first century. He also continued the trust-breaking work started by Roosevelt, though progress in this area was slow. In 1914 Progressives in Congress were intent on establishing an industrial trade commission to oversee business activities and suppress unfair labor practices. Wilson, on the other hand, wanted limited government intervention. Eventually they arrived at a compromise with the Clayton Antitrust Act. This act outlawed monopolistic practices such as price discrimination and allowing executives to sit on the boards of two or more competing companies. A Federal Trade Commission (FTC) was created to investigate corporations and issue cease-and-desist orders against unfair trade practices.

The Clayton Antitrust Act included clauses allowing workers to unionize and strike. With its declaration that "the labor of a human being is not a commodity or article of commerce," the Clayton Act for the first time legitimized the existence of unions. Its critics, however, pointed to the cautious wording of the act, which could lead to a variety of interpretations. Their concerns soon were proved correct. The courts had long been opposed to government interference in private industry, and their interpretations of the act weakened its labor provisions.

Reforms at the state level

Even with high popular support for laborers in the Progressive Era, attempts by the states to regulate working hours and conditions were resisted as fiercely by the courts as they were by employers. Under the Fourteenth Amendment to the U.S. Constitution, states could not deprive any person of life, liberty, or property without due process of law. In case after case the courts interpreted this to mean that states could not limit an individual's liberty to make a contract, and that when a state tried to set limits to the number of hours a person worked in a day or a week, the state was infringing on his or her liberty.

Working hours

Workers had been seeking a shorter workday since the early nineteenth century. By 1900 many industries and occupations had achieved a ten-hour day and a sixty-hour week. Cigar makers, in fact, had gotten their workweek below fifty hours in some states. Workers in other occupations were less fortunate. They were required by their employers to work eleven- to thirteen-hour days and sixty-five or more hours per week. Those who refused to work long hours were often fired. Bakers were one group that worked long hours in unhealthy and uncomfortable conditions. In 1895 the reform-minded New York State legislature passed the Bakeshop Act, limiting the bakers' workweek to sixty hours. When a bakeshop owner

In the glass industry, young boys molded glass in front of hot furnaces. *(© Corbis.)*

was charged with violating the act, he took his case to the Supreme Court. In the case of *Lochner v. New York* (1905) the Supreme Court held the maximum hours provisions in the Bakeshop Act to be in conflict with the Fourteenth Amendment. The *Lochner* decision continued to halt legislation to improve the conditions of American labor until it was finally overruled in 1937. There were some exceptions, however, such as the 1908 court ruling that found that Oregon could limit the working hours of women to ten each day. This ruling was based on the belief that women occupied a special place in society and needed the law to protect them.

Child labor

The employment of children as a ready and cheap source of labor continued well into the twentieth century. Exhausting and dangerous conditions in the canning industry, the glass industry (where boys were hired to mold glass for hours on end in front of blistering-hot furnaces), the coal mining industry, and the textile industry began to attract considerable attention from reformers after 1900. (For more information on child labor, see Chapter 9.) Most legislation against child labor took place at the state level, but in 1904 the National Child Labor Committee was formed by Congress to promote the welfare of America's working children and investigate conditions in a number of states. The committee was not authorized to act against the abusive situations it found, and its efforts to improve conditions on a state-by-state basis were not effective. In 1910 it was estimated that there were still more than two million U.S. children employed in industrial settings.

Congress passed the law establishing the Children's Bureau as an agency in the Department of Commerce and Labor in 1912, but the bureau had no power to enact or enforce legislation. Then, in 1916, Congress passed the Keating-Owen Child Labor Act. The act barred the interstate shipment of goods made in whole or in part by children and prohibited children under sixteen from working in dangerous locations such as mines and quarries (open excavations), from working longer than eight hours a day, and from working at night. It also set the minimum age for other types of work at fourteen. In 1918 the Supreme Court, citing states' rights, declared the law unconstitutional. It was not until 1938 that Congress passed the Fair Labor Standards Act (FLSA), which set a minimum wage for all workers, set a maximum workweek of forty-four hours, and prohibited interstate shipment of goods produced by children under the age of sixteen. After decades of ruling against attempts to regulate child labor, the Supreme Court allowed this act to stand.

Minimum wage

In 1912 Massachusetts became the first U.S. state to pass a minimum wage law, and in 1918 Congress authorized minimum wage levels for female workers in the District of Columbia. Five years later, however, the U.S. Supreme Court ruled that minimum wage laws infringed on the freedom of businesses and workers to form contracts as they saw fit. In 1938 the Supreme Court changed its views and the FLSA soon followed, setting the first minimum wage at twenty-five cents an hour.

Workers' compensation

By 1900 industrial accidents killed thirty-five thousand workers each year and maimed five hundred thousand others. In the nineteenth century, workers injured on the job had little choice but to sue their employers in court. Courts often ruled against workers, declaring that they had assumed the risk of injury by taking the job. Workers' compensation laws, by awarding set amounts of monetary compensation for various injuries, brought relief to workers and employers. Workers received money for injuries, and employers no longer needed to worry about being sued for work-related accidents. By 1916 thirty-five states had passed workers' compensation laws, but there was no law for federal workers. The 1916 Kern-McGillicuddy Act filled this gap by establishing a system of compensation for federal workers.

For More Information

Books

Brody, David. *Workers in Industrial America: Essays on the 20th-Century Struggle.* 2nd ed. New York: Oxford University Press, 1993.

Diner, Steven J. *A Very Different Age: Americans of the Progressive Era.* New York: Hill and Wang, 1998.

Summers, Mark Wahlgren. *The Gilded Age or, the Hazard of New Functions.* Upper Saddle River, NJ: Prentice-Hall, 1997.

Wagenknecht, Edward. *American Profile: 1900–1909.* Amherst: University of Massachusetts Press, 1982.

Web Sites

"America 1900." *American Experience: PBS.* http://www.pbs.org/wgbh/amex/1900/index.html (accessed on June 30, 2005).

Progressive Era History Resources. http://www.snowcrest.net/jmike/progressive.html (accessed on June 30, 2005).

Industrialism in the Twentieth Century

The scale of industrial enterprises in the United States increased during the early years of the twentieth century, making the American workplace very different from that of the preceding century. During the period of the Industrial Revolution known as the Gilded Age (the era of industrialization from the early 1860s to the turn of the century in which a few wealthy individuals gained tremendous power and influence; see Chapter 5), manufacturers in the largest industries, such as steel and oil refining, were pushed aside by enormous new factory complexes sometimes employing fifteen thousand to twenty thousand workers. These new plants produced automobiles, farm machinery, electrical equipment, textiles, and many other goods.

During the twentieth century the nature of manufacturing gradually changed. American consumers had more money to spend and wanted to be able to choose from a variety of products. To remain competitive, corporations had to respond to consumers' desires. Gradually, in the

The Ford Automobile Plant in Highland Park, Michigan. *(© Bettmann/Corbis.)*

Words to Know

antitrust laws: Laws opposing or regulating trusts or similar business monopolies.

aviation: The operation and manufacture of aircraft.

conveyor belt: A moving belt that carries materials from one place to another.

depression: A period of drastic decline in the economy.

foreclosure: A legal process in which a borrower who does not make payments on a mortgage or loan is deprived of the mortgaged property.

gross national product (GNP): The total of all goods and services produced each year.

labor union: An organization of workers formed to protect and further their mutual interests by bargaining as a group with their employers over wages, working conditions, and benefits.

laissez-faire: An economic doctrine that opposes government regulation of commerce and industry beyond the minimum necessary.

machine tool: A machine that shapes solid materials.

machinist: A worker skilled in operating machine tools.

mass production: The manufacture of goods in quantity by using machines and standardized designs and parts.

New Deal: A set of legislative programs and policies for economic recovery and social reform initiated in the 1930s during the presidency of Franklin Delano Roosevelt.

pension: A fixed sum paid regularly, usually as a retirement benefit.

postindustrial era: A time marked by the lessened importance of manufacturing and increased importance of service industries.

productivity: The amount of work someone can do in a set amount of time.

robots: Machines that automatically perform routine, often complex, tasks.

stock: An element of ownership of a corporation that has been divided up into shares that can be bought and sold.

stock market: A system for trade in companies, ventures, and other investments through the buying and selling of stocks, bonds, mutual funds, limited partnerships, and other securities.

last decades of the century, the heavy industries such as steel and auto manufacturing went into a slow decline, and the U.S. economy passed into a postindustrial era—a time marked by the lessened importance of manufacturing and increased importance of service industries such as food and custodial services, health, finance, recreation, engineering, and computers.

Efficiency management

By the turn of the century, the use of advanced machines and technology dominated factories even more than it had in the nineteenth century. Machines were designed so that workers with little training and experience could operate them. Since they were hiring more unskilled labor, factories needed more management to oversee the work process. To remain competitive, they needed to keep their costs low and their productivity (the amount of work they could get done in a set amount of time) high.

In the late nineteenth century, Frederick Winslow Taylor (1856–1915), a machinist (someone skilled in operating machine tools, which are machines used to cut or shape metals) was working as the foreman, or overseer, of work crews at a large Philadelphia machine shop. Taylor studied all the steps accomplished on the work floor, and then tried to find ways cut down on the number of steps in order to increase the productivity of

Frederick W. Taylor tried to find ways to increase worker productivity. *(© Bettman/Corbis. Reproduced by permission.)*

the workers. At first the workers resisted Taylor's efforts, but eventually he won their support. He began publishing essays about his scientific analysis of the individual steps involved in cutting metal most effectively and about incentives (something that moves someone into action) for workers. In 1903 he combined these interests in an essay presented to mechanical engineers that would stand as his most complete report on scientific management. This publication began to receive widespread attention among other industries, and by the 1910s, it had become the basis of a new movement known as scientific management, or Taylorism.

Under Taylor's scientific management principles, managers first studied a job and paid special attention to the minimum number of necessary steps needed to complete the task. Each step was then analyzed to determine the most time-saving means of performing it. Although workers who could not finish a step in the allowed time were in danger of losing their jobs, the primary reason for the laborers to perform well was money. Taylor argued that managers should determine a standard day's output from an excellent worker and then set up pay incentives to reward workers for meeting those standards.

Taylor believed that a worker should never have to think about what he or she was doing. All tasks should be repetitive and automatic, with every movement and motion having a specific purpose. Under the Taylor system, all thinking in the workplace would be done by management, which would then assign the tasks. The ideal worker would perform his task with little or no need for brainwork. New types of record keeping and inspection were developed to measure the workers' production. The tests to determine productivity were scientific. Managers would use a stopwatch rather than judging for themselves how long a task was taking. Specific movements were counted. Nothing was to be left to the individual judgment of managers.

Labor union organizers did not like scientific management, arguing that it was simply an attempt to give the managers more control over the workforce. A labor union is an organization of workers formed to protect and further their mutual interests by bargaining as a group with their employers over wages, working conditions, and benefits. Craft workers, people who were skilled in producing things, tried to maintain some control over their work, but this became more and more difficult. Under the division of labor imposed by the Taylor system, each worker performed only a small part of the work needed to create a product.

Henry Ford and mass production

Automobile designer and mechanic Henry Ford (1863–1947) was using some of Taylor's efficiency principles to build a car industry beginning in 1903. From childhood, Ford had displayed a marked mechanical aptitude. Though his father wanted him to be a farmer, like himself, Ford left the farm in 1891 for an engineering job in Detroit, Michigan. In 1899, with the support of a group of investors, he established the Detroit Automobile Company, the

Workers assemble a Model T automobile at the Ford plant in Highland Park, Michigan. *(© Bettman/Corbis. Reproduced by permission.)*

first company organized in Detroit for the manufacture of autos. The company turned out twelve unreliable vehicles and went out of business in the fall of 1900. Ford began building successful racing cars, and after a couple of failed attempts to get an automobile manufacturing company established, the Ford Motor Company opened its doors in 1903.

In the first decade of the twentieth century, cars were new and far too expensive for the average person. Ford set out to change this, by producing a practical car for a reasonable price. He studied the principles of Taylorism to learn how to reduce the number of steps in a task and to get the most productivity out of workers. He also worked with the principles of mass production, the manufacture of goods in quantity by using machines and standardized designs and parts. This system of manufacturing uses specialized labor and machinery, as well as a smooth and logical flow of materials, to produce large volumes of the same product at the lowest possible cost. By 1908, Ford had designed the Model T, the practical car he wanted to manufacture. He went on to build a Model T factory in Highland Park, Michigan, designed to use mass production and carefully managed work systems that saved workers' steps and promoted streamlined production. By 1913 a finished Model T left the factory every forty seconds. Production went from 14,000 cars in 1909 to 189,000 in 1913, while the price of a Model T dropped from $950 to $550.

The assembly line

When Ford's factory first opened, a stationary line of car parts was set up. Groups of workers moved down the line, each worker carrying out specific assembly tasks on each of the parts. The management soon found that some workers and groups were faster or slower than others, and they often got in each other's way. Ford and his technicians decided to move the work instead of the workers. If engines in need of assembly were moved by a conveyor belt (a moving belt that carries materials from one place to the next), the speed of work would match the speed the conveyor belt moved. After months of experimenting with various lengths and rates of speed for the assembly line, Ford switched to assembly line production in 1913. By 1914 six hundred cars were completed each day on Ford's assembly line. The amount of time required to build a car was reduced to about one-third of what it had been, and production increased greatly. Soon other manufacturers were using methods like Ford's.

Working at Ford

Workers at Ford grew tired of repeating simple movements over and over again. As their boredom increased, productivity decreased and many workers quit their jobs. In 1914 Ford announced the five-dollar day for Ford workers, a very generous salary at a time when the average weekly pay was about eleven dollars. It was an effort to keep good workers productive, on the job, and perhaps buying Fords for their families, but it was also considered by some as an attempt to control their lives.

The company divided the employee's five dollar daily income in two: half was considered wages and the other half profits. Workers received their regular wages for showing up at work but only got their profits when they met specific standards of efficiency and followed guidelines set at Ford for their home lives. The Sociological Department was established to advise employees on how to live in order to receive their profits. Its advice on everything from personal finances to drinking, gambling, and how immigrant workers could adapt to American culture intruded on the privacy of the employees. Unions were against Ford policies. Spies from the department spotted union organization and fired those who joined. Thus, the Ford worker traded privacy for a job with high pay. The five-dollar day system was abandoned by the 1920s, when Ford set its pay at market rates and dropped its Sociological Department activities.

Making changes at Ford

Ford's early mass production system made one unchanging product, and each copy of that product was exactly the same. Customers had no choices about the cars they purchased from Ford. By the time fifteen million Model Ts had been built in 1927, the design was twenty years old. When Ford finally switched from the Model T to the Model A in 1927, the entire factory had to be shut down for six months to accommodate the change. Ford had become so good at producing one product that changing to a new one was very difficult.

One of Ford's rivals, General Motors (GM), designed and expanded a more flexible mass production system during the 1920s. GM used general purpose machine tools that could be adapted quickly to design changes. It also built the parts that went into its cars at a variety of locations, rather than all in the same factory as at Ford. In the 1920s GM began creating a new version of its cars each year, partly to give customers more choices, and partly to give those who already owned a car a reason to buy another. In the 1930s Ford, too, adopted this practice. Most consumers were happy to have more choice in what they bought. The Model T had been designed purely to function well, and many people found it ugly. The Model A was considered far more visually appealing. Industrial design became increasingly important in attracting customers.

Industry after World War I

During World War I (1914–18; a war in which Great Britain, France, the United States and their allies defeated Germany, Austria-Hungary, and their allies) the relationship between industry and government changed. In order to meet its own military needs, the U.S. government spent vast sums for the development of technology in American factories. The wartime government helped big business in many ways, one of which was to suspend antitrust laws (laws opposing or regulating trusts or similar business monopolies) for American firms operating overseas. Secretary of Commerce Herbert Hoover (1874–1964) called the government's assistance of big business "the American System." In his opinion the government should step aside to allow corporations to grow and succeed, which he believed would benefit all. Indeed, industries did grow at a great pace during the war and by its end they had reshaped the economy. Advanced new factories were in place, thousands of rural workers had moved to the industrial centers, and there was a large new class of executives in corporate America.

In 1925 pro-business president Calvin Coolidge (1872–1933; served 1923–29) voiced the theme for the decade when, according to Arthur Schlesinger Jr. in *The Age of Roosevelt: Crisis of the Old Order,* he declared: "The business of America is business. The man who builds a factory builds a temple. The man who works there worships there." Businessmen often expressed the belief that their material success confirmed their innate ability to lead the rest of society. Conversely, they believed that poor people were responsible for their poverty because they had not taken advantage of available opportunities. They argued that the government should not burden the honorable rich to help the undeserving poor.

Throughout the 1920s the American economy remained strong. Technological advances and mass production brought financial stability and a sense of well-being to the average American family. With new lending policies offering consumers the chance to pay for their purchases in installment payments, more people were able to buy such luxury items as automobiles, radios, vacuum cleaners, and electric iceboxes, all of which were just coming into widespread use.

The Great Depression

In the fall of 1929 the United States entered the worst economic depression (period of drastic decline in the economy) it had ever experienced. On October 29, 1929, American stock prices fell sharply. Stocks are an element of ownership of a corporation that has been divided up into shares that can be bought and sold. The life savings of many small investors were depleted and many businesses and banks failed. The Great Depression of the 1930s followed, and the American economy struggled. The gross national product (GNP), the total of all goods and services produced each year, fell from $104.4 billion in 1929 to $74.2 billion in 1933. Industrial production declined 51 percent before rising slightly in 1932. Before 1929 there had been nearly 1.5 million people without jobs in the country. After 1929 the unemployment figure dramatically increased; at its peak in 1933, more than 12.6 million people were unemployed, although some estimates placed the number as high as 16 million. By 1933 farmers, perhaps the hardest hit economic group, saw their total combined income drop from $11.9 billion to $5.3 billion.

Changing to consumer industries

Even without the stock market crash of 1929, the 1930s would have been difficult. Many heavy industries had reached the limits of their production. Domestic railway construction had long since peaked, and in 1931 more railroad cars were scrapped, replaced, or stored by owners than were manufactured. Oil production far exceeded the demands of consumers. Agricultural prices dropped due to overproduction. While heavy industries, such as rail, steel, and textiles, were declining, other industries were just beginning to grow. These included the new mass-based consumer industries, or service industries, such as trade; health and social services; business services; accommodation and food services; amusement, recreation, and personal services; education; finance, insurance, and real estate; government services; transportation; and communications. In time, jobs in the service industries would outnumber those in heavy industry. When these new industries were forming in the 1930s, however, most people could not afford their services. The gap between the establishment of these newer industries and the collapse of older industries led to a temporarily inactive economy that made life difficult for millions.

One of the changes being introduced to the U.S. economy was a large proportion of women in the workforce. In 1920 women composed 23.6 percent of the labor force, and 8.3 million women older than the age of fifteen worked outside the home. By 1930 the percentage of women in the work force rose to 27, and their numbers increased to 11 million. World War I had expanded women's employment in new sectors of the economy, and by 1920, 25.6 percent of employed women worked in white-collar office-staff jobs, 23.8 percent in manufacturing, 18.2 percent in domestic service, and 12.9 percent in agriculture. While the first generation of college-educated women entered professions in the 1920s, they found opportunities only in nurturing professions, such as nursing, teaching, social work, and pediatrics. In factories, while male factory workers on federal contracts in 1920 started at forty cents an hour, women started at twenty-five cents.

An example of the change to a more consumer-focused economy that took place in the 1930s could be seen in the processed foods industry. Lower food prices and an increasing number of women working outside the home resulted in more Americans eating canned and processed foods, which were quicker and easier to prepare than cooking meals from scratch. Retailers responded by greatly expanding the grocery business. The first true supermarket was opened in 1930, and by 1939 nearly five thousand existed around the country. Concerns about the cleanliness of products that were loosely wrapped in paper led to an increase in glass products used for packaging. Demand for canned and frozen foods rose sharply. Many large new industries arose as a response to changing consumer needs.

Roosevelt and the New Deal

In 1932 Franklin Delano Roosevelt (1882–1945; served 1933–45) won the presidential election, taking office during the Great Depression. An estimated thirteen million people were out of work, many large industries—like steel—were barely operating, and banks were failing. Roosevelt won the election on the strength of his promises for a "New Deal," a set of legislative programs and policies for economic recovery and social reform. To accomplish his social and economic goals, Roosevelt tried to overcome the intense public prejudices

Franklin Delano Roosevelt. *(© Bettmann/Corbis.)*

against a strong federal government. Roosevelt created federal jobs for the unemployed, assisted farmers ruined by the Great Depression, and protected citizens against the loss of their homes by mortgage foreclosures (legal process in which a borrower who does not make payments on a mortgage or loan is deprived of the mortgaged property). He also passed the Social Security Act, which created an old-age pension system (a fixed sum paid regularly, usually as a retirement benefit) and paid benefits to the disabled and widows with children.

Roosevelt and supporters of the New Deal believed that one primary cause of the Great Depression was the low wages of workers. Therefore, in addition to limiting work hours and improving workplace conditions, the New Dealer sought to raise pay, believing that the higher wages would be used to purchase consumer goods, thus increasing production and helping the economy. The Roosevelt administration attempted to distribute wealth in America more evenly, but the New Deal alone did not solve the economic crisis. In 1941 around 40 percent of all American families lived below the poverty level. Nearly eight million workers earned less than the legal minimum wage of thirty cents an hour, while another eight million Americans were unemployed.

World War II

World War II (1939–45; a war in which Great Britain, France, the United States, and their allies defeated Germany, Italy, and Japan) changed the economic forces at work in the United States. Soon after the nation entered the war in 1941, the armed forces drafted (selected for service in the armed forces) ten million men to fight. The war effort demanded increased production at home to supply the military and maintain civilian needs. American industry limited or suspended the production of consumer goods to focus its efforts on making weapons and war materiel. No civilian automobiles and trucks were manufactured from 1942 until after the war. Other steel, rubber, or electrical consumer goods were hard to get or completely unavailable. The government abandoned its laissez-faire policy, an economic doctrine that opposes government regulation of commerce and industry beyond the minimum necessary. The government was involved in people's daily lives, raising taxes, rationing (distributing equally) some commodities, controlling prices, assigning people to work for military and civilian production, and even restricting where individuals lived or worked.

In the expanded industrial production during the war the gross national product and manufacturing output doubled. The labor force expanded from around 56 million workers in 1940 to over 65 million in 1945. Average yearly earnings rose. While more than half of all Americans lived in poverty during the Great Depression, by the end of the war just over one-third were classified as poor. Another third earned wages that gave them significant disposable income for the first time.

Women's roles changed drastically during the war. Once women's employment became vital to the war effort it was applauded as patriotic. Government posters featured women rolling up their sleeves and affirming "We Can Do It." The number of workingwomen rose about 50 percent, from 11.9

The Airline Industry Partners with the Government

On May 20 and 21, 1927, Charles A. Lindbergh (1902–1974) captured the imagination of the American people when he made his famous 2,610-mile transatlantic (spanning the Atlantic Ocean) solo flight from Long Island, New York, to Paris, France. Afterwards, there was a frenzy to get into the aviation industry, the flying and manufacture of aircraft. Early airplane manufacturers such as William Boeing (1881–1956) and Donald Douglas (1892–1981) began making airplanes designed specifically for passenger travel. By 1930 there were forty-three scheduled airlines (airlines that fly scheduled flights for passenger service) in the United States, necessitating some form of regulation or organization amidst the increasingly crowded skies.

Regulation of the airlines posed new problems. Allowing competing airlines to fly in the same airways (routes along which airplanes fly) without central control was wasteful and extremely dangerous. While the Interstate Commerce Commission had long regulated railroads and motor carriers, airlines were judged to be a substantially different industry requiring different rules.

In the late 1930s airline officials approached the federal government, asking it to formulate a basic set of guiding principles for all airlines to follow. It was one of the first times in history that an industry had requested to be regulated by the government. After several months of study by industry leaders and government officials, the Civil Aeronautics Act was introduced into Congress in 1938. It established three agencies: the Civil Aeronautics Authority (CAA), which established policies for regulation of safety and economics; an administrator of aviation appointed to carry out the safety policies of the CAA; and an air safety board, formed as an independent group of three persons responsible for the investigation of aircraft accidents.

million in 1940 to 18.6 million in 1945. By the end of the war women comprised 36.1 percent of the civilian workforce and they were enjoying increases in income created by the wartime economy.

When the war came to an end in 1945, many Americans feared that there would not be enough jobs in the United States to support the millions of soldiers reentering the civilian workforce. No new crisis occurred. During the war Americans had saved billions of dollars, which they spent afterwards on new homes, cars, and appliances. Wartime profits allowed businesses money to invest in plants and equipment for civilian production. The Servicemen's Readjustment Act of 1944 gave

Passengers boarding a plane. (© H. Armstrong Roberts/ Corbis.)

number of daily flights. Air accidents became more frequent and more deadly, leading to the demand for a single aviation agency to oversee the operation of airports and airways and all services related to air traffic control. The Federal Aviation Agency (FAA) was established in 1958 to regulate the use of air space, to establish and operate air navigation facilities, to set air traffic rules for all aircraft, to conduct research and development, and to suspend or take away safety certificates.

Government regulation led to better radio communications, safety improvements at airports, and more accurate weather services, all of which contributed to an increase in air traffic and profits. The American economy flourished as passenger sales rose dramatically from $17.3 million in 1950 to $38 million in 1955. The airliner was well on its way to replacing the train and the ocean liner as the top transportation choice for long distance travel.

In the decades that followed, there was a tremendous increase in the flying speed of aircraft and rapid growth in the

veterans one year of unemployment pay, financial assistance for job training and education, and low-interest loans to buy homes, farms, and businesses. This aid to veterans and their families, known as the GI Bill of Rights, was granted to nearly one-fourth of the population and further stimulated the economy. Postwar wealth paired with continuing New Deal policies became the basis of long term prosperity, insuring a quality of life from 1945 to 1972 never before seen in American history.

It is worth noting, however, that after World War II ended, a woman's average weekly pay fell from $50 to $37, a decline of 26 percent that contrasts sharply to an overall postwar decrease of four percent. Although three-quarters of women employed in war industries were still employed in 1946, 90 percent of them were earning less than they had earned during the war. Faced with a postwar decrease in the already inadequate number of childcare facilities many working mothers withdrew from the workforce. Nevertheless, after World War II women entered the U.S. workforce in steadily increasing numbers.

The computer age

Americans of the 1950s witnessed the dawn of the information age, although many were probably not aware of it. During the decade the computer developed from its earliest models—hundreds of square feet of flashing neon bulbs, dials, cables, and clicking switches—to relatively small units that were affordable to academic and business communities. The first real computer was called the Electronic Numerical Integrator and Computer (ENIAC). It had been developed by scientists at the University of Pennsylvania for the government during World War II. The ENIAC, which weighed thirty tons and occupied eighteen hundred square feet, was first demonstrated to the public in 1946. By 1950 there were twenty computers in the United States, worth a total of one million dollars.

As the first electronic machine that could solve mathematical problems quickly, ENIAC was a marvel of the time. The scientists who created the computer were aware of its problems, however, and immediately began work on a better machine. What the ENIAC lacked was stored memory, or the ability to save and retrieve previous instructions or calculations. In the late 1940s several different groups of researchers built new computers, each one a slight improvement over ENIAC. In these years the development of computers split into two branches: business machines, which processed great volumes of data; and scientific machines, which completed long, complex calculations with only small amounts of data. The business machines came to dominate the computer market while scientific computers evolved into pocket calculators. Early customers for the business machines included the U.S. Census Bureau, several large insurance companies, and Northrop Aircraft. The early machines were built on

The Electronic Numerical Integrator and Computer (ENIAC) was the first real computer. *(© Bettmann/Corbis.)*

commission, at a cost to the customer of between $100,000 and $150,000.

In 1951 ENIAC's original designers, who were then working for Remington-Rand (now called Sperry Rand), introduced the Universal Automatic Computer, or UNIVAC I. UNIVAC was one-tenth the size of ENIAC, much easier to program, and capable of storing information on magnetic tape. It became the first computer to capture widespread public attention when the CBS television network used it to predict the outcome of the 1952 presidential election. The success of UNIVAC prompted International Business Machines (IBM), the leader in the office equipment field, to enter the computer market. Throughout 1953 and 1954 IBM introduced the 700 series computers. They were technologically less advanced than UNIVAC, but IBM's sales force stole the consumer market from Remington-Rand. Within five years of its entrance into the market IBM was selling more than half of the computers in America.

Although the computer might appear to "think," it could not. It was a machine that had to be instructed to undertake its every action. The method of writing these instructions was immediately seen as an important key to increasing the possible operations and uses of the computer. As a result, the profession of computer programming arose. Programmers created software, detailed programs that translated the instructions of human operators to the basic level needed to make all programmable computers work.

Dramatic advances in design and major changes in the materials and techniques used for construction made the computer smaller and much more efficient. The speed with which a computer could complete a calculation rose from thousandths of a second to millionths of a second during the 1950s and 1960s and to billionths of a second by the 1970s. As they improved, the cost of computers steadily decreased. The result was a rapid spread of computer use. While at the start only institutions and corporations could afford to lease and use computers, within thirty years private personal use became common.

Mass production in the computer age

In the computer age, mass production became far more intricate. To increase productivity managers focused on planning and scheduling. Production became a carefully managed flow of parts, materials, and employees. Sales and marketing developed into a scientific process that helped management to determine how many copies of a product to make.

By the early twenty-first century, mass production had become so sophisticated that it was no longer true mass production. Many products came with a variety of options for the customer. When buying a computer from some manufacturers, for example, a customer could choose the size and make of the hard drive, how much memory the computer had, what kind of screen and printer they wanted, and many other details. Choosing the different parts was called customizing one's product; in effect, the customer was having a product built for him or her.

In the 1980s Japanese and Italian automobile manufacturers so successfully automated, or operated with automatic machinery, their assembly lines that some of their factories consisted almost entirely of robots (machines that automatically perform routine, often complex, tasks) doing the jobs. Starting with the bare frame of the vehicle, major parts (which themselves had been automatically assembled elsewhere) were attached by robots, and a computer kept track of exactly what was to be added to each step of the process. The central computer assured total assembly of each car. Though this worked in foreign plants, American auto makers were more resistant to the use of robots and were not as quick to adapt to the new technology. In the early 2000s, though, U.S. carmakers are once again trying to use robots in their manufacturing products, often successfully.

The postindustrial era

During the rise of industrialism, manufacturing on a large scale was the key to success in industry, but after the 1980s, in what is now called the postindustrial era, scaling back was the main industrial goal. Many companies analyzed their productivity and then laid off, or eliminated, a certain percentage of their workers. This procedure was frequently repeated over the years, as companies sought to employ only minimal workforces. Downsizing (reducing the workforce through lay offs) became the dreaded word among laborers of all types who feared for their jobs. Laid-off workers with few skills were often forced to seek jobs in lower paying service industries. There were many inter-related reasons for the loss of industrial work in the United States.

After World War II, the United States became involved in an increasingly global, or worldwide, market. Easy air travel made distances between countries less of a barrier. The Internet provided instant communication among computer users and made it possible to move money anywhere in the world at a moment's notice. At the beginning of the twenty-first century, multinational corporations accounted for some 20 percent of the world's production. These companies, many funded by American investors, were often able to avoid national laws regulating corporations. American capital, or the wealth that is put into building industries, was spent on factories worldwide, and much less investment went into industries in the United States.

During the 1980s the availability of low-cost import items such as cars created strongly competitive conditions for U.S. industries. As imports cut into their profits, many industries could no longer support their large workforces. Some U.S. corporations began to shut down their plants and move them to newly industrialized nations such as South Korea, Hong Kong, Taiwan, and Singapore, where workers accepted much lower wages. As steel and auto factories in the United States deteriorated, industrialists frequently decided against spending the money to make the needed improvements to them.

Nevertheless the United States remained the leading industrial nation in the first years of the twenty-first century, maintaining its position as the richest, most powerful and technologically advanced economy in the world. Though it is correct to call the United States an industrial nation, many historians and economists also call it a postindustrial economy, noting the decline of heavy industries in the 1980s, and the nation's decreased focus on mass production and manufacturing, and increased focus on service industries.

For More Information

Books

Brody, David. *Workers in Industrial America: Essays on the 20th-Century Struggle.* 2nd ed. New York: Oxford University Press, 1993.

Lacey, Robert. *Ford: The Men and the Machine.* New York: Little, Brown, 1986.

Porter, Glen. *The Rise of Big Business, 1860–1920.* Arlington Heights, IL: Harlan Davidson, 1992.

Schlesinger, Arthur, Jr. *The Crisis of the Old Order : 1919–1933, The Age of Roosevelt.* Vol. 1. Boston, MA: Houghton Mifflin, 1957.

Web Sites

Fingleton, Eamonn. "In Praise of Hard Industries." *Industry Week,* October 18, 1999. http://www.industryweek.com/CurrentArticles/asp/articles.asp?ArticleID=643 (accessed on June 30, 2005).

"Great Depression and World War II, 1929–1945." *The Learning Page.* http://memory.loc.gov/ammem/ndlpedu/features/timeline/depwwii/newdeal/newdeal.html (accessed on June 30, 2005.)

Robot Hall of Fame; Carnegie Mellon. http://www.robothalloffame.org/ (accessed on June 30, 2005).

Where to Learn More

Books

Bagley, Katie. *The Early American Industrial Revolution, 1793–1850.* Bridgestone Books, Mankato, MN: 2003.

Calhoun, Charles W., ed. *The Gilded Age: Essays on the Origins of Modern America.* Wilmington, DE: Scholarly Resources, 1996.

Cashman, Sean Dennis. *America in the Gilded Age: From the Death of Lincoln to the Rise of Theodore Roosevelt.* New York and London: New York University Press, 1984.

Clare, John. D. *Industrial Revolution.* San Diego: Harcourt Brace & Co., 1994.

Faler, Paul. *Mechanics and Manufacturers in the Early Industrial Revolution: Lynn, Massachusetts, 1780–1860.* Albany: State University of New York Press, 1981.

Foner, Philip S., ed.*The Factory Girls.* Urbana, IL: University of Illinois Press, 1977.

Hindle, Brooke, and Steven Lubar. *Engines of Change: The American Industrial Revolution, 1790–1860.* Washington, D.C. and London: Smithsonian Institution Press, 1986.

Kornblith, Gary J., ed. *The Industrial Revolution in America.* Boston, MA: Houghton Mifflin, 1998.

McCormick, Anita Louise. *The Industrial Revolution in American History*. Berkeley Heights, NJ: Enslow Publishers, 1998.

Olson, James S. *Encyclopedia of the Industrial Revolution in the U.S.* Westport, CT: Greenwood Press, 2002.

Orleck, Annelise. *Common Sense and a Little Fire: Women and Working-Class Politics in the United States, 1900–1965*. Chapel Hill: University of North Carolina, 1995.

Rivard, Paul E. *A New Order of Things: How the Textile Industry Transformed New England*. Hanover, NH: University Press of New England, 2002.

Ruggoff, Milton. *America's Gilded Age: Intimate Portraits from an Era of Extravagance and Change, 1850–1890*. New York: Henry Holt and Company, 1989.

Smith, Page. *The Rise of Industrial America: A People's History of the Post-Reconstruction Era*. Vol. 6. New York: McGraw-Hill, 1984.

Summers, Mark Wahlgren. *The Gilded Age, or, the Hazard of New Functions*. Upper Saddle River, NJ: Prentice-Hall, 1997.

Web Sites

"The Industrial Revolution." http://www.bergen.org/technology/indust.html (accessed on July 8, 2005).

"Rise of Industrial America, 1876–1900." *The Learning Page*. http://memory.loc.gov/learn/features/timeline/riseind/riseof.html (accessed on July 8, 2005).

"Technology in 1900." *Way Back: U.S. History for Kids*. http://pbskids.org/wayback/tech1900/ (accessed on July 8, 2005).

"Transcontinental Railroad." *American Experience: PBS*. http://www.pbs.org/wgbh/amex/tcrr/index.html (accessed on July 8, 2005).

"Wake Up, America." Webisode 4 of "Freedom: A History of US." http://www.pbs.org/wnet/historyofus/web04/ (accessed on July 8, 2005).

Index

M

Machine shop, apprentices in, 29 (ill.)
Macy's, 115
Mann, Horace, 124
Mantle clock, 34
Manufacturing, Hamilton's views on, 10
Marshall Field's, 115
Martin, Pierre Émile, 92
Marx, Karl, 143
Mass production
  adaptation to clock making, 34
  in computer age, 214–15
  Henry Ford and, 201–4
Matzeliger, Jan Ernst, 53
McClure, Samuel S., 185–86
McClure's (magazine), 185–86
McCormick, Cyrus, 171
McCormick Harvester Company, 141
  strike at, 141–42
McCormick reaper, 37–38
McCoy, Joseph G., 172–73
McKinley, William
  antitrust policy under, 99
  assassination of, 187
  in election of 1896, 180
McParlan, James, 139
Meat Inspection Act, 187
Meatpacking industry
  in Chicago, 88, 163
  conditions in, 88
  investigation of, 186–87
Mechanical reapers, 171
Mechanicians, 28
Mechanization of farming, 35–39
Memphis, Tennessee, growth of, 103
Mercantile, 7–8
Metalworking, 10
Metropolitan Museum of Art, 94
Michigan Central, 167
Michigan Salt Association, 87
Michigan Southern, 167
Migration
  of African Americans, 107–8, 163
  from farm to cities, 106–8
Milwaukee, Wisconsin
  growth of, 103
  immigrants in, 105
Minimum wage, 195
Mississippi River, early traffic on, 17

Mitchell, John, 189 (ill.), 191
Model A automobiles, 204
Model T automobiles, 202 (ill.), 203, 204
Molders Union, 136
Molly Maguires, 138–39, 138 (ill.)
Monopolies, 64, 87, 182
  early response to, 96–97
Montgomery Ward and Company, 176
Morgan, J. P., 64, 82, 98, 188
  Morganization and, 157
  philanthropy of, 94
  U.S. Steel and, 95
Morganization, 82, 157, 188
Morse, Samuel F. B., 25, 26 (ill.)
Mortgage foreclosures, 208
Muckrakers, 97, 185–87
Muskets, manufacture of, 31–32
Myers, Isaac, 149

N

National Bank Act (1863), 61
National Cash Register Company (Corning, New York), 103
National Child Labor Committee, 123, 195
National Farmers' Alliance & Industrial Union, 164
National Grange of the Patrons of Husbandry, 175–77, 176 (ill.)
National Labor Union, 136, 149
National Monuments Act (1906), 190
National Road, 17
National Steel, 95
Nebraska, settlement of, 59 (ill.)
New Deal, 207–9
New Haven, Connecticut, growth of, 103
New immigrants, 105, 120
New Orleans, Louisiana, 102, 168
New York Central Railroad, 79
New York City, 101 (ill.), 102
  garment industry in, 127
  growth of, 103, 167
  immigrants in, 105
  political machine in, 110–11
  population of, 7, 103, 108
  slums of, 111–12
  streetcars in, 107

Y

3/06

$55.00

LONGWOOD PUBLIC LIBRARY
Middle Country Road
Middle Island, NY 11953
(631) 924-6400

LIBRARY HOURS

Monday-Friday	9:30 a.m. - 9:00 p.m.
Saturday	9:30 a.m. - 5:00 p.m.
Sunday (Sept-June)	1:00 p.m. - 5:00 p.m.